The German Constitution

SOME RECENT BORZOI BOOKS

IN DAYS TO COME
By Walter Rathenau

EARLY CIVILIZATION:
AN INTRODUCTION TO ANTHROPOLOGY
By Alexander A. Goldenweiser

HUMAN NATURE IN POLITICS
By Graham Wallas

HOW ENGLAND IS GOVERNED
By Rt. Hon. C. F. G. Masterman

PRINCIPLES OF SOCIAL PSYCHOLOGY
By James Mickel Williams

THE HISTORY OF SOCIAL DEVELOPMENT
By Dr. F. Müller-Lyer

THE FOUNDATIONS OF SOCIAL SCIENCE
By James Mickel Williams

For sale at all bookshops
For further particulars address
ALFRED A. KNOPF, *Publisher* **NEW YORK**

The New German Constitution

by
René Brunet

Professor of Constitutional Law in the Faculty of Law at the University of Caen, formerly legal advisor to the French Embassy at Berlin

Translated from the French by Joseph Gollomb
Foreword by Charles A. Beard

New York   Mcmxxii
Alfred · A · Knopf

COPYRIGHT, 1922, BY
ALFRED A. KNOPF, Inc

Published April, 1922.

JN
3953
.B7

*Set up, electrotyped, and printed by the J. J. Little & Ives Co., New York, N. Y.
Paper furnished by W. F. Etherington & Co., New York, N. Y.
Bound by the H. Wolff Estate, New York, N. Y.*

MANUFACTURED IN THE UNITED STATES OF AMERICA

FOREWORD

It is a pleasure to introduce M. Brunet to the American public. He is a French scholar of the finest type, careful, objective, and sincere. The present work on the German constitution bears the impress of these high qualities. In this volume we find the scientific spirit that was to be expected, combined with an intimate, first-hand knowledge of the forces and materials which are described. All this is very significant. The long night of the Great War was hardly over before M. Brunet began an impartial and thorough-going study of the state of affairs created in Germany by the revolution of November, 1918. If a Frenchman who suffered so much can display such good sense and sobriety, then surely American scholars ought to give more than a hearty welcome to this volume. It is an excellent beginning in the reconstruction of the republic of letters.

In this book we have a plain and simple account of the German revolution and the conflict of forces which ended in the establishment of the republic. The balance of parties is examined. The results of the elections to the national assembly are summarized. Then follows a systematic analysis of the new plan of government, illuminated by continual reference to the concrete historical circumstances in which the makers of the German constitution had to operate.

M. Brunet has tried to steer his way on an even keel between the highly theoretical methods of the German political philosophers and the hard, matter-of-fact methods of the Anglo-Saxons. He has succeeded admirably. Accordingly, the usefulness of his volume extends beyond the information which it presents. It affords an interesting model to young American writers who have occasion to deal with constitutional and legal matters. There is no reason why a doctor of philosophy should not love insight and form as much as the poet does. The great English doctor of law, Maitland, certainly did.

M. Brunet's excellent qualities have enabled him to write the best treatise on the German constitution which exists in any language. Any one who will spend a day comparing this volume with Dr. Fritz Stier-Somlo's *Die Verfassung des Deutschen Reichs vom 11, August, 1919,* for example, will soon discover how much more ingenious and penetrating is the French commentator. M. Brunet's volume is to be commended on other grounds than those of intrinsic excellence. It brings information to the American public on a subject concerning which very little is known at present. The new German constitution has been translated into English and there are a few stray articles by the way of commentary available to Americans, but this is the first systematic treatise on the topic in our tongue.

It would not be fitting to give in this foreword a résumé of M. Brunet's volume. The admirable survey presented in the analytical table of contents can be seen at a glance. It may not be out of place, however, to indicate some points of contact between the present course of American thinking and the system of government here described. Notwithstanding the curious constitution worship that flourishes in many places in the United States, there are signs of fresh currents of thinking. Mr. Woodrow Wilson, in his remarkable essay, *Congressional Government*, set in train new opinions as to our constitutional system which have by no means been lost to view in the general revulsion of feeling that followed the war. Only recently Professor Lindsay Rogers, of Columbia University, took occasion to remark, in the course of an interesting article on modern French politics, that we ought to have a more lively and intelligent discussion of constitutional questions in America. The ink was hardly dry on his paper before Professor William Macdonald accepted the challenge by bringing out his highly suggestive book, entitled *A New Constitution for a New America*.

The rhythm of human affairs is such that we may reasonably expect a return to the constitutional searchings of 1912 on a higher and different plane. Those who fix their eyes not upon the written letter of our Constitution, but upon judicial decisions, political practice, and congressional procedure are never under the delusion that our constitutional system does not change. If, as Professor Seligman long ago pointed out, economic conditions are rapidly becoming the same all over the world with similar legal results, then we may, with proper warrant, expect very soon a new and lively examination of constitutional principles to break in upon us. M. Brunet's book fits in with the signs of the times. No person who pretends to be intelligent about constitutional matters can neglect it.

It would be difficult to imagine anything more illuminating than a comparison of the Constitution of the United States drawn up in 1787, the fundamental law of the Australian Commonwealth adopted in 1900, and the new German *Reichsverfassung* of 1919, which vibrates with the tramp of the proletariat. In the attempt of the Germans to combine the strength of Hamilton's government with the democratic control so vaunted by Jefferson we have an experiment that ought to stir our deepest interest. In the provisions for social, not to say socialistic, enterprise, both the Australian and the German constitutions offer noteworthy contrasts to our own fundamental law. It will not escape the close observer that the Germans have not created a supreme court, on the model of our own, endowed with power to set aside acts of the executive and legislative branches of the government. The relations established by the Germans between the federal government and the states, ingenious compromises all must admit, ought to be studied in connection with Mr. Roosevelt's "New Nationalism"—not as an echo of a dead past but as a prophecy of the future.

FOREWORD

The science of comparative government is as fruitful to-day as it was a generation ago when it flourished in such vigour. A teacher who will place M. Brunet's book and "The Federalist" in the hands of a college class cannot fail to evoke a lively interest in politics and a more intelligent consideration of American constitutional problems.

To the historian, the introductory part of M. Brunet's volume will afford food for thought. There is no doubt that the new German constitution is the product of a sharp and determined conflict of classes. M. Brunet records the fact and gives the alignment of parties. No sophisticated person will ever imagine (whatever he may say) that the German fundamental law was drawn from abstract political thinking, theories about the rights of states, or reflections on the fate of Greek democracies and ancient Rome. The pressure of class interests is evident in almost every line. If one should underscore the socialist sections with red, the Centre clauses with yellow, and the capitalist phrases with black, one would have an interesting study in constitutional artistry. From time to time, M. Brunet makes specific references to the precise effect of party pressures upon legal phraseology. It would, however, be a work of supererogation to point out to American scholars the relevancy of these passages. Having recovered from the shock of learning that the Fathers of our Constitution were made of mortal clay, they are prepared to receive M. Brunet's book with open minds.

My hearty thanks are due to Mr. Knopf, who, on my suggestion, undertook to make this volume available to the American public. I am indebted to Professors Munro and Holcombe for the right to use their translation of the "Constitution of the German Commonwealth" issued by the World Peace Foundation. Especially am I under obligation to Mr. Joseph Gollomb for undertaking the translation of M. Brunet's text. Mr. Gollomb was himself a witness at many of the scenes described in these pages. He has first-hand knowledge of European politics. His long residence in Paris gave him a

FOREWORD

mastery of the French tongue. In making this English version, he has kept in mind the requirements of the general reader as well as those of technical students.

CHARLES A. BEARD.

New Milford, Conn.,
December 14, 1921.

CONTENTS

FOREWORD   v

CHAPTER I
THE ORIGINS
SECTION 1
THE REVOLUTION

The Constitution of April 16, 1871, and the reforms of October, 1918	1
The fall of the old régime	12
The republic of councils	16

SECTION 2
THE NATIONAL CONSTITUENT ASSEMBLY

The composition of the Assembly	24
The Provisional Constitution of February 10, 1919	28
The adoption of the Constitution and supplementary laws	35

CHAPTER II
TOWARD A UNIFIED STATE
SECTION 1
TERRITORIAL STATUS OF THE STATES

The problem of the dismemberment of Prussia	43
Modifications of the territories of states	53
The creation of a state—Thuringia	57

CONTENTS

Section 2
DIVISION OF POWER BETWEEN THE REICH AND THE STATES

The constitution of the states	59
The legislative power of the *Reich*	61
(1) Fundamental limits of power	61
(2) Supremacy of national over state laws	65
Administrative services of the government	65
Justice and the High Court	68

Section 3
JURIDICAL AND POLITICAL STRUCTURE OF THE REICH

Is the *Reich* a federal state?	69
Prussia and the *Reich*	72

CHAPTER III
THE DEMOCRATIC PRINCIPLE

Section 1
THE PRINCIPLE

The power of the state is derived from the people	75
The system of councils, or the dictatorship of the proletariat	77
The Chamber of Labour, or the Vocational Parliament	82
The Political Activity of the Unions	91

Section 2
THE APPLICATIONS

The republic	98
Universal suffrage, the political parties and the electoral law	100
General principles	103
The electorate and eligibility	109
Preparations for elections	112
Distribution of seats	113
The actual working of the law	115
Direct government	118

CONTENTS

CHAPTER IV
PARLIAMENTARY GOVERNMENT

Section 1
THE REICHSTAG

Privileges and guarantees accorded to the Reichstag	131
The rules of the Reichstag	135
The duration of the powers of the Reichstag	137
Powers of the Reichstag	138
1. Powers of the Reichstag, as principal holder of sovereignty	138
2. Legislative powers; how laws are proposed and passed	139
3. Power of control; interpellations and committees	147

Section 2
THE PRESIDENT OF THE REICH

The need for a strong president	153
The election of the President and the length of his term	156
The powers of the President	162
The responsibility of the President	168

Section 3
THE CABINET OF THE REICH

The Chancellor and the Ministers according to the Constitution	172
The working of constitutional rules; how a Ministry is formed, how it works and is dissolved	177

Section 4
THE REICHSRAT

General features of the Reichsrat	186
The composition and the functioning of the Reichsrat	188
Powers of the Reichsrat	192

CHAPTER V

FUNDAMENTAL RIGHTS AND DUTIES OF GERMANS

Legal and political aspects of fundamental rights and duties	195
Fundamental rights and duties of the individual	202
Fundamental rights and duties of communities	216
Religion and the churches	222
Instruction and the schools	226

CHAPTER VI

THE ECONOMIC CONSTITUTION AND SOCIALIZATION

Section 1

THE ECONOMIC CONSTITUTION

The "anchorage" of the Councils in the Constitution	236
Constitutional provisions relative to the Councils	244
Factory Workers Councils	248
The Trade Unions and the Councils	257
The Provisional Economic Council	263

Section 2

SOCIALIZATION

The problem of socialization	269
Collective economy	275
The regulation of the coal industry	280

CONCLUSION

APPENDIX

The Constitution of August 11, 1919 (text)	297

The German
Constitution

CHAPTER I

THE ORIGINS

Up to the autumn of 1918 Germany was under the Empire of the Constitution of April 16, 1871. Then in November, 1918, the work of Bismarck was suddenly overthrown and military defeat and revolution plunged Germany into chaos. How she worked out of it, through what vicissitudes she passed and with what groping she finally achieved her new Constitution is the question to examine first.

SECTION I

THE REVOLUTION

The revolution of November, 1918, was preceded by partial reforms embodied at a late hour in the Constitution of 1871; and when it broke out, in a few hours it completely threw over all the apparatus of the old régime. A new government sprang up which for several weeks held power in the name of a minority and without any right other than that of force.

1.—THE CONSTITUTION OF APRIL 16, 1871, AND THE REFORMS OF OCTOBER, 1918.

The principal characteristics of the Constitution of April 16, 1871, are well known.

Germany was a federal state, that is to say, above the member states, which renounced a part of their individual independence to strengthen their collective political and economic power, there existed a central state in whose favor they had given up that degree of independence—the German Empire.

In the Reich sovereign power belonged to an assembly of

Princes and of governments represented by the Bundesrat or Federal Council. This council which consisted of representatives of all the member states shared with the Reichstag the power to initiate and vote legislation. It promulgated the general administrative measures necessary for the execution of the laws; and with the consent of the Emperor it could dissolve the Reichstag.

The nation was presided over by the German Emperor. He exercised generally the rights which modern nations reserve to the executive power. In particular he represented the Empire in its international relations; promulgated its laws; watched over their execution; appointed civil and military officials, etc.

Several remarkable details have to be pointed out. Although in principle the Emperor's actions had to be countersigned by a minister he was free from that restriction in such matters as concerned military affairs, particularly in the nomination of the superior officers of the army and the navy. The German Emperor was the absolute chief of the forces of the Empire on sea and land. Furthermore, although he could not declare war without the consent of the Bundesrat he could act on his own authority in case of attack by a foreign power against the territory or the coasts of the German Confederation.

The Emperor nominated the Chancellor, who was after the Emperor himself, the sole chief of the political and administrative organization of the Empire. "The Chancellor," says Article 15, "presides over the Bundesrat and directs its labours." But as he clearly could not himself assume such an overwhelming task, he was authorized by the law of March 17, 1878, to call assistance and be supplemented at need by high functionaries placed at the head of Imperial departments— those of foreign affairs, of the interior, justice, treasury, railroads, marine, colonies, posts and telegraphs. These officials carried the title of State Secretaries, which seemed to give

THE REVOLUTION 3

them something of the nature of ministers, though in reality they were completely subordinated to the Chancellor.

Just as the Bundesrat represented the federated Princes so the Reichstag represented the German people. Elected by direct and universal suffrage the Reichstag had the right to initiate legislation; and no law was operative unless it had obtained a majority both in the Bundesrat and in the Reichstag. Furthermore the Reichstag had the right to interpellate, not the Secretaries of State but the Chancellor himself and to ask questions; and discussions of a question could be closed by voting an expression of the confidence of the Assembly.

Under the Empire there were twenty-five states [1] and the territory of Alsace-Lorraine.

These states were governed by constitutions of the greatest variety. There were three free cities, Hamburg, Bremen and Lübeck; twenty-two monarchies, which carried different titles; Kingdoms—Prussia, Bavaria, Saxony, Wurtemberg; Grand Duchies—Baden, Hesse; Duchies—Saxe-Coburg-Gotha, Saxe-Meiningen; and Principalities—Waldeck, Schaumburg-Lippe, etc.

Among these states some, a large majority but the least important, had adopted the system of the single legislative chamber, which, with one or two exceptions, comprised, beside the deputies elected by universal suffrage, members named by the princes of the state, or by special electoral colleges such as groups of the heaviest tax payers, chambers of commerce, industrial and agricultural organizations, the clergy, the professions, etc.

The other states, four kingdoms and the Grand Duchies of Baden and of Hesse, had two chambers each. The upper

---

[1] Prussia, Bavaria, Saxony, Wurtemberg, Baden, Hesse, Mecklenburg-Schwerin, Saxe-Weimar, Mecklenburg-Strelitz, Oldenburg, Brunswick, Saxe-Meiningen, Saxe-Altenburg, Saxe-Coburg-Gotha, Anhalt, Schwarzburg-Rudolstadt, Schwarzburg-Sondershausen, Waldeck, Reuss (elder line), Reuss (younger line), Schaumburg-Lippe, Lippe, Lubeck, Bremen and Hamburg.

house was almost entirely composed of members of the reigning families or their kin and of personages charged with representing the nobility or the great landed proprietors. The lower house was elected sometimes by universal suffrage, sometimes by a system of plural voting; or by a system that divided the population in such a way that the voice of the people was nullified almost entirely in favor of the big taxpayers as in Prussia.

All this would present an erroneous and incomplete picture if one did not take the precaution to search beyond the letter of these constitutions and inquire how the government of Germany was actually conducted. The political institutions of Germany presented a certain number of aspects which it is important to bring out clearly: [1]

1. *These institutions were anti-democratic.* It is true the Reichstag was elected by universal and direct suffrage. But, on the one hand the electoral legislation of the Reich contained certain provisions which were singularly behind the times, such as the denial to the poor of the right to vote, the fixing of the voting age at twenty-five, etc. On the other hand, the Bundesrat, which was not elected, possessed powers superior to those of the Reichstag; and the latter could do nothing without the Bundesrat. The same situation existed within the individual states, which either did not have a chamber elected by universal suffrage or else limited it in power by the check of an upper house, feudal and conservative in character.

2. *These institutions were anti-parliamentary.* The Reichstag could interpellate the Chancellor but could not depose him. To a question or to an interpellation the Chancellor was always free to respond that he did not wish to reply; or he could fix his own time for replying; and finally, if he was in the minority in the house he did not have to resign.

[1] See Joseph–Barthelémy, *les Institutions politiques de l'Allemagne contemporaine*, Paris, Alcan, 1915.

3. *The Reich encroached more and more on the domain of the individual states.* This encroachment, this evolution toward unitarism, manifested itself in most divers ways. In military matters it took the form of a fusion of fighting contingents which belonged more or less nominally to the various states, but which, with the exception perhaps of Bavaria, placed their whole force at the direct command of the Emperor. As for Bavaria, at the outbreak of the war its "reserved rights" had almost completely disappeared. The development of the legislation of the Empire had accentuated this evolution toward unitarism. In the measure that the Reich legislated in a large number of domains, it wiped out in these matters the different regulations that existed up to then in the individual states. It is true that the execution of the national legislation was entrusted to functionaries within these states; but these officials were under the control of the Bundesrat and subject to the supervision of the Reich. Even in financial matters the liberty of the individual states was more and more limited. While it is true that they conserved their autonomy in matters of duties and taxes, the more the Reich discovered new sources of revenue the more the legislation of the Empire imposed on the several states the task of collecting this revenue and the more narrow became the scope in which the states could manage their own financial affairs, and the dependency of the states grew the more on the financial legislation and the budgetary dispositions allowed them by the Reich.[1]

4. In contrast to the other federated states whose Constitutions were based on the principle of equality of the component states, Germany was based on the notion of the inequality of the states federated in it. *Prussia exercised a true hegemony in Germany.* In the Bundesrat it was represented by 17 votes whereas the other most favoured state, Bavaria, had but 6; two others, Saxony and Wurtenberg, had only 4

[1] See Laband, *Die geschichtliche Entwicklung der Reichsverfassung* in the *Jahrbuch des oeffentlichen Rechts*, 1907, p. 1, *et seq.*

each; two, Baden and Hesse, 3 each; Mecklenburg and Brunswick, 2 each; and all the others but 1 apiece. In addition the Rhineland was also represented by 3 votes in the Bundesrat but these votes were instructed by Prussia. The latter, therefore, had 17 votes, 20 with those of Alsace-Lorraine, 21 with that of Waldeck, since the latter by its treaty of entry into the Confederation had abandoned its governmental rights to Prussia. It had therefore numerically a third of the total strength of the Bundesrat, while in actual influence it counted much more. Only Prussia could feel assured that its representation made it mistress of the situation in the Bundesrat; fourteen votes were sufficient to head off a constitutional change. Consequently Prussia possessed absolute veto power. It must not be forgotten that the representatives of the Princes in the Bundesrat received imperative mandates from them and that the representatives of the state had to cast their votes as a bloc—that is, as a unit. It mattered little, therefore, that such and such was the numerical representation in the Bundesrat of the particular states, that Prussia had 17 votes, Bavaria 6, etc. As to legislative changes relating to the army or the navy, and to taxes feeding the treasury of the Empire, nothing of this kind could be enacted if it was opposed by the "presidency." And the "presidency" belonged by undisputed right to Prussia.

In the Reichstag Prussia exercised the same preponderance. The Reichstag was composed of deputies, one for each 100,000 inhabitants. There Prussia counted much more than half, for its population was nearly two-thirds that of the whole Empire—40,165,217 out of 64,925,933. She also elected 236 deputies out of the 397 that made up the Reichstag.

To the same degree she was in control of executive action. While sovereignty nominally resided in the assemblage of Princes in the Bundesrath, it resided no less in the hands of the King of Prussia who had full rights as the German Emperor; and it was he who nominated the Chancellor, the sole responsible minister of the Empire. The Chancellor was almost always a subject of the King of Prussia and, following a rule to which there were few exceptions, at the same time the Prime Minister of Prussia.

Thus, therefore, Prussia elected a majority in the Reichstag, and if by some extraordinary chance the latter voted against the desire of Prussia the decree could be nullified by the Prussian representative in the Bundesrath. The King of Prussia was Emperor. He nominated the Chancellor, chief of all the administrative machinery of the state. The King of Prussia was master of the government of the Empire. Germany was a veritable Prussia enlarged.

We can now distinguish the essential traits that characterized constitutional Germany on the eve of the war. There was in Germany, under the infinite complexity of written provisions, behind a deliberately effected juxtaposition of the most modern formula by the side of some of the most archaic, a living reality. It was a despotic organization that placed full power in the hands of a feudal monarch. It was, to put it in the words of President Wilson, the largest enterprise of domination that the world has ever known.

Such a system and that which made it such an anachronism could not survive the test of war and still less that of defeat.

Already during the war several demands for reforms made themselves felt. In proportion as the war was prolonged and the heavier became the burdens that weighed on the people together with the sacrifices that were imposed upon them, there developed a pressure on the part of the people for recognition, for compensation, for the right to participate in a more effective fashion in the conduct of public affairs. The Reichstag appointed a commission to investigate to what extent it was possible to modify the Constitution of the Reich in conformity with the desires of the people. On his part the Emperor in a message on April 7, 1917, declared that it was the duty of the Chancellor to satisfy the exigencies of new times with every means appropriate; and to reconstruct the constitutional edifice in such a way as to insure a free and spontaneous collaboration of all the elements of the nation. The Chancellor seemed to be in accord with the Emperor on the necessity and urgency of a "new orientation."

On the 15th of May, 1917, Bethmann-Hollweg spoke of realizing a programme of "trusting collaboration of the Emperor and the nation." On July 19, 1917, Michaelis foreshadowed the establishment of a close contact between a government and parliament, the creation of a bond of mutual confidence between the government of the Empire and the Reichstag, in the sense that the management of various affairs should be entrusted to men who, aside from their professional abilities, would enjoy the full confidence of the great parties in the popular branch of the government.

They were nothing but vague words; and this "parliamentarization" of the government of the Reich did not commence to show itself until the pressure of defeat came, such as was felt in the summer of 1918. The adoption of a parliamentary régime then seemed the sole means of obtaining from the masses the sacrifices which were still expected of them both on the firing line and in the interior.

The true reforms commenced with the letter which the Emperor wrote on September 30, 1918, to the departing Chancellor von Hertling, and which was a real message to the German people and to the Reichstag. "I desire," said the Emperor, "that the German people shall collaborate more effectively than in the past in the determination of the destiny of our Fatherland. It is my wish therefore that men invested with the confidence of the people shall participate in a large measure in the rights and duties of the government." Legally it was only an expression of the hitherto recognized imperial will. But from a political point of view this message constituted the recognition of a new system of government, in virtue of which the centre of gravity of political institutions passed from the organs of the government, the Bundesrath and the Emperor, to the popular assembly, the Reichstag.

The spirit in which the new reforms were to be carried out and the importance which they were to assume were made clearer several days later when, on October 5, 1918, Chancellor Maximilian of Baden in a programme speech addressed in the Reichstag said, "It is in the essence of the system of the government which we are now instituting that I now state clearly and without reservation the principles by which I shall seek to fulfil my heavy responsibilities. These principles were accepted before I assumed my duties as Chancellor in an agreement reached between confederated governments and the chiefs of the parties of the majority of this Chamber. . . . It is only when the people take an active part to the largest measure in the determination of the destiny of the nation; and when the sense of responsibility is also shared by the majority of the political chiefs freely elected, that a statesman can accept direction of the helm with confidence and himself participate in this responsibility. Otherwise the shoulders of one man will be too feeble to support the immense responsibility that now confronts our government. I am convinced that the manner in which the directing government has been formed to-day with the collaboration of the Reichstag is not temporary in its nature and that in times of peace hereafter no government can be formed that has not the support of the Reichstag, that does not lean on the Reichstag, and that does not take from the Reichstag its principal chiefs."

As a consequence two laws were passed which carried the date of October 28, 1918. They were designed to meet the three most important exigencies of the hour:

1. *They realized the parliamentarization of the government of the Reich.* Article 15 of the Constitution of 1871, which

dealt with the nomination of the Chancellor had the following amendment added: "The Chancellor in order to continue direction of the affairs of the Reich must have the confidence of the Reichstag. The Chancellor is responsible for all the political acts of the Emperor performed in the exercise of his constitutional rights. The Chancellor and his representatives are responsible for the conduct of affairs to the Bundesrat and the Reichstag."[1]

This text established not only the responsibility of the Chancellor; it also recognized constitutionally the right of parties or their parliamentary groups to participate in the nomination of the Chancellor and it specified that when the confidence of the Reichstag is withdrawn from the Chancellor he must resign.

The responsibility of the Chancellor, who was answerable both to the Reichstag and to the Bundesrat, extended not only to the general and particular decrees issued by the Emperor and countersigned by the Chancellor but also to acts of a political nature on the part of the Emperor; and it followed from this that the Chancellor and his representatives were also responsible for their own actions of the same character.

Further, one of the laws of October 28, 1918, in abrogating paragraph 2 of Article 21 of the Constitution of 1871, permitted thereafter members of the Reichstag to become secretaries of state while fulfilling at the same time their functions as members of the Reichstag. On the other hand the incompatibility between the Bundesrat and the Reichstag (article 9, paragraph 2, of the Constitution of 1871) was not abolished. It followed from that, therefore, that while a member of the Reichstag could become a Secretary of State, he could not become a member of the Bundesrat and therefore could not

---

[1] Piloty, *Die Umformung der Reichsregierung und die Reichsverfassung, Deutsche Juristen Zeitung*, 1918, p. 651, *et seq.*; Stier-somlo, *Reichsverfassung*, p. 6.

Page 13, footnote 1. See the text of these claims in Gentizon, *la Révolution allemande*. 1 vol. Payot, Paris, 1919, p. 222.

become Chancellor; for that office was open only to members of the Bundesrat.

2. The laws of October 28, 1918, broadened considerably the authority of the Reichstag and diminished correspondingly the Imperial authority in the right to declare war and conclude treaties. The Emperor could never again under any circumstances declare war in the name of the Reich without the consent of the Reichstag and the Bundesrat. He was required to obtain the same consent of the two assemblies to conclude treaties of peace and all other treaties that touched matters in which either of the assemblies had competence.

3. *The authority of the Emperor as military commander was put under parliamentary control.*

These reforms constituted certainly important progress along the road of parliamentary rule and it can be said that it placed Germany thereafter among the nations that are governed by such a system.

The texts of the laws of October 28, 1918, were accompanied by a letter of the Emperor to the Chancellor in which he wrote: "Prepared by a series of governmental acts a new order comes into being in which fundamental rights of the Emperor pass to the people. After the events of these our times the German people must not be denied a single right that is needed to guarantee them a free and happy future. I acquiesce together with my highest colleagues in the decisions of the representatives of the people and do so with the firm determination to co-operate to the greatest effectiveness, convinced that I will thus serve the welfare of the German people. The Emperor is at the service of the people."

German jurists with good reason characterized this letter as a "political abdication." But the changes which went with it came too late, and a simple "political abdication" appeared thereafter as strikingly insufficient. The German Empire was falling into ruin and it was no longer a question of partial reforms.

2.—THE FALL OF THE OLD RÉGIME.

Revolution broke out in Germany at the beginning of November, 1918.

From the end of October riots and revolts had been taking place on board the vessels of the Imperial navy. But on November 4 at Kiel there broke out a revolt among the sailors, who became masters of the situation. They formed a Council of Soldiers which presented to the mayor of the city a list of demands—the liberation of arrested sailors; the suppression of a military hierarchy outside of the service; a demand that the approval of the Council of Soldiers be necessary for all military measures, etc.

The next day the workers of Kiel declared a general strike and formed Workers Councils which united with Councils of Soldiers consisting of the marines of the city.

From Kiel the movement spread the same day to Lubeck and to Hamburg. On the 6th, a general strike was proclaimed in the dock yards of Hamburg and revolution broke out in Bremen.

Simultaneously revolution won other cities: Hanover, Cologne, Magdeburg, Brunswick, Leipzig, and Dresden, where Councils of Workers and Soldiers were formed. From November 4th to the 9th all North Germany, the South and the Centre fell into the hands of the Councils.

The movement, which at its beginning could be considered as principally a military revolt, took on for the first time a political character most clearly marked in Munich, where in the night of the eighth of November after a great manifestation by the Independent Socialists serious disturbances broke out. The royal family was expelled and the Republic proclaimed.

With few exceptions the revolutionists met with no opposition. The bourgeoisie did not react. It was enough for some thirty marines from Kiel to enter a town or for a group of soldiers returning from the fighting front to present themselves at the city hall. Immediately every one yielded to their orders and the Councils were able to install themselves in power without firing a shot. In this revolution, to which no serious opposition had been presented and which appeared rather as the collapse of an old régime whose reason for existence had vanished, there lacked only to complete it the fall of the capital and the abdication of the monarch.

At Berlin the military power devoted itself to the defence of the city. On the fifth a state of siege was proclaimed and on the seventh a decree forbade the formation of Councils of Soldiers and of Workers "on the Russian model."

But the same day the Social Democrats sent to Chancellor Maximilian of Baden the Secretary of State Scheidemann, the bearer of an ultimatum demanding the immediate abrogation of the decree forbidding meetings; such a transformation of the government of Prussia that those in control of it should be of the same political complexion as the majority of the Reichstag; the strengthening of the Social Democratic influence in the government; and finally the abdication of the Emperor and the renunciation by the Crown Prince of all claims to the throne.

Although confronted with imminent revolution only officials and functionaries were overthrown. The bourgeoisie here as elsewhere looked on passively and attempted no resistance.

As for Maximilian of Baden he hoped to find a basis for negotiation. He pondered measures to parliamentarize still further the old government and contemplated the immediate convocation of a constituent assembly to develop a new constitution. Meanwhile he did not reply to the ultimatum of the Social Democrats. Whereupon there were organized Councils of Workers and Soldiers in Berlin who made themselves felt with their first act on the morning of the ninth of November by declaring a general strike.

The Chancellor could no longer delay action. On the ninth at two o'clock in the afternoon, after a telephonic conversation with William II, he announced officially that the Emperor had abdicated and that the Crown Prince had renounced the throne. He declared that he, Maximilian of Baden, would remain in office until the installation of the Regent. He would propose to the Regent the nomination as Chancellor of the Social Democratic leader Ebert, and the convocation of electoral colleges with the view of choosing a national constituent assembly to which would be given the task of directing the future of the state.

Thus the Chancellor hoped to the last moment to effect in an almost legal manner the transition from the old to the new Germany. But the pressure of events was too strong for him and he was not able to realize his hope.

In the early part of the afternoon, Ebert accompanied by Scheidemann appeared at the Chancellery and declared in the name of their party that in order to avoid bloodshed and to maintain public order they considered it necessary to take power in their hands and assume the direction of the government. When Vice-Chancellor von Payer asked Ebert if he intended to conduct the government on the basis of the Constitution or in the name of the Councils of Workers and Soldiers, Ebert replied, "Within the frame work of the constitution." After short deliberation and in view of the fact that the troops in Berlin had deserted the old government the cabinet of Maximilian decided to place in the hands of Ebert the powers of Chancellor of the Empire "subject to the approval of the legislature." Ebert at once entered into office without the question of the regency being decided.

But the Socialist parties pressed for the proclamation of a republic. This proclamation took place several minutes after the installation of Ebert as Chancellor. In answer to the clamor of a great gathering of the people in front of the Reichstag Scheidemann appeared on the terrace and declared

THE FALL OF THE OLD RÉGIME

in substance, "We have conquered everywhere along the line. The old régime is no more. Ebert is Chancellor. Our deputy, Lieutenant Göhre, is associate minister of war. We must now strengthen our victory and nothing will stop our march. The Hohenzollerns have abdicated. Let us see to it that this magnificent day is marred by nothing. May this be a day of eternal glory in the history of Germany. Long live the German Republic!"

The same day and almost the same hour similar events took place in all the states of Germany. Everywhere under the threat and under the pressure of the Councils of Workers and Soldiers the old Diets and the old governments vanished. The kings, the grand dukes and the dukes resigned or were simply replaced. The republic was proclaimed. One can say that on November 9, 1918, when at two in the afternoon in front of the Reichstag Scheidemann proclaimed the Republic, the ancient régime had fallen in Germany.

From this date on all the organs of government which had incarnated the old régime disappeared or were entirely transformed.

The Bundesrat, in which the sovereignty of the old Reich was incorporated, ceased to exist as such. It is true that the new leaders of the Reich permitted the Bundesrat "the right to continue the exercise of administrative powers according to laws and regulations" (decree of November 14, 1918); and thus there continued a Bundesrat of limited power. But it was no longer the old Bundesrat, for the governments of the individual states, having changed through revolution, sent new delegates who no longer represented princes but republics.

Naturally there was no longer any question of the Emperor. Having lost his crown on November 9, he fled across the Dutch frontier on the 10th, as a private individual and his letter from Amerongen on November 28, 1918, in which he, William II, declared that he expressly renounced for all time the crown of Prussia and thereby "the Imperial German crown," had only, so to speak, a moral effect.

After the resignation of Maximilian of Baden there was no longer a Chancellor of the Empire. It is true that he had passed on his powers to Ebert but we will see shortly that Ebert did not consider himself as such except for a few hours.

As for the Reichstag whose last session ended on October 26, 1918, it was not exactly dissolved after the revolution. At the same time no formal dissolution was necessary, for a new sovereignty had been installed and had taken the place of the old Reichstag. Meanwhile, taking advantage of the fact that no formal decision had been made as to the old Reichstag the chairman of that assembly, Fehrenbach, refused to recognize its implied dissolution. On November 12, 1918, he addressed a circular to the deputies in which he declared that owing to the exigencies of the hour and without the consent of the government he would convoke the Reichstag, reserving to himself the right to announce later the time and place of the assembly. The revolutionary government thereupon notified Fehrenbach that a conflict would ensue thereat. Notwithstanding this Fehrenbach several days later repeated the announcement of the convocation. But the old Reichstag never met again. In February, 1919, it was dissolved by decree which also declared that its last session was dated as of November 9, 1919.

3.—THE REPUBLIC OF THE COUNCILS.

While the Empire was collapsing there arose quickly on the ruins of the old edifice a new structure. In place of the Empire, the government of a bourgeois and military oligarchy, came the dictatorship of the proletarian masses at one blow, the republic of the working class. Everywhere Councils of Workers and Soldiers were formed, which, taking political power in their hands, appeared to be thereafter the only and real holders of sovereignty.

THE REPUBLIC OF THE COUNCILS 17

But the Councils lacked the needed agreement in aim and action. Two diametrically opposed tendencies divided the new powers in control. On the one hand the members of the Social Democratic party within the Councils pursued a purely political goal—the creation of a German republic on a democratic basis to be effected by a Constituent Assembly to be convoked as soon as possible. On the other hand the Independent Socialists, the Communists, the Spartacists and other left wing elements set up as the principal aim an economic change—the quick and complete socialization of all means of production. But they also had in view a political objective, the establishment of a dictatorship of the proletariat on the model of the Russian Soviet Republic, by the complete organization of the system of Councils of Workers and Soldiers. The particular question on which the antagonism between these two groups broke out was whether or not there should be called a new constituent assembly.

The revolution was undoubtedly the work of the Independents. Their leader, Ernest Daümig, had been to Moscow to study the Bolshevist movement, and Russia had come back with him in the persons of Joffe and his agents of propaganda. Already during the strikes of January, 1918, which had been organized by them, there had appeared for the first time in Germany Workers Councils; and in the days preceding the insurrection of November, 1918, Councils of Workers and Soldiers had been secretly organized at Kiel as well as in Berlin. The Social Democrats, on the other hand, to the last moment warned the people against the consequences of an ill-considered insurrection. But when the success of the revolts seemed assured it was seen that many who had condemned it were now joining it. Thanks to Maximilian of Baden it was the Social Democrats, Ebert and Scheidemann and the trade unions that were installed in power on the 9th of November, 1918. The history of the German revolution is the story of a revolution made by one political group and its fruits garnered by another. At first the two Socialist parties divided power equally. But after several weeks of collaboration the Social Democrats eliminated the Independents and remained in sole control of the government.

1. AT FIRST THE TWO SOCIALIST PARTIES PARTICIPATE EQUALLY IN CONTROL.—On the 9th of November early in the afternoon Ebert had received from the former Imperial cabinet his functions of Chancellor of the Empire. He considered himself such at the time. His intention was to nominate Scheidemann and Landsberg as secretaries of state, but to keep in the cabinet the old state secretaries; in addition to which the Independent Socialists were to enter the government. He proclaimed immediately several decrees signed, "Chancellor of the Empire, Ebert."

It must be observed that up to then the change which had been brought about constituted without doubt a revolution, but a revolution remarkably moderate. It is true that constitutional right did not give the Chancellor the authority to name his successor; from the legal point of view the nomination of Ebert certainly constituted a violation of the old constitutional law. Nevertheless in its outer aspect the new government with Ebert at the head sought to appear as the expression of the will of the former government. The idea of a radically new law had not yet made its appearance.

In the course of a few hours, however, the situation completely changed. The Independents submitted as the condition of their entry into the government the following twofold demand: The cabinet was to consist only of socialists, and it was to recognize officially that political sovereignty resided in the hands of the Workers and Soldiers Councils. The next day the Social Democrats accepted these conditions —for the Independents were still the actual power in control and "the street belonged to them"—and a government of six chiefs was constituted. It comprised three Socialist Democrats, Ebert, Scheidemann and Landsberg, and three Independents, Haase, Dittmann and Barth.[1] In the evening there was held at the Busch Circus a plenary session of the Workers and Soldiers Councils of Berlin. This assembly passed a resolution which declared among other things the following: "Old Germany is no more. The dynasties are gone forever. The holders of thrones are stripped of their power. Germany is now a Republic, a Socialist Republic. The Workers and Soldiers Councils are now the holders of political power." Then the assembly nominated an executive committee (Vollzugsrat) of twenty-four members, six Social Democrats, six Independents, and twelve Soldiers, and they proclaimed as the men in control of the government the six named above.

Following this meeting the cabinet was constituted. It formed a "college" of which all the members had equal rights and which took the name of "Council of Commissars of the People (Rat der Volksbeauftragten); Ebert and Haase were nominated chairmen. All the decrees of the government would have to be promulgated by these two in accord and signed jointly by them. It was, so to speak, a Chancellorship of two.

The Council of Commissars of the People thus found itself invested with political power by the General Assembly of the Councils of Workers and Soldiers of Berlin. Making immediate use of its power the Council of Commissars issued on November 12, 1918, a proclamation which constituted a declaration of rights of the new régime: The state of siege was revoked. Freedom of assembly and meeting were restored without restriction. All political offences were amnestied. The eight-hour day went into effect on January 1, 1919. All elections thereafter would be held on the basis of equal, direct, universal suffrage based on proportional repre-

[1] It is interesting to note that with the exception of Barth all these men were members of the Reichstag before the Revolution.

sentation for all men and women who had passed the twentieth birthday, etc.

But difficulties arose soon between The Council of Commissars of the People and the Executive Committee of the Workers and Soldiers Councils of Berlin. Each of these two bodies considered itself the chief holder of sovereignty and launched proclamations issuing orders. It became absolutely necessary to put precise limits to their respective powers. That was the object of an agreement reached by these two bodies November 22, 1918.

According to the terms of this agreement sovereignty belonged wholly to the Executive Committee. The Council of Commissars was to exercise executive power under the permanent control of the Executive Committee.

The latter had the power to nominate or recall members of the Council of Commissars. In reality the situation was somewhat different; for the Council of Commissars exercised to some extent legislative powers according to which it claimed the right to issue decrees that had the force of laws.

For a month the two bodies worked in this accord. Collisions occurred, of course. The functionaries of the old régime endured impatiently the supervision of the Councils of Workers and Soldiers. Inflaming rumours circulated of the extravagance with which these Councils managed the public finances. Worst of all was the increasing opposition that developed all over the country to the Executive Committee of Workers and Soldiers Councils, which, consisting exclusively of Berlin members, claimed to represent the Councils of all Germany and which acted in effect as though it were delegated by the Councils of the whole country. The fact that on November 23 this Executive Committee had added to itself a certain number of delegates of Workers and Soldiers Councils of states other than Prussia, delegates who had authority to deliberate in matters that concerned all of Germany, did not

THE REPUBLIC OF THE COUNCILS 21

strengthen the position of the Executive Committee. Meanwhile, however, its machinery appeared to be functioning.

2. THE SOCIAL DEMOCRATS ELIMINATE THE INDEPENDENTS AND REMAIN IN SOLE CONTROL.—In the struggle that ensued among socialists, the Social Democrats brought to their side the support first of individual states, then that of a general Congress of Workers and Soldiers Councils.

1. From November 10 Ebert and his party showed an increasing determination to call a constituent assembly. However, they did not attempt to act upon it at once, being restrained by the strength that still lay in the hands of the Councils. But on November 25 under the name of "the conference of German Federated States" there was held at Berlin a meeting of representatives of the revolutionary governments of several states. It was presided over by the Commissar of the People, Ebert.

Speaking of the forthcoming constitution, Ebert declared, "The system of collaboration between the government of the Reich and the Federated States, which should be very definitely specified, must be established by a National Assembly. The government has firmly resolved to call this National Assembly with the least delay. Till then nothing but a provisional agreement can be effected between the Reich and the States." In the course of the discussion the most conflicting opinions possible were expressed; but finally the immense majority of the delegates present adopted the following twofold resolution:

"It is to a National Assembly that the power of establishing the constitution of the Reich should be entrusted. Till such a time, however, the Workers and Soldiers Councils are the representatives of the will of the people."

Strengthened by this decision the Council of the Commissars of the People promulgated on ·November 30 a decree for the election of a National Assembly.

2. It was the general congress of Workers and Soldiers Councils at its meetings in Berlin from December 16 to 20, more than any other factor, that gave the Social Democrats the opportunity they had been seeking to disembarrass themselves of the Executive Committee of the Workers and Soldiers Councils of Berlin; and by this means to deliver a decisive blow at the system of Councils as a whole. The Social Democrats had an overwhelming majority in this congress and the delegates, well disciplined and little familiar with parliamentary debate, carried out punctiliously the instructions which had been given them by the official spokesmen.

The congress passed a number of important resolutions:

a. *The Councils or Soviet System is rejected.*—On December 19 by a vote of 334 against 98 the congress rejected the motion made by Daümig that "under all circumstances the Councils system shall be adhered to as the basis of the Socialist Republic in the sense that the Councils shall possess supreme legislative, executive and judiciary powers."

b. *The Council of the Commissars of the People is strengthened.*—The congress, which declared itself invested with complete political power, delegated legislative and executive power to the Council of Commissars of the People up to the time the National Assembly convened. Further, it nominated a central committee (Zentralrat) of the Workers and Soldiers Councils of Germany, consisting of twenty-seven members which was to exercise parliamentary control over the German and Prussian cabinets; that is to say, according to the official explanation of Commissar of the People Haase, all projects of law must be submitted by the Council of the Commissars of the People to the Central Committee and discussed by them. The Central Committee had the right to appoint and recall Commissars of the People for Prussia and for the Reich. Finally the Council of the Commissars of the People was to appoint to each Secretary of State two delegates, a Social Democrat and an Independent, who would be charged

THE REPUBLIC OF THE COUNCILS 23

with the conduct of affairs within the ministries. As for the Executive Committee of the Workers and Soldiers Councils of Berlin it was limited by the congress to authority only in matters pertaining to the Berlin group.

c. *Elections for the National Assembly are held January 19, 1919.*—The victory of the Social Democrats was complete. The Independents, because of the small number of representatives they had elected, refused to form a part of the Central Committee, which thereupon consisted only of Social Democrats and was presided over by Leinert, then by Max Cohen, both very moderate in their opinions. The conflict between the Executive Committee of Workers and Soldiers Councils of Berlin and the Central Committee never gave the government any trouble.

But the Independents and the Spartacists had not at all decided to give up the game, for they believed themselves to be at least "masters of the street." And Christmas week of 1918 in Berlin was a bloody one. A detachment of marines which had installed itself in the royal castle and had refused to leave it in spite of the orders of the government of Prussia had tried to capture Commissars of the People, Ebert and Landsberg, to keep them as hostages against the non-payment of wages due them. Their attempt failed and troops were summoned by the government to force the sailors to leave the castle. Bloody fights ensued in Berlin which lasted till Christmas.

These events produced a crisis in the government. On December 29 the Independents, Haase, Dittmann, and Barth, resigned from the Council of the Commissars of the People; whereupon the remaining three Commissars immediately handed their resignations to the Central Committee. The latter reappointed the three Social Democrats and completed the Government by adding to them three new Commissars, all Social Democrats, Noske, Wissel, Löbe. Löbe declined and his post remained vacant; but Noske and Wissel entered the

Government. Scheidemann replaced Haase as co-president with Ebert.

The Independents and the Communists made another attempt. On January 3, the Independents who had entered the Government of Prussia handed in their resignations. But Eichhorn, since the revolution president of the Berlin police, refused to resign his powers and, being recalled, refused to relinquish his post. That was the signal for a veritable insurrection which had been called, not without reason, "the second revolution." Troops of Spartacists met in bloody encounters in the streets with the troops of Noske and the affair ended with the assassination of Karl Liebknecht and Rosa Luxemburg.

When, three days later the elections for the National Assembly took place, Germany found itself under an exclusively Social Democratic Government.

SECTION II

THE NATIONAL CONSTITUENT ASSEMBLY

The National Assembly elected on January 19, 1919, had as its foremost task the conclusion of peace and the creation of a new constitution for Germany. But in view of the problems that it was confronted with, it will be difficult to understand precisely how it was led to take this or that position and to know how to reconcile the intent of the different resolutions voted if one does not keep constantly in mind the spirit in which they were drawn up, the forces that met in conflict within the Assembly, and the proportion of strength they bore to one another—if one does not follow at least in its ensemble the long process of elaboration in the midst of which the work of the Assembly was accomplished.

1.—THE COMPOSITION OF THE ASSEMBLY.

The Constituent Assembly had been elected according to what was perhaps the most democratic suffrage ever known.

NATIONAL CONSTITUENT ASSEMBLY 25

All Germans were electors, men and women, soldiers and officers, poor and feeble, provided they had passed the twentieth birthday. All electors were eligible to vote who had been Germans for at least a year.

The election took place on the basis of general tickets which could not be "split," that is, an elector could not vote for candidates of different tickets; but facility was offered for parties to present lists in common.

The distribution of seats followed the system of proportional representation known under the name of Hondt.

These elections sent to the Assembly 423 deputies, of whom 39 were women.

At the extreme right were the German Nationalists (Deutschnationalen) with forty-two members. They were the former Conservatives of whom the least one can say is that they had learned but little from the war. It was the party of the big landed proprietors and the big manufacturers. Politically they declared themselves in December, 1918, in favour of the restoration of the monarchy and willing to accept a parliamentary monarchy. Economically they did not ask a single reform. Reactionary in politics they were in economic matters strongly conservative. Their leaders, Clemens von Delbrück, former minister of the Emperor and former chief of the Emperor's civil cabinet, Düringer, raised their voices whenever it was necessary to defend the old régime, opposing all diminution in Prussia's share of the government, and combatting every democratic institution.

To the left of them sat twenty-two members of the German People's Party (Deutsche Volkspartei). The name is new; their ideas resembled those of the former National-Liberals.[1] It was the party of business men. Of the future form of government they said nothing. In fact, most of them remained monarchists, but that was a minor question. Their

[1] See Jean de Granvilliers, *Essai sur le libéralisme allemand*, Paris, 1914.

main concern was to establish in a tranquil and well regulated state freedom of commerce and a guarantee of protection for private property. They did not shut their eyes completely to the realities of the hour and intended to scrutinize certain reforms which it would be useless to oppose; such as new governmental monopolies, the participation of workers in industry control, etc. They were nationalist in feeling and would not sign a peace except one that safeguarded the economic prosperity of Germany. They were democrats in the sense that they were in favor of a strict legal equality for all persons. This group was presided over by Stresemann, whose cleverness in manipulating the parliamentary game was widely recognized.

Then came the Centre with eighty-nine deputies. Of all the parties it was this one that remained since its inception most faithful to itself. Its programme had not changed. It contained several propositions which formed its solid framework and for which the party was prepared to fight with all its power: the union of Church and State, confessional public schools, liberty of instruction, etc. On the political and economical problems of the hour the Centre certainly had its opinions; but it always ended by conceding whatever was necessary to safeguard the essential principles of a religious state and of freedom of instruction. Among those elected to the Centre there were Fehrenbach, who presided over the Assembly, Trimborn, Professor Beyerle, and Erzberger, whose indefatigable activities and limitless fertility of resources assured him perhaps a preponderant rôle in the government for some months, and who as much as the Minister of Finance was to effect a fundamental reform in the German fiscal system.

Then came seventy-four Democrats. Their party was born after the revolution of 1918 of a fusion of the old Progressives with the group of National-Liberals who did not go with the *Volkspartei*. Their program was that of the classic liberal-

NATIONAL CONSTITUENT ASSEMBLY 27

ism: national sovereignty, universal suffrage, equality of right of all citizens, individual rights, the right of private property and commerce. They opposed the intervention of the State except in extraordinary circumstances. This party attempted to group about itself all Germans in favour of a bourgeois republic, and was resolute in its opposition to both reaction and revolutionary socialism. This group counted among its members some of the men whose personal worth impressed itself on the assembly and who played rôles perhaps the most important in the development of the constitution—Haussmann, president of the committee on the Constitution; Frederick Naumann, whose idealism had free reign when he proposed with Beyerle the list of fundamental rights and duties of the Germans; Dernburg, Minister for the Colonies under the old régime and Minister of Finance under the Revolution; Koch of Cassel, future minister, and others.

There were 163 Social Democrats. They formed the most numerous group in the Assembly but, accustomed to the facile negations of opposition they seemed little prepared for the constructive rôle, at that time particularly difficult, which their electoral success suddenly called upon them to exercise. Theoretically they declared themselves faithful to the programme of Erfurt and to the Marxian theory of the class struggle. But at the same time they declared their faith in democracy, opposed all dictatorship and counted only on universal suffrage and the parliamentary régime to effect their socialistic reforms. It is from this Social Democratic group that there came the three Chancellors who governed Germany while the National Assembly sat—Scheidemann, Bauer and Hermann Müller. It is to this group that belonged Legien, president of the German Federation of Labour, Wissel who as Minister tried in vain to organize systematic control of business, and the Ministers Noske, David, the deputy Sinzheimer, who drew up the remarkable report on the Workers Councils, and others.

Finally there came the group of Independents of whom there were twenty-two. They accused the Social Democrats of having betrayed the cause of Socialism. As for their own program they did not specify any measures more definite than did the Social Democrats. They contented themselves with demanding that socialization be immediately commenced in order to break capitalist domination, to promote production to the highest possible degree and to distribute the fruits thereof among all citizens. Their spokesmen were Cohn and Haase, former Commissar of the People, who was later assassinated in July, 1919.

To sum up one can present the following table of the forces of the respective parties in the National Assembly:

PARTY	VOTES	DEPUTIES
German National People's Party	3,200,000	42 (3 women)
German People's Party	1,200,000	22 (1 woman)
Centre	6,000,000	89 (6 women)
Democrats	5,600,000	74 (7 women)
Social Democrats	11,400,000	163 (17 women)
Independents	2,300,000	22 (3 women)
Other parties	500,000	9 (2 women)

Besides these, troops from the Western front sent two deputies, both Social Democrats.

2.—THE PROVISIONAL CONSTITUTION OF FEBRUARY 10, 1919.

The National Constituent Assembly met at Weimar February 6, 1919. It wisely avoided meeting in Berlin where it would be tempting prey for organizers of revolts and insurrections.

Elected by the people the Assembly incorporated the sovereignty of the people. It was the supreme power. That power was universally accorded to it.

The first question that had to be dealt with by the Assembly was that of a provisional government of Germany. It was true that a Constitution was to be adopted by the Assembly eventually; but that would be a labour of several months at least. Meanwhile it would be necessary for Germany to be governed in its internal affairs by some authority created in the spirit of democracy, one which could be represented abroad by delegates of the German people. A provisional constitution would have to be adopted, and adopted at once.

On February 8 Secretary of State of the Interior Preuss submitted a draft of a provisional government of the Reich. It was only an improvisation. Commencing with January 25, 1919, a conference of more than one hundred representatives of different states met with the Minister of the Interior to consider the project of this provisional constitution. The draft presented by Preuss was approved by them. This gave assurance that no fundamental objections would be raised. On the other hand, to assure a quick vote on it the author of the project had prudently avoided all vexing questions whose immediate settlement was not indispensable; and on the questions which he had to treat he wisely did so in the spirit of compromise. Thanks to these precautions the draft by Preuss was adopted on February 10. It dealt with these four points:

1. CONSTITUTIONAL LAWS.—The National Assembly was to retain all power in dealing with this province. Elected above all to furnish Germany with a constitution this was its essential work.

Only the Assembly could decide constitutional questions and could do so without consulting anybody else. Meanwhile, however, although keeping control the members could limit themselves, if they wished, in authority—and this is one of the instances in the provisional constitution characterized by its spirit of compromise—if this limitation seemed to them in the general interest and necessary to the prompt accomplishment of their work. In fact, the National Assembly limited itself in this matter of the constitution only on one point, a fundamental one—the territorial status of the states. According to Article 4, paragraph 2, of the law dealing with that question "the territories of the component republics cannot be modified except by their consent." This meant that the sovereign National Assembly did not permit even itself to change the territorial map of Germany. Minister Preuss explained to the Assembly that he had to make this concession, for they could not with a stroke of the pen and by a simple decision change the boundaries of the respective states without their consent. This provision was necessary to reassure the states, being given especially in view of the announced intentions of the government of the Reich on a territorial regrouping and a partition of Prussia. But it was distinctly specified by Preuss that this provision would hold only until the definitive action on the Constitution by the Assembly. For in this Constitution the National Assembly could of its own accord and without limitations take whatever decision it wished. In other words after the definite adoption of the Constitution the states could no longer invoke article 4, paragraph 3 of the law of February 10, 1919, in order to oppose the operation of article 18 of the Constitution of Weimar,[1] in case an individual state were so minded.

2. ORDINARY LAWS.—The National Assembly had other work to do besides the Constitution. They recognized (Article 1 of the law of February 10, 1919) that beside the Constitution they had to vote "other urgent laws for the Reich." But here in contrast to the procedure in the adoption of constitutional laws the National Assembly did not adopt laws except in agreement with the representatives of the individual states. No project could become a law until it was accepted both by the representatives of the individual states and by

[1] See page 73, *et seq.*, of this book.

the National Assembly. For this purpose the law of February 10, 1919, created a Commission of States.

This Commission recalled in several respects the old Bundesrat but differed fundamentally in certain other respects. It was composed of representatives of all the German states whose governments were based on the confidence in them of their representative assemblies elected by universal suffrage. Each state had at least one vote; but the more important states could have additional votes; one vote for every million inhabitants, and a fraction in excess would be counted as a supplementary vote provided that fraction was equal at least to the number of inhabitants of the least populous state in the Reich. No state was allowed more than two-thirds of the total number of votes. Some writers find this reform important. "The traditional proportion of representation is broken," writes Apelt in "Das Werden der neuen Reichsverfassung, Deutsche Juristen Zeitung," 1919, p. 205. "It has been replaced by the modern principle of the distribution of influence according to the number of inhabitants." But we must not delude ourselves. The application of paragraph 2 of the law of February 10 resulted in the following: Prussia had 19 votes, Bavaria 7, Saxony 5, Wurtemberg 3, the Grand Duchy of Baden 3, the Grand Duchy of Hesse 2; the other states one each, in all 58, and after the fusion of the two states of Reuss, 57. Thus Prussia had two votes more than in the Bundesrat, Bavaria and Saxony each one vote more, Wurtemberg, Hesse, Mecklenburg-Schwerin and Brunswick each at least one vote. If one considers the loss of Alsace-Lorraine and the disappearance of the two Reuss states it is quite remarkable to note that in the Bundesrat and in the Commission of States the total number of votes was exactly the same and the distribution almost the same in both.

However, the Commission of States differed in other respects from the Bundesrat, especially in authority. It is true that as formerly no law could be enacted except with the approval of the Assembly. But now the centre of gravity of political power passed from the Assembly of States to the popular assembly. From this came the following consequences: formerly if a projected law emanating from the Presidency of the Empire did not secure a majority in the Bundesrat it could not be considered by the Reichstag, and was thereby definitely buried. Whereas now the government could submit for decision by the National Assembly a project which had been rejected by the Commission of States. Formerly, too, in a disagreement between the two assemblies over a projected law which the Reichstag had accepted but the Bundesrat had rejected, the last word rested with the negative party, that is to say, the Bundesrat, where naturally the project was buried. Now, however, the government was never bound by a decision of the majority of the Commission of States and it could always bring a project up again before the National Assembly, which had been defeated in the Commission. The members of the government of the Reich and those of the Commission of States had the right to participate in the National Assembly and defend their respective points of view; but it was the National Assembly that always made the final decision. If, however, a discord between the two Assemblies could not be broken the President of the Reich had the right to submit this difference to a popular referendum for decision. This situation, however, has not as yet presented itself.

The differences between the former Bundesrat and the new Commission of States were considerable. The champions of a united Reich criticized the Commission as an obstacle to the foundation of a united German Republic and this objection seemed from their point of view justifiable. It must be noted also that the provisional constitution does not specify which, the state's parliament or its government, in each member state nominates the delegates to the Commission. We know only that the members of the Commission of States had an imperative mandate, for its representatives defended the point of view of their governments.

A law became operative when it was adopted by both the National Assembly and the Commission of States.

3. THE PRESIDENT OF THE REICH.—The Provisional Constitution placed at the head of the Reich a president.

The president of the Reich had to be elected by an absolute majority of the National Assembly. He was to remain in power until the inauguration of the president elected in conformity with the permanent constitution.

To avoid discussions which would retard the adoption of the law and not to have to specify the powers of the president the provision attributed to him generally the powers of a chief of state in a modern republic.

However, the Provisional Constitution specifically described the authority of the president on certain particular points which because of special circumstances and on account of German traditions were especially delicate. The right to declare war and to conclude peace was taken away from him and given to the National Assembly. He represented the Reich, however, in foreign relations, accredited and received ambassadors and signed treaties. But in this last respect his right was limited by two restrictions. He could not without the consent of the National Assembly and of the Commission of States conclude any treaty containing matters on which the authority rested with these bodies; and were Germany to enter a league of nations that excludes secret treaties, all the treaties with states which are members of that league would have to be submitted to the approval of the National Assembly and the Commission of States. In other words, secret treaties were in principle forbidden; but in order not to place Germany in a disadvantageous position with regard to other states it was specified that this prohibition would be effective only in regard to treaties with other states that forbade secret treaties.

4. THE MINISTERS.—The president of the Reich nominated a ministry charged with the government of the Reich.

The law specified nothing on the organization of the ministry. However, there were several provisions which clearly indicated an essentially parliamentary régime. Thus ministers could remain in power only as long as they had the confidence of the Assembly. Decrees and ordinances of the president were operative only when signed by a minister. The ministers were responsible to the National Assembly for the conduct of their departments.

The provisional constitution of February 10 became operative immediately upon its adoption.[1] Two series of acts thereupon naturally followed.

First the authorities who received their powers from the Revolution resigned these into the hands of the National Assembly. On February 10, Commissar of the People Scheidemann declared before the Assembly, "Since the National Assembly is in session and the Provisional Constitution is adopted the historic mission which had been entrusted to us as a provisional government is terminated. We return the powers which we have received from the Revolution into the hands of the National Assembly."

The next day, February 11, there was read before the Assembly a letter from the Central Committee of the German Socialist Republic in which three propositions should be noted. First, the Central Committee returned to the German National Assembly the powers which it had held by virtue of the authority given it by the Congress of Workers and Soldiers

[1] German jurists get much pleasure in pointing out the following constitutional curiosity: the condition necessary for a law enacted by a parliament to become operative is that this law shall be promulgated, that is to say, authenticated and published. But these operations suppose a government. Now, the law of February 10, created the government; but this law could not be promulgated by a government which this very promulgation would create. It was decided, therefore, that the law should become operative immediately and be authenticated by the President of the National Assembly.

Councils. Secondly, it demanded the incorporation of the Workers and Soldiers Councils in the future Constitution of the Empire to strengthen the representation of the workers and to defend the interests of the producers as well as to assure a popular organization of the Empire's armed forces. Thirdly, it opposed with utmost energy the dangerous reappearance of the rights of sovereignty of individual states when these rights went beyond the domain of questions affecting the autonomy and the culture of the states.

There remained the task of organizing the new government in conformity with the provisions of the law. On February 11, Commissar of the People Ebert was elected President of the Reich by a vote of 277 out of a possible 328. He resigned as deputy and named a ministry headed by Scheidemann. As David, who had been elected President of the Assembly, was also appointed member of the Ministry without portfolio he was replaced as President of the National Assembly by Fehrenbach on February 12.

3.—THE ADOPTION OF THE CONSTITUTION AND THE SUPPLEMENTARY LAWS.

The elaboration of the permanent Constitution lasted nearly seven months. There were preliminary drafts, drafts and supplementary drafts; which were studied in conference with the states, in sub-committees and committees, and in full session of the National Assembly with countless changes and modifications up to the last minute.

The man who was constantly in the breach throughout all this labour and who may be considered the principal author of the Constitution was Professor Preuss.

Before the Revolution he belonged to the Progressive Party; after which he joined the Democrats. Under-secretary of State for the Interior, on February 15, 1918; Minister of the Interior in Scheidemann's cabinet of February, 1919; representative of the government at the National Assembly to discuss the Constitution when, in June, 1919, he left office; it was on him from the beginning to end that the chief burden of these discussions rested. Master of constitutional law he showed himself in politics essentially a realist. He fought stubbornly for the ideas he put forward in his first draft—the necessity of unifying the Reich and dismembering Prussia, the need of creating confidence in democracy, the superiority of a parliamentary régime. He fought for these to the very end with vigour of argument and such fertility of resources that the greater part of his ideas survived every attack. Certainly the definitive text of the Constitution is quite different from his original project; Preuss did not underestimate the forces and influences with which he had to deal; nevertheless he won great support on his principal issues and he is really the chief artisan of the work of Weimar.

The Constitution was adopted on July 31 by a vote of 262 for and 75 against. Those who voted against it were the German Nationalists, the German People's Party, The Independents, The Bavarian Peasant Union, and several members of the Bavarian People's Party, among them Dr. Heim.

It was promulgated and published on August 11, 1919, and became operative at once.

Having concluded peace and adopted the Constitution the National Assembly, it would seem, should have dissolved. But it did not. It had the authority to fix the duration of its mandate. The Assembly considered that its work was not finished on August 11, 1919, two tasks still remaining to be accomplished; the first of these to draw up and pass the principal laws needed for the application of the constitution. The latter in a number of its provisions necessitated the passing of a series of special laws and ordinary laws regulating details which, in the course of the deliberations on the Constitution, the members could not find time to enact or on which they had not been able to agree. Among such were laws regulating the election of the Reichstag and of the President of the Reich, laws on initiative and referendum, on the state of siege, the army, Workers Councils, and Economic Councils, laws regulating the transfer of railroads and postal systems of the various states to the control of the Reich, etc.

The Assembly in addition considered itself bound to study and pass laws of a character not necessarily constitutional but urgently needed by the Reich. In the front rank in importance were the laws designed to create the financial resources of which the Reich had great need in order to meet the enormous charges imposed upon it by the treaty of peace, the losses of five years of war and the increased public expenditure. It was also urgent to enact laws governing pensions and indemnities to the wounded, the mutilated, and the widows of the war, etc.

But from the moment the Constitution entered into force on August 11, Germany was under a new constitutional régime. It was no longer the régime of the Provisional Constitution of February 10, 1919; that Constitution was abolished by the definitive one. Nor had it as yet entered on the complete régime of the definitive Constitution; for that provided for a Reichstag, and no one would dream of calling a Reichstag to sit at the same time as the National Assembly. It was a transitional régime; from August 12, 1919, to June 6, 1920, the Constitution of August 11 was in force but the National Assembly performed the function of the Reichstag, and the President of the Reich, elected by the National Assembly, remained in office until the people should elect his successor (Article 180 of the Constitution).

In conformity with this decision on August 21, 1919, President of the Reich, Ebert, took the oath of allegiance to the new Constitution before the National Assembly in the course of its last session at Weimar.

From September 30 on, the Assembly sat in Berlin in the palace of the Reichstag, where it discussed and passed important financial legislation, which included "a law on the income tax"; another "on a consumption tax on liquors"; and still others dealing with "factory councils and with the relief of public distress throughout the Reich."

In the early part of March, 1920, the parties of the Right, who hoped by means of new elections to obtain considerable increase in strength, submitted a proposal in which the Reich was asked to make known at once what projects for laws it expected to submit to the Assembly before its dissolution; and demanding that the Assembly submit as soon as possible proposals regulating the elections to the Reichstag, the election of the President, on initiative and referendum; and in addition proposing that the Assembly declare itself dissolved on May 1, 1920. This motion was defeated on March 10 after the Minister of Interior, Koch, had indicated the laws which still remained to be enacted. He insisted on the necessity of a profound study of the project of the law governing the election of the Reichstag; and that the first Reichstag of the Republic should not be elected according to the provisions of a temporary and little studied law. He declared that the National Assembly could not be dissolved nor the elections held before the autumn of 1920.

But two days later came the *putch* of Kapp and Lüttwitz. Berlin fell into the hands of a military faction who announced openly their determination to bring back the old régime. The regular government fled to Stuttgart, where it hastily convoked the National Assembly. A general strike was declared everywhere. Defeated by this, Kapp and Lüttwitz fled and the regular government came back to Berlin. But the workers refused to resume work without receiving first the guarantees they considered necessary against the return of the military dictatorship. Then followed also troubles in the Ruhr and the occupation of German cities on the right bank of the Rhine by Franco-Belgian troops.

All these events were too important and upset too profoundly the political situation to make it feasible to go on without an immediate consultation with the people of Germany. Therefore, after hastily enacting the last of the immediately urgent laws, particularly electoral provisions, the Assembly dissolved at the end of May, 1920.

CHAPTER II

TOWARD A UNITARY STATE

The first question with which the National Assembly found itself confronted and which had to be decided was whether the German Reich was to remain a federated state or whether it was to become a unitary state; or, supposing that an intermediate solution were obtainable, to what extent it could partake of the characteristics of one or the other type of state.

The unitary state possesses an undivided and exclusive sovereignty. There is unity of law, of power and of will with one Constitution, one administration and one authority. The type of such a unitary state is France. To the unitary state is opposed the composite state in which co-exist several sovereignties, those of the member states as well as that of the central government.

For, there are two principal types of federated states: the confederation of states, which has as its basis an international treaty and the expression of whose will is only the sum total of the wishes of its member states; each component state retains its sovereignty, but certain attributes of that sovereignty are exercised in common through the confederate organs. The other type is the federal state, which has as its basis a constitution and which possesses a sovereignty necessary for the performance of its duties, the exercise of its rights and its independent will.

But it goes without saying that these concepts are essentially relative. Between the unitary state and the confederation of states lies a whole series of state types, one merging by imperceptible nuances into the other, types which differ one from another according to the extent to which the member states are called upon to collaborate in the formation of the common will. Further, the federal state is never static, in the sense that its institutions never cease to change, tending either toward unitarism—that is to say, toward the tightening of the federating bonds or even toward their disappearance through the complete fusion of the component states; or tending toward federalism, that is to say, toward a loosening of the bonds, or even their disappearance by the dissolution of the composite state.

There are undoubtedly in every composite state at the same time tendencies of both kinds. Theoretically they may even act as balances to one another. But this equilibrium is never completely realized and according as one of these tendencies gains over the other, the composite state tends more or less rapidly toward unitarism or toward federalism.[1]

Before the war the German Empire was a federated state with unitary tendencies. Since the war these tendencies have strengthened. For, the downfall of the Empire and its army, the economic catastrophe which followed the war and aggravated the revolution, the separatist tendencies which have shown themselves here and there on German soil, and the financial burdens which have weighed on Germany all have

[1] These concepts of "unitarism" and "federalism" must be compared with "centralism" and "particularism," which correspond to them, but which, nevertheless, also differ from them. When one speaks of "particularism" one means, beyond the legal and political differences which may exist between the member states of a federated state, the peculiarities of race, special traits of culture, geographic and ethnographic characteristics which give to populations their own stamp and a distinct collective sentiment. Political "particularism" and federalist tendencies may co-exist naturally; but "particularism" is not necessarily anti-centralistic: a "particularism" inspired by the love of a little fatherland and its individuality gives to the population a certain national consciousness which is not necessarily antagonistic to the establishment of a strong central power. On the other hand "unitarism," if it preserves for the state the character of a federated state and does not tend to a complete fusion of the member states, may well recognize that races and provinces wish for individual existence and may be ready to accord them corresponding liberty.

convinced its leaders that to save Germany and to build it up there was but one means possible—to concentrate all the powers in the hands of those at the helm of the Empire, and as a consequence, to diminish to the greatest possible measure the powers of the member states (if not actually to suppress them completely) in order to give all efforts available a single direction and to utilize them to the maximum, avoiding at the same time all unproductive energy and all scattering of forces.

By what means did this evolution manifest itself? How far did the Constituent Assembly go toward unitarization of the Reich? Will the German Reich remain a federated state?

To answer these questions we must successively examine: (a) whether the states still exercise self-determination and particularly whether they remain masters of their territory; (b) whether the states retain the right to give themselves their individual constitutions and laws and to govern themselves; (c) and finally whether the states participate, as such, in the formation of the will of the Reich. This last problem will be examined in studying the organization of the public powers, particularly those of the Reichsrat. The present chapter will be devoted to the study of the first two considerations.

SECTION I

TERRITORIAL STATUS OF THE STATES

Territory is one of the essential elements of a state. In a confederated state the central government cannot force on the member states changes or exchanges of territory, fusions or parceling of their respective holdings. Such was in principle the régime prevailing in the old German Empire. The historic composition of the individual states as they were when their princes signed the federal pact in 1871 was guaranteed, and the territories of individual states were protected by the

THE DISMEMBERMENT OF PRUSSIA

Constitution in the geographic integrity they had when they entered the Empire.

The Constitution of Weimar on the other hand put forward the principle *of the mobility of frontiers.* But it was not until after the most violent and passionate discussions that this was adopted, and not without modifications that peculiarly limited its operation. For, what was foremost in the deliberations and constantly dominated them was neither more nor less than the question of the dismemberment of Prussia. The cardinal consideration was this: legally the majority of the problems of organization that the Constitution had to solve would depend for their solution according to whether Prussia would or would not retain its territorial integrity. But the political problem was also grave. Prussia remaining as such, would it not exercise again its former hegemony over Germany with all the attendant dangers to the domestic and foreign policies of the Reich, dangers of an obstinate reaction at home and of an insatiable pan-Germanism abroad?

1.—THE PROBLEM OF THE DISMEMBERMENT OF PRUSSIA.

In November, 1918, there was felt throughout Germany a very powerful centrifugal movement. The masses of the people saw in the Reich nothing more than an alliance of princes and Prussian domination. It was to the princes and to Prussia that they attributed the inexpiable fault of having begun the war and lost it. During several weeks of limitless despair, two cries were raised, "Down with the Princes!" and above that, "Separation from Prussia!" It must be added that behind these cries was partly the unavowed hope that by abandoning the Reich one could more or less escape the menacing consequences of defeat. The Reich seemed on the point of dissolution.[1]

But some men at once realized that if Germany was to be saved the one efficacious remedy was to revive in the people

[1] See Preuss, *Deutschlands republikanische Reichsverfassung,* p. 8.

the sentiment of national unity and to reconstruct the Reich on new bases. A unitary republic would have to be created and the domination of Prussia overturned.

These two fundamental objectives were self-explanatory and mutually compulsory. For, given the disproportion in power that existed between Prussia and the other states, the more one increased the power of the Reich to the detriment of the states the more one strengthened the domination of Prussia, for thereby Prussia was made all powerful within the Reich. If, therefore, the centralizing character of the Constitution was to be accentuated, the following dilemma would have to be confronted. Either Prussia as it was would have to be accepted by the Reich, in which case the German Republic would in reality become a unitary Prussian Republic in which non-Prussian parties would be subjected to the will of Prussia. Or, if this state of affairs was to be avoided and a unitary state with central will was desired, Prussia would have to be suppressed, either by a partition of her own accord or one imposed upon it by the Reich.[1] It was this latter alternative that Under-Secretary of State Preuss chose when he was put in charge of the drafting of the Constitution.

The individual states, he pointed out, were the products of purely dynastic politics which almost everywhere ran counter to the natural relations of populations and races, separating what should have been united and uniting elements that had nothing in common. Only the republic has the possibility—it is also its duty—to reunite what belonged together. The fundamental question of the internal organization of Germany is, can a centralized Prussian State be maintained within the future German Republic? This question Preuss, after philosophical, historical considerations, answered in the negative. He demanded the territorial redistribution of the states on the basis of the right of populations to self-determination, according to their needs and their political and

---

[1] See Jacobi, *Einheitsstaat oder Bundesstaat*, Leipzig, 1919.

THE DISMEMBERMENT OF PRUSSIA

economic inclinations, with the intervention, by the sanction and under the direction of the Reich. Preuss insisted throughout on the fact that Prussia is not a nation, but that she constitutes an artificial formation, due to the political hazards of a reigning house, purchases, marriages, conquests, etc. The Prussian state does not form an organic whole and is bound together neither by economic nor cultural relations. It is an incomplete German state, "an edifice of fortune." Even admitting that it had been for a time indispensible, in that it constituted to a certain measure an internal bond, it has now outlived its usefulness as a state. The national unity of Germany as a whole is a vital question for the German people and therefore for the German Republic. It is imperative that the diverse races who lived in forced unity in Prussia should be at once placed under the sovereignty of the Reich instead of being "mediatized" by a state that interposes itself between them and the Reich. It is only by the suppression of Prussia that these populations can secure that equality which is their right by the side of the other German states. It is only by the dismemberment of Prussia that the small states of North and Central Germany can make themselves communities able to survive. That an incompletely unified state of forty million Germans, that is to say, Prussia, could co-exist with a more complete unity of seventy million Germans, is contrary to nature and is a political contradiction. The German people, therefore, must be free to erect within the Reich new German republics without regarding the actual boundaries of the existing German states, as far as economic conditions and historical considerations permit the formation of new states. Newly created states will have to have at least two million inhabitants each. The fusion of several member states into a new state can be effected by an interstate treaty drawn up by the states in question, and approved by their parliaments as well as the government of the Reich. If the population of a territory wishes to separate itself from the state to which it belonged in order to unite with one or more other German Republics, or to form for itself an independent republic within the Reich, a plebiscite must be resorted to.

These proposals aroused most violent opposition. In the meetings of the committees as well as in plenary sessions of the Assembly two declarations were constantly emphasized. On the one hand, matters could not remain as they were, for the interior boundaries of the country were too entangled and there were states too small and powerless to discharge conveniently their obligations. On the other hand, it was impossible to conceive a radical transformation and to hope to see realized a completely new regrouping if this had to be done on purely rational principles. Revolution could perhaps effect this transformation, but the Republic was not yet strong enough to undertake this task, particularly as it was so preoccupied with the problem of a constitution. Insistence on the complete solution of this problem, even if it did not invite complete failure, would mean too much loss of time. A compromise had to be found.

The terms of such a compromise were extremely difficult to find. For no change in the territories of the various states could be effected without encroaching on the territory of Prussia, which has "enclaves" or domains in most of the states whose transformation was contemplated. If even one were to content oneself with the fusing of several small states—which it was unanimously agreed was highly desirable—it could be done only by taking from Prussia such and such piece of its territory. No matter from what side, therefore, the problem was attacked one came to the question of the dismemberment of Prussia. And over this question came conflict.

Some of the members followed the lines of the proposal submitted by Preuss on the partition of Prussia; but they went much further and indicated precisely what territory they found necessary to take away from it.

THE DISMEMBERMENT OF PRUSSIA 47

It was above all the question of the Rhineland. Through Trimborn, spokesman of the Centre, deputies of Cologne and Aix-la-Chapelle, the inhabitants of the Rhine country presented their claims. Prussia, product of a political dynasty, is an aggregation of different races, for there is no Prussian nation. The people who live on the banks of the Rhine feel themselves handicapped in comparison with the other German races, since they are not in direct contact with the Reich, and are represented in it only through the medium of Prussia. It follows from this that the people of the Rhine cannot have free expression of their native tendencies nor develop their own culture. They suffer in every way by not having their own administration and by having to endure Prussian functionaries over them.

The objections which came from the Prussian side to the formation of a Rhine state were not valid, insisted the partisans of the latter. The separation of the Rhineland from Prussia need not entail in itself a separation from the Reich. On the contrary, the Rhineland would be more solidly and intimately welded to the Reich if they belonged to it directly instead of being only part of Prussia. Nor would they admit the argument that the Rhineland should belong to Prussia to supplement economically the relatively poor Eastern provinces of Prussia. "The old cry of the poor East and the rich West is to-day dead," the Rhinelanders insisted. War and revolution have done infinitely more damage to industrial Rhine than to the rural Eastern provinces. Finally, while it is possible that for a certain period, undoubtedly short, there might be disturbances in Germany caused by the creation of a new state, these would be less harmful than leaving on the Rhine a situation that would remain a permanent source of trouble. In conclusion, the representatives of the Rhineland demanded the creation of a Republic of the West, which should take in the provinces of the Rhine, a part of Westphalia and the territories of Oldenburg and Bremen.

On the other hand, the representatives of Hanover demanded justice against the violent annexation to which it had been subjected in 1866. There was formed in the Assembly a "German-Hanoverian" group which demanded "a free Hanover within a new Germany." It involved the fusion of Lower Saxony with Hanover and Brunswick.

In the same way the small states of Central Germany wanted to fuse into a single state which would take in also part of the territory of Prussia and the region of Erfurt, and would form the state of Thuringia.

To these claims the representatives of Prussia, particularly the Prussian Minister of Justice, Heinze, and the German Nationalist, Düringer, replied, that the separatists were rats who were deserting a sinking ship; and they presented a vigorous defence of Prussia.

Firstly, they insisted, Prussia is no longer what it was before the Revolution. Formerly it was a powerful state enjoying all the advantages of hegemony and all the privileges which came from the fact that the German Emperor was the King of Prussia. To-day, said they, Prussia, whose military backbone is broken, finds itself economically and financially ruined and all its ancient perogatives taken away. Furthermore, its former electoral system based on a class suffrage is gone and all the elements, including those of the Rhine, can make themselves equally felt thereafter.

Prussia as it now exists should be maintained, they went on. Its dismemberment would hurt the Reich more than it would serve it. Only powerful states, in command of important financial resources, can discharge the innumerable duties that to-day are incumbent on public organisms. Not only is Prussian culture necessary for the development of German culture, but the downfall of Prussia would involve the downfall of Germany; for Prussia is the cement that holds together the unity of the Reich, and renders services proportional to its greatness. Then, too, what would be the result

THE DISMEMBERMENT OF PRUSSIA 49

of a dismemberment of Prussia? Aside from the fact that the advocates of dismemberment are absolutely unable to indicate the number and extent of the states into which they would carve Prussia, its parcelling out would involve a considerable loss in power and spirit, in time and in money. For each new state will want to have new administrative apparatus complete in every respect, a separate constitution, a separate parliament, a separate legislature, and so on. These states by reason of their weakness will be unable to discharge the obligations that would fall upon them. Still further, nothing was more illogical than to create new states if one wants to realize some day or other the unity of the Reich; for, each of these states will constitute later on just one more obstacle to such a unity.

Finally, said the Prussians, Prussia, which has already given all and sacrificed all to the greatness of the Empire, is ready to renounce still more, for the benefit of the Reich, what still remains of its independence, provided, *that the other states do as much.*

But it was precisely this demand that made the proposition impossible of acceptance by the others. In "sacrificing to the Reich all that remained" of the ancient rights of Prussia, the latter in reality sacrificed nothing; on the contrary, it gained a great deal. For, mistress of the Reich as it would be, it would secure thereby not only everything it brought to it, but also all that the other states contributed to it. It was thus, therefore, that Preuss always came back to the same dilemma: either a Germany under Prussian hegemony or a Prussia dissolved into the Reich.

Following the position which they took on this question, the members of the Committee on the Constitution supported either the text adopted by the conference of States or the project put forward by the government.

It became indispensable to know who in the last instance would decide on the territorial distribution. The conference of states replied, that only the states concerned should have the decision, otherwise there remains no such thing as states. The government insisted that it alone should be the deciding power, for it was the natural arbiter between the states, and only it controlled the situation sufficiently to resolve the problem in accordance with the political and economic considerations that were involved. Only the Reich can accomplish the necessary redistribution according to a consistent plan. Such a redistribution would have to be regulated by a law. A third current of opinion in this question came particularly from the champions of the creation of a Rhine republic, who pressed for the submission of the question of territorial redistribution to popular referendum and insisted that the will of the population thus expressed should be the ultimate guide for territorial redistribution.

After a preliminary examination of the question the committee to which it had been submitted presented a project according to which territorial changes would be regulated by a law, which, however, would have to be demanded either by the people involved or by a predominant general interest. It would be the Reich that would decide this in the last instance. Against this first project of the committee, objections were raised on March 29 by the states of south Germany; and negotiations began between the government, the representatives of these states and those of the majority parties. On May 29, a compromise was signed which, after slight alterations on June 5 by the Committee on the Constitution, provided that territorial changes must be accepted in principle by the states involved, and approved by the Reich. If the states refused their consent these changes could not be effected except by a law that took the form of a Constitutional provision; but this law could not be enacted unless the populations affected demanded it or unless the preponderant general interest required it. This new version increased the rôle of the states but also augmented the difficulty of pro-

THE DISMEMBERMENT OF PRUSSIA

cedure in any dismemberment whatsoever. It did not, however, exclude the hypothesis of a dismemberment effected in opposition to the wishes of the interested states.

The debate came back again and again to this version; and when the question reached the second reading before the National Assembly there was presented an amendment drawn up by Löbe of the Social Democrats, Trimborn of the Centre, and Heile of the Democrats, which after very much discussion among the government and the representatives of the states modified considerably the version of the Committee on the Constitution. On the one hand, territorial modifications were facilitated in the sense that new states could thereafter be created, even against the desires of the interested states, by a simple law; for they wanted to avoid, for example, the situation in which Prussia or another state could completely prevent all territorial modification by rendering impossible the necessary majority for the vote needed to enact a constitutional law. On the other hand, the creation of such a new state was rendered more difficult in the sense that it considerably complicated the conditions according to which the populations affected could express their desires. But most important of all—and that was the principal provision of the amendment—it was specified that no territorial change could be effected against the wish of the states concerned before a period of two years after the formal adoption of the Constitution.

Thus Prussia was guaranteed for at least two years against dismemberment.

This last provision was aimed at the Rhineland whose situation, as it was clearly indicated at the Assembly, was at the bottom of all the discussion. It was declared that the Rhineland needed above all tranquillity in the particular circumstances in which it found itself; that occupied by foreign troops it could decide its territorial needs only with difficulty; and that, above all, the creation of a state on the banks of the Rhine would be considered abroad as a preliminary to the complete independence of this state from the German Reich; and that it was "necessary to maintain a unity of front against French imperialism." Along this line of argument it was further insisted that the dismemberment of Prussia has been the chief aim of the war waged by the enemies of Germany and the creation of a Rhenish Republic would be exploited by them as an additional victory. This resulted in the deputies from the Rhenish provinces declaring in the tribune of the Assembly their loyalty to the Reich and that whatever were their desires to see the Rhineland organized into a state, they would support the Löbe-Trimborn-Heile amendment including the postponement for two years of their justifiable claims.

The amendment was adopted by vote of 169 to 71, with 10 abstentions.

This version could not yet be considered as definitive, since when it came up for the third reading before the Assembly a new version was presented in the form of a new amendment by Löbe, Trimborn and Heile, which modified the original version. The changes proposed dealt with the method of calculating the majorities necessary in a popular vote to determine territorial changes. The Prussian Minister of the Interior Heine complained that the compromise previously adopted after such long debate had been modified at the last moment in the course of conferences to which the representatives of the states concerned had not been summoned. He preferred the original version; nevertheless he accepted the new one since he was convinced that the Constitution would have to be revised in several of its parts. He added several interesting declarations. It would be dangerous, he said, to seek to realize unity within the Reich by creating new states, which would almost immediately after have to abandon their newly won sovereignty and dissolve themselves into the Reich as a whole. That would be a useless detour. Heine pledged

CHANGES IN STATE TERRITORIES 53

himself to facilitate the creation of the state of Thuringia and to give up to it a part of Prussian territory on the condition that prior to this a treaty would be enacted between that state and Prussia regulating the administrative and economic relations between the two. But he opposed with vigor the proposition to create the state of Upper Silesia and above all opposed the creation of a Rhenish Republic. This Republic, he pointed out, would unite the territories of the left bank of the Rhine occupied by the enemy and the territories of the right bank administered by Prussia. Such a union far from safeguarding the German spirit on the left bank would incur the risk of submitting the right bank to the same influences that prevailed on the other, and thus create a considerable danger of infection to the right bank.

Finally the Löbe-Trimborn-Heile amendment in its new version was adopted by the Assembly.

At the same time the Assembly passed a resolution which invited the Government to institute a central office where the different states would be represented; one which would have as its function to prepare programmes for regrouping the territory in accordance with a general plan. In July, 1920, a commission was formed in the Reichsrat with the consent of the states to devote itself to this task. The Minister of the Interior for the Reich, Koch, summed up its programme as "federation and decentralization."

2.—CHANGES IN STATE TERRITORIES.

The territorial status of states is regulated by Article 18 of the Constitution.

This, as we have said, is a compromise; its leading idea is to fortify and draw closer the bonds of unity within the Reich on the basis of a new redistribution of territory according to economic and social interests and taking into account the wishes of the population. It is true that this has the value only of a programme without positive legislative force; nevertheless it has its importance; it presents the principle of a progressive revision of the territories of the states, a revision whose new unities would form organic divisions of the Reich such as would serve to a maximum degree the interest of the whole German people. The idea which should direct this territorial regrouping must be exclusively the interest of the German nation in its ensemble. The territorial status of the states no longer has as formerly a value absolute in itself, but is thereafter subjected to the condition that it assures in the largest measure possible the highest well-being of the Reich as a whole. There is in this undoubtedly a victory for the unitary idea.

Frontiers, therefore, will be "mobile" and their modification will have to serve the development of the general welfare. It will have to be the Reich that will be called upon to preside over the question of new repartition of territories, because it alone is the holder of sovereignty in Germany, and because it alone is in position to maintain an equal balance between the varied and particular interests of the states. No territorial change whatsoever, whether a fusion, a separation, or the creation of a state, will be possible or operative no matter what conditions exist for its consummation, *without a law enacted by the Reich.*

In addition—and this general rule must be followed every time that a change is envisaged which does not constitute an exception expressly provided for—such a law of the Reich must be enacted in the *form of a constitutional law.*

This rule has three exceptions in which an ordinary law of the Reich suffices, provided that a certain number of other conditions are realized.

(1) An ordinary law is sufficient when the change, the separation or the union of territories takes place *with the consent of the interested states.* This consent manifests itself in the form of a declaration of the governments of the states; for these governments by virtue of the constitution enjoy

the confidence of the people, since they are supposed to be both democratic and republican; in which case a plebiscite is superfluous.

(2) But cases may present themselves in which populations wish to separate from a state to which they belong, against the desires of the government of the state. The Constitution provides that the wish of these populations must be followed. According to Article 18 an ordinary law is sufficient to permit territorial changes or the creation of states if the interested states do not consent to it, but *if the wish of the population demands it and at the same time the preponderant interest of the Reich requires it.* This provision is evidently directed against Prussia; for should in such a case a constitutional law be demanded Prussia would command a sufficient number of votes in the Assemblies to prevent changes it did not wish. The dismemberment of Prussia is thus rendered theoretically possible by this provision. But we know that this provision is not applicable before August 12, 1921.

It remains to be seen how the wish of a population can manifest itself in the operation of the latter provision.

The population may either be consulted by the government of the Reich, which can order an immediate plebiscite; or the population can take the initiative and impose on the government of the Reich the obligation of ordering the plebiscite. This initiative must be signed by a third of the inhabitants of the territory whose separation is asked for. The plebiscite in such a case must be ordered by the government of the Reich.

Whether the plebiscite is ordered by the government or results from popular initiative, it must, to be effective, satisfy the following conditions of majority. They must obtain (a) three-fifths of the total number of votes cast; (b) a majority of the votes of the inhabitants entitled to suffrage; (c) and finally when the question is one of dividing a territory which wishes to separate from its state, the population of the whole district or administrative division of which it was a part must be consulted; this in order to avoid break-ups due to parochial quarrels. In other words, the plebiscite must extend to the whole district even if the part that wishes to separate forms only a fraction of this district. Nevertheless Article 18 provides for practical purposes one exception to this third condition. This refers to exceptional districts, that is to say, sections of territory that have no geographical kinship with the district to which they belong. In such a case a special law of the Reich could decide that the wish of the population of this special district is sufficient and that the entire population of the district to which it belongs need not be consulted.

The plebiscite having rendered an affirmative verdict the government of the Reich must submit to the Reichstag the project of law necessary to effect the changes in territory desired by the population.

(3) An ordinary law is sufficient *to modify the outer boundaries of the state*, that is to say, the frontiers of the Reich itself, when these are necessitated by a treaty of peace. When these modifications are to be effected otherwise than by the special case of a treaty of peace, the consent of the state affected must be obtained (Article 78).

Such are the provisions of the Constitution relative to the territorial status of the states, but it must be recalled that certain of these provisions—those which aim at territorial change based on the desires of the population but against the wishes of their state government—do not become operative until two years after the adoption of the constitution. Thus up to August 12, 1921, no parcel of the territory of Prussia, Bavaria, Hesse, Oldenburg, occupied by foreign armies, could be constitutionally taken away from their states without their wish. The aim pursued by the constituent Assembly in adopting this provision was to combat separatist attempts of powers whose armies occupy German soil, and to avoid all appearances and possibilities of dismemberment until revolu-

THE CREATION OF A STATE—THURINGIA

tionary effervescence and political disorders shall have come to an end.

3.—THE CREATION OF A STATE—THURINGIA.

The provisions which we have elucidated have already been put into operation. A new state has appeared in the Reich created by the fusion of several former states.

Almost immediately after the revolution of November, 1918, a project was born in central Germany to fuse several states there and to form of their territories the state of "Thuringia."

First the two states of Reuss reunited. On December 21, 1918, they organized an administration in common and the fusion became operative on April 4, 1919. This new state appeared thereafter as a sort of centre for crystallization. The first state to join this movement was the Republic of Altenburg, with which Reuss had many interests in common.

But this development toward the federation of states of central Germany was soon interrupted and seemed for a time even definitely arrested. The men who were pushing the project of extending this movement conceived the idea of the creation of a "Great Thuringia," which would comprise important parts of Prussian territory and which would have as the economic and political centre and as capital the Prussian city of Erfurt.

The execution of this plan aroused violent opposition on the part of the government of Prussia, such as it manifested whenever the question came up of the separation from it of any part of its territory. It encountered also the strong objection on the part of the authorities and the population of Erfurt who preferred the present advantage of belonging to the most powerful German state rather than the possible benefit of becoming an important element in a new state. The project of a "Great Thuringia" was abandoned and the effort continued as before to form a state which should comprise all the states of Thuringia without appropriating any Prussian territory.

Of the eight republics of central Germany included in this plan of fusion one, that of Coburg,[1] refused to join the movement. This republic, having on October 30 inaugurated a plebiscite to find out whether the population wished to belong to Bavaria or to the future "Thuringia," obtained 3,460 votes for Thuringia and 16,102 votes for Bavaria. This reunion with Bavaria was then consummated, with the consent of Bavaria, by a law of the Reich of April 30, 1920.

As for seven other republics—Saxe-Weimar-Eisenach, Saxe-Altenburg, Reuss, Saxe-Gotha, Schwarzburg-Rudolstadt, Schwarzburg-Sondershausen and Saxe-Meiningen—they concluded a "treaty" by which they combined in a "community" to prepare their complete fusion.

To this effect the treaty provided two organs:

(a) A popular Council, the legislative organ of the "Community," composed of representatives of each of the seven Diets;

(b) A Council of States, the executive organ, consisting of representatives of each of the seven governments.

These organs had as their mission to study and take all preliminary measures necessary for the fusion. To permit the accomplishment of this mission the states transferred to them all their legislative and administrative powers necessary. The laws voted by the popular Council were therefore compulsory in the territory of all the seven states. They were particularly operative over the governments and the administrative authorities of these states.[2]

[1] Since the Revolution, Coburg has detached itself from Saxe-Coburg-Gotha and become a distinct state without the decision of any authority whatsoever sanctioning this situation.
[2] There was in this a true provisionally federated state within a federal German state. For several months there was thus, in central Germany, a triple superposition of states.

The common organs were in addition instructed to prepare the Constitution of their future state.

When all these necessary preliminary provisions had been taken the Reich declared the fusion in being. All the interested states being in agreement with this step an ordinary law sufficed; and it carries the date of April 30, 1920.

SECTION II

THE DIVISION OF POWER BETWEEN THE REICH AND THE STATES

The unitary character of the Constitution appeared not only in the fact that it recognized in principle the right of the Reich to regulate the territorial status of the states. It appeared also in the clauses relating to the division of authority between the Reich and the States, provisions that took from the latter and gave to the Reich a considerable quantity of powers of a constitutional character as well as legislative and administrative.

1.—THE CONSTITUTION OF THE STATES.

The Constitution of the German Empire of 1871 recognized the right of the member states to choose whatever constitutions they desired.[1] The Empire never concerned itself with the form of government chosen by any of its states nor with the different provisions they inserted in their constitutions.

Germany was thereby the only federated state which thus left, theoretically at least, such a latitude to its member states. The United States and Switzerland, for instance, impose certain fundamental provisions on the constitutions of their component states, relating to the form of their State.

This latitude could not exist in the new Germany for the

[1] It must be recognized nevertheless that with the exception of the Hanseatic cities the monarchical form was implied. For Prussia it was obligatory.

Reich, having adopted a democratic and republican constitution, could not, without condemning the very principles on which it had been built, agree that such and such of the member states should remain monarchical. Proscribed in the Reich, monarchy would also have to be barred in the states. Also the co-existence of both monarchies and republics within the Reich would have something so inconsistent within itself that it would run particularly counter to the centralizing tendency which was being so eagerly promoted.

Article 17 therefore indicates to the states the bases on which they must erect their future constitutions, in order to insure a harmony of principles between the Constitution of the Reich and the constitutions of the states. These bases would have to be analogous to those serving as the foundation of the Constitution of the Reich. One can group these principles under three heads:

1. THE DEMOCRATIC PRINCIPLE.—All power springs from the people; as a consequence national representatives must be elected by popular vote; that is to say, they must be elected by all the Germans, men and women, by universal, equal, direct and secret suffrage following the rules of proportional representation. The same applies for municipal councils. On the other hand the states remain free to provide different modes of suffrage in elections in wards, districts and provinces.

2. THE REPUBLICAN FORM OF THE GOVERNMENT.—All monarchical restoration is forbidden.

3. PARLIAMENTARY GOVERNMENT.—But this provision was only desired by the Constituent Assembly; it is not strictly imperative. Preuss formally declared in committee meeting that any constitution, for example such as that existing in Switzerland, which provided for a council elected by popular vote, would be admissible; but there would be excluded a régime of despotism in which the government was completely

THE LEGISLATIVE POWER OF THE REICH

independent of the popular Assembly. It mattered little otherwise whether the state adopted the one-chamber system or that of two chambers.

These three principles were accepted without serious difficulty. A twofold point must, however, be noted. First that all Germans could vote in all the states for the election of the popular Chamber, that is to say, for example, a Bavarian could vote at the election of the Prussian Diet. This provision is one of the principles that suppressed almost entirely the nationalistic motive of the individual states; it is clearly characteristic of the unitary tendency of the constitution. In addition to this, Article 17 adds to the general conditions a special condition in the case of local elections: a year's residence in the district is necessary for the right to vote.

In the National Assembly the speakers for the parties of the Right insisted at great length on the difference that exists between political elections and purely local elections. In the latter it was necessary above all that the elector choose men known to be familiar with local needs and competent to satisfy them. These propositions are undisputable, but the conclusion which the German Nationalists drew from them was that to be an elector in a district one must be a holder of property in it. These conclusions were rejected by the Assembly as contrary to the democratic principle, and a year's residence was the only condition finally adopted.

2.—THE LEGISLATIVE POWER OF THE REICH.

The states are limited not only in their right to adopt whatever constitution they desire; they are also limited considerably in legislative power by that of the Reich.

I.—FUNDAMENTAL LIMITS OF POWER.

Already the Constitution of 1871 had reserved to the Reich a certain number of matters on which only it had the right to legislate. It was thus that foreign affairs, citizenship, customs, indirect taxes, railroads, post and telegraph, legislation, civil, penal and commercial, the army, the navy, the police and regulation of the press, all were included in the legislative authority of the Reich. In the memorandum submitted by Preuss in his draft of the Constitution, he insisted on the necessity of revising this division of authority. He submitted as a principle that all state functions belonging naturally to the national collectivity as such should be concentrated in the hands of the Reich more strongly, more exclusively and more clearly than in the preceding constitution. On the other hand, the autonomy and free administration of the smaller collectivities, from the communes up, would find their consummation and their most complete development in the republics, which should be constituted in united groups according to the nature of their populations and their economic structure.

In the course of this work two tendencies clashed: the necessity for the development and strengthening of the unity of the Reich; and the necessity, on the other hand, of assuring the states a sufficiently individual existence. A compromise was effected; but more than ever before perhaps the centralizing tendency was accentuated; and it has gone as far as possible without completely suppressing the reason for the existence of the states.

The authority of the Reich is more or less extended according to circumstances. It can be, to use the technical expressions employed in Germany, exclusive, concurrent, and normative.

1. The competence of the Reich is *exclusive,* when *it alone has the right to legislate,* in the respect that the states cannot pass laws on the matters touching this authority of the Reich, even if the Reich abstains from using that right. These matters are enumerated in Article 6, which contains, as compared with the former constitution, important innovations.

The relations with foreign nations are hereafter the exclu-

THE LEGISLATIVE POWER OF THE REICH

sive province of the Reich. The states lose the active and passive rights of legation, and they cannot enter into relations with foreign states except through the intermediacy of the Reich. However, Article 78 gives them the right to conclude treaties with foreign powers on matters which belong to their own proper legislative domains, policing of the frontier problems, for example. But these treaties must secure in addition the consent of the Reich.

Another novelty is the unification of the army. In place of the former contigents there is hereafter an army of the Reich in the hands of which is concentrated all the means of defence of Germany. The army is hereafter from this point of view placed on the same basis as the navy.

In the same way there is an increase in the authority of the Reich over the interior situation, the provisions according to which the Reich only has the power to legislate on posts, telegraphs, and telephones. It is true that the former constitution had put forward the principle that the posts and telegraphs of the German Empire should be organized and administered in a uniformed manner; but this provision and principle was nullified by the fact that it was not applied in Bavaria and in Wurtemberg, these states having in virtue of special treaties "particular" rights. But these rights were annulled by the present constitution.

Finally it must be noted that Articles 89 and 97 of the Constitution granted the Reich the right to administer the railroads and the waterways that served the general commerce. This right the Reich made use of in appropriating in April, 1920, the railroads belonging to the various states.

2. The second group of subjects entering the province of the Reich's authority consisted of matters on which the Constitution gave to the Reich the right to legislate *by priority*, without thereby excluding the legislative authorities of the various states, so that there could exist *concurrent legislation* in the Reich and in the States, the states retaining

the right to legislate as long as the Reich does not use its own right to legislate on these matters.

This group is defined in the Constitution by Articles 7, 8 and 9.

Article 7 sums up briefly, as did Article 4 of the old Constitution, the province of concurrent legislation, but adds considerably to the enumeration strengthening here the unity of the Reich and adding to the subjects which enter into the concurrent legislative competence of the Reich all such important matters as assistance and care to be given to mothers, infants, children and youths; also questions relating to professional representation, to the socialization of natural wealth, to economic enterprises as well as the organization of collective enterprises. To this, strengthening still further the competence of the Reich, Article 12, Section 2, adds that the government of the Reich has the right to veto laws passed by the states dealing with socialization, if these laws touch the well-being of the whole population of the Reich.

Article 8 introduces in the Constitution, in spite of the violent opposition of the states, the principle of financial sovereignty of the Reich and fiscal centralization therein. This article gives to the Reich the right to take possession of all sources of revenue, stipulating, however, that it must leave to the states resources sufficient for their existence. This provision constitutes an important advance along the road to the unity of the Reich and strengthens considerably the financial competence of the Reich compared to its former situation.

Article 9 also deals with the concurrent authority of the Reich in matters concerning the public weal and the protection of order and public security; but under this head there is the limitation, "to the extent that it shall become necessary to pass uniform legislation." This limitation, however, is of no particular importance, for as with the matters dealt with in Article 7 the Reich does not make use of its right of legislation except as it feels the need for it. The restriction provided by Article 9 is explained by the fact that the authority of the Reich in these matters naturally met resistance on the part of the states and that a compromise had to be effected; they came to the agreement that the Reich would not take up these questions in advance and in the first instance.

3. Besides "exclusive" and "concurrent" legislation there is also "normative" legislation. This is provided by Articles 10 and 11 and consists in the right of the Reich to *"lay down principles simply leaving the details to be enacted and carried out by the legislators of the state."*

According to Article 10 in this kind of legislation are included matters of vital importance from the points of view of culture and of social considerations. Already in its second part the Constitution enacts a certain number of principles to which both the legislators of the Reich and of the states are subjected.

Article 11 deals with the "normative" competence of the Reich over financial legislation of the states. It was necessary that the Reich legislate on this question for otherwise there was the fear that the states, in attending to their own financial needs, would drain sources of revenue needed by the Reich.

II.—AUTHORITY OF NATIONAL OVER STATE LAWS.

However precise and rigorous may be the division of the authority between the Reich and the states, conflicts may nevertheless arise between the two. In such cases it was natural that the Reich should claim for its laws, "the authority of Empire surpasses the authority of states."

3.—THE ADMINISTRATIVE SERVICES OF THE REICH.

Before the Revolution the Reich did not have in principle an administration proper to it; the execution of the laws of the Empire were as a general rule assured by the functionaries of the member-states under the control of the Reich. The new Constitution continued, it is true, the same principle but it provided exceptions of the first importance. Three hypotheses must be noted here:

1. Certain powers belong exclusively to the Reich. They are those which we have enumerated as contained in Article 6. The Reich has the exclusive right to legislate on these matters, but in addition it has also the sole right to execute these laws; that is to say, it creates and directs the administrative services necessary to assure the application of the provisions which it has the exclusive right to promulgate. Foreign affairs, the army, the navy, etc., are administered directly by the Reich. But in addition in matters that belong concurrently both to the Reich and to the State and which have been placed in the hands of the Reich the latter has created a special administration which it directs itself, that of finances.

2. In other cases in which the Reich has the right to legislate and uses it, *it yet leaves the care of the execution of these laws to the functionaries of the State.* Although these public services are instituted and organized according to the laws of the Reich the functioning is assured exclusively by the officials of the state. There was formerly, and there still is to-day, the hypothesis of authority in common in matters of public security, assistance and the Reich.

3. In a third series of cases, finally, the states have exclusive competence. *They may both legislate and administer.*

Of these three hypotheses the one most important from our present point of view is the first. The recognized right of the Reich to have public services designed to apply its laws and acts, permits it to organize public administrations and to have functionaries subordinate directly to the Reich throughout the whole German territory. The unity of the Reich is greatly strengthened by the fact that the principal public services—the army, finances, diplomatic corps, postal telegraphs, railroads—are hereafter completely concentrated in its hands.

In addition when the Reich fails to organize its own administration or when it has left to the states the task of legislating on subjects that are contained in the legislative competence of the Reich, the latter is far from being weakened in its power therein. For it possesses in such cases the *Right of Control* over the administrative authorities of these states, and this right was notably strengthened by the Constitution of 1919 as compared to its former power.

According to the terms of Article 15, paragraph 2, control by the Reich may be exercised by the government of the Reich in matters on which the latter has the right to legislate. That means that control on the part of the Reich extends not only to the domains which have been already assigned to it by the legislation of the Reich, but also to matters in which it has the right to legislate even though it has not yet made use of such right.

The means by which these rights of control are exercised are the following:

(a) General instructions addressed to the authorities of the states for the execution of the laws of the Reich. These instructions of the government of the Reich are compulsory on the different authorities of the states. But instructions to subordinate authorities of these states must not be given in particular applications of these laws, for otherwise these authorities might receive contradictory orders from different sources; and in that way the governments of the state might lose all authority.

(b) The control of the Reich is exercised in addition by sending to the governments of the states commissioners charged with the supervising of the execution of the laws of the Reich. Such commissioners may even be sent, with the consent of the governments of the states, to subordinate authorities. In the latter case it must be admitted even that the Reich has the right to demand that the files of the state authorities be opened to it and with the consent of the governments of the states the Reich may examine witnesses, take testimony and make surveys within the provinces of the state.

(c) Finally the Reich may demand that lapses observed in the execution of its laws be corrected.

The ensemble of all these measures constitutes a strengthening of the right of control by the Reich as compared to the former régime. On the one hand, the recognized right of the Reich to send commissioners to subordinate authorities with, it is true, the consent of the governments of the states, is new. Formerly such imperial commissioners were received only by the governments of the states themselves, instead of allowing immediate access to subordinates as to-day. In addition and above all when difficulties arise especially from the insufficiency of the measures taken by the authorities of the states, the power to settle these difficulties no longer belongs as formerly to a college constituted by the representatives of states, such as was the Bundesrat; but is now the function of the independent organs of the Reich, such as the government of the Reich or the High Court of Justice of the Reich.

4.—JUSTICE AND THE HIGH COURT OF JUSTICE.

The centralizing influence of the Constituent Assembly is manifested, finally, in the provisions which it adopted relating to the organization of justice. We know that in Germany justice, particularly such as is regulated by the laws on the organization of justice, the Code of Civil Procedure, the Code of Criminal Procedure, is administered by the tribunals of the states. The Reich had only one judicial organism, the *Reichsgericht,* whose powers are in principle similar to those of the *Cour de Cassation* (the highest court of appeal in France). The new Constitution has changed nothing in this system. A proposal submitted in committee for the purpose of giving the Reich full control over the administration of justice and making all judges functionaries of the Reich, was defeated. Now as before the sole authority of the Reich in this domain lies in the *Reichsgericht.*

But the Constitution has introduced a new judicial or-

JURIDICAL AND POLITICAL STRUCTURE 69

ganism whose authority extends over all important cases of a national scope, and constitutes thereby a powerful element in centralization: that is the High Court of Justice. The task of organizing this Court is left by the Constitution to a special law. Until this law enters into effect the powers of this Court are entrusted to a senate of seven members, of which four are nominated by the Reichstag and two by the Reichsgericht.

The authority of the High Court of Justice is regulated by the Constitution. It is this Court that passes on the difficulties that may arise between states in the cases of division of patrimony where changes or separations of territories are involved. It is this Court also that decides constitutional difficulties within a state when there is no competent tribunal within the state to deal with such a question. It is this Court that adjudicates disputes as to public rights that arise between different states or between a state and the Reich, when there is no other tribunal of the Reich that has jurisdiction over such a dispute. This Court in addition presides over actions instituted by the Reichstag against the President, the Chancellor and the Ministers of the Reich for culpable violation of the Constitution or the laws of the Reich.

SECTION III

THE JURIDICAL AND POLITICAL STRUCTURE OF THE REICH

Having described the provisions which regulate the distribution of authority and territory and mark the reciprocal relations of the Reich and the States we may now attempt to define the Reich and to give precision to its relation to the States, politically and juridically.

1.—IS THE REICH A FEDERAL STATE?

Formerly when one spoke of the German Constitution the question was, "Is the German Empire a federal state or a confederation of states?" To-day when speaking of the Constitution of Weimar the question is asked, "Is the Reich a federal state or a single state?"

Nearly all the German jurists have attempted to answer this question and are almost equally divided in the answer. Some of them observe that the states have no longer the power to fix the form of their governments and that they can no longer change the organic provisions of their Constitutions; that the Reich can prescribe changes in territory against their will and even order new formations of the country. The Reich is in control of sovereignty and of the life and death of German states. It may against their will deprive them of their sovereignty. The new financial constitution of the Reich, which entered into operation on October 1, 1919, has taken away finally whatever had remained of their state rights, and all financial powers of the states have passed into the hands of the Reich. The states are no longer independent states, they are only autonomous administrative bodies within the Reich. The Reich has become a single decentralized state.[1]

The other jurists emphasize the characteristics of the States which bring them nearer in nature to states properly so called. The Constitution has recognised that if sovereignty in the Reich emanates from all the people, sovereignty in the states also emanates directly from the people of those states. From this it follows as a logical consequence that this power is exercised within the states, in the matters within their jurisdiction and through the organs of the states on the basis of their Constitution. The Constitution has admitted that the states have their own proper territory since the territory of the Reich is composed of the territories of the state. The latter have also their own individual legislative and administrative

---

[1] See Giese, *Die Reichsverfassung, vom II, August, 1919*, p. 65; Jacobi, *Einheitsstaat oder Bundesstaat*, p. 6, et seq.; Poetsch, *Handausgabe der Reichsverfassung*, p. 25, et seq.; Wenzel, *Festgabe für Bergbohn*, 1919, p. 159, et seq.

JURIDICAL AND POLITICAL STRUCTURE 71

organizations. It need only be added that if the Reich disappeared the states could still subsist and continue to live according to their Constitutions, which proves that their sovereignty belongs to them and is not surrendered to the Reich. Finally, and this is the essential argument, in the Reichstag the states are represented as such and as such they participate in the formation of the will of the Reich. This makes it, therefore, a federated state.[1]

The National Assembly did not want to take a position on this question and of its own accord adopted an entirely colourless declaration on it which left the doors open to all opinions. While the individual states were called in the Constitution of 1871 "federated states," they were thereafter called "republics" in the Preuss draft, "member-states" in the draft submitted by the government and finally "länder" in the draft of the constitutional commission and in the definitive text.

Actually, however, it is difficult to understand the interest in this question. What difference does it make whether the states are states or provinces, so long as their powers and obligations are strictly defined by the Constitution? From their names alone we can deduce nothing practically informative about their nature. It is an academic question which has not progressed one step in three generations, which one studies but does nothing about, for there is no reality in it.

In fact it is not possible to indicate a precise and material criterion according to which one should differentiate between a state and an autonomous province which is not entitled to the name of state.

There are no clearly defined categories which one can label once for all and among which one can distribute the different state and provincial collectivities.

There are only collectivities that are according to different circumstances more or less broad in power. They differ one

[1] See Stier-Somblo, *op. cit.*, p. 79, *et seq.*; Walter Jellinek, Revolution und Reichsverfassung, in Jahrbuch des öffentlichen Rechts, p. 81; Arndt, Reichsverfassung, 1919, p. 35.

from another not in quality or in nature but in the quantity, in the total powers which they may exercise. Here all one can ask is, whether the states, as they are defined by the Constitution, resemble more the type generally called a state, or the type generally called autonomous province; and one can say, if one wishes, that they are more the former than the latter.[1]

2.—PRUSSIA AND THE REICH.

There is a second question of more immediate interest; and that is to know how the political forces in the Reich are divided and in what relation they find themselves one to another.

The Constitution has increased the power of the central state already great under the old régime as compared with the individual states; the states have lost considerably in their importance and this in the measure that the Reich has gained. They have undoubtedly the theoretical right to legislate; but the Reich legislates on all matters of any importance and the legislative domain of the states is thereby reduced almost to nothing.

They have in principle judiciary and administrative services, but in all important respects such as relations with foreign states, military administration, railroads, waterways, posts and telegraphs, their authority has been taken away; the whole domain of financial legislation has also passed to the Reich and they can no longer exist except through subsidies from the Reich.

They have a territorial sovereignty; but a constitutional

---

[1] In reality the states still exchange ambassadors and, in the official German language, the agreements reached either between two states or several carry the name of Staatsverträge (international treaties). See particularly the international treaty adopted between the Reich on the one hand, and Prussia, Bavaria, Saxony, Wurtemberg, Baden, Hesse, Mecklenburg-Schwerin and Oldenburg on the other, concerning the transfer to the Reich of the railroads of these states, the treaty approved by the National Assembly, April 30, 1920.

PRUSSIA AND THE REICH

law, and in certain cases even an ordinary law may modify that territory against their will.

They still have their citizens; but every German may exercise in every state of the Reich the same rights and duties as those exercised by a citizen of his own state.

In reality the states no longer count and the Reich is all powerful. Such is the situation in which the centralizing tendencies of the Constituent Assembly have culminated. But we come back to it in a problem that presents itself as follows: Has Prussia retained the hegemony which it exercised actually under the Empire and has it kept it to the extent that any increase in the centralizing character of the republic will only increase the power of Prussia in the Germany of to-day? Professor Schücking said one day to the National Assembly that all history of Germany past and future can be summed up with, "Up to 1867 Prussia was against the Reich; from 1867 to 1918 Prussia was above the Reich; the Reich must hereafter be above Prussia."[1] Will this consummation ever be attained? To what extent has the Prussian hegemony been diminished since November, 1918?

The Constitution embodies several important provisions affecting this question. Prussia has lost all the advantages it derived from the fact that the German Emperor was the King of Prussia; the privileges it enjoyed in the legislative initiative, in military matters and in fiscal affairs have disappeared; the Bundesrat, in which it played a preponderant rôle, and which was in itself the most powerful organ of the Empire, is now reduced to a Reichsrat which can no longer prevent anything. There is no longer a Chancellor nominated by an Emperor-King and chief of all the *politique* of the Empire and of the entire administration; the powers of the Emperor have been transferred to the President of the Reich elected by all the people; Prussia may even against its will—though not

[1] See Heilfron, *Die deutsche Nationalversammlung im Jahre,* 1919, vol. ii, p. 1176.

for two years, it is true—be deprived of several sections of its territory and see them erected into new states or attached to still other states. All these diminutions of right have been consented to by Prussia itself. Are they sufficient to suppress totally the political domination which Prussia exercised over the German states, small and great? It does not seem so, for there still remains this paramount fact: *Prussia represents four-sevenths of the total population of the Reich;* that is to say, Prussia alone has the majority. The Reich being a democracy wherein the majority is sovereign Prussia is assured in important questions of the opportunity to impose its will always on Germany.

The remedy is evidently to divide Prussia into several states. But the Constituent Assembly did not have the desire —or the force—to resort to this; so that to-day Prussia is still above the Reich.

Perhaps another remedy is possible; and it is on this that those who wish to place the Reich above Prussia base all their hope. That is to give to Prussian provinces a very broad autonomy in such a way that their powers being progressively increased, they will join little by little the states whose powers are diminishing. There must be effected a decentralization as complete as possible, in such a way that these provinces while still remaining in the state of Prussia will have sufficient means to be able to live individual lives and to impress their special temperaments on the different acts of their political life. It would be necessary—and it is there that the problem is most difficult—to maintain in these provinces Prussian legislation and at the same time give them the right also to legislate and assure them a sufficiently independent administration.

These are only projects and one cannot tell to what extent they are realizable. We shall see, however, that the Constitution of Weimar has timidly commenced an effort to realize them.

CHAPTER III

THE DEMOCRATIC PRINCIPLE

If the National Assembly has not completely realized the unitary state and has allowed traces of the federal régime to remain, it has fully admitted the principle of national sovereignty and has applied it to a greater extent than any other country in the world.

SECTION I

THE PRINCIPLE

The democratic principle was adopted by the majority of the National Assembly without any difficulty. But in the public opinion there became manifest certain tendencies which are either directly contrary to this principle or whose consistency with this principle is debatable; and some of them have received and are still gaining active and influential adherence.

It is important therefore to define in reference to the principle of national sovereignty the theories to which it finds itself subjected in practice.

1.—THE POWER OF THE STATE IS DERIVED FROM THE PEOPLE.

Democracy is defined as government by the people; a democratic government is a government in which sovereignty resides in the people, or, to speak more precisely, one in which the will of the majority determines sovereignty.

That this principle was completely ignored in practice in Germany before the Revolution we already know. According to the Constitution of 1871 sovereignty belonged to the ensemble of confederated princes, Germany being governed by an association of monarchs under the all-powerful direction of one of them, the King of Prussia.

Such a system obviously could not survive the disappearance of the monarchs themselves; and after the Revolution the democratic principle, to which Bismarck had given the semblance of expression in creating a Reichstag elected by universal suffrage, became fully applied. One consideration contributed above all to the establishment of government by the greatest number: The German Princes had governed and had conducted themselves as monarchs by divine right; under their régime no social class could develop to which a certain political power could be given over, which the people would become accustomed to regard as authoritative. There was in Germany no political nobility, no bourgeoisie invested with political power. So that when sovereignty fell from the weakened hands of the monarchs it could be taken over only by the people.

The people are therefore sovereign. German jurists go on to say that the people cease to be the object of sovereignty and become the subject of sovereignty.

But we are here in a federal state, and the problem becomes more complicated because of the particular form of the state. For there are here, in theory at least, two sovereignties: that of the Reich, and that of the State. Which is the primary sovereignty?

In committees the representatives of the states naturally supported the latter of these alternatives. For them the former states at the moment of signing the confederate pact gave up to the federal state a certain number of their powers; but they have kept others. The Revolution has changed nothing in this situation; it has thrown out the dynasties, but it has not at all changed the integrity and the rights of the individual states. It is in these states therefore that sovereignty originally resides. The sovereignty of the Reich is only derived; although the Reich is no longer an alliance of Princes, it is certainly an alliance of the Republics that compose it.

This theory has not prevailed. It is true that one could not go so far as to admit that the sovereignty of the states is derived from that of the Reich and is given to them by the latter; but it is equally true that it cannot be admitted that the sovereignty of the states is expressly limited by the rights that the Reich attributes to itself. It has been admitted, therefore, that the people is sovereign in the Reich, but that it is equally and by the same title sovereign in the states in the spheres of action which are left to the states.

Such is the principle proclaimed by Article 1, paragraph 2, of the Constitution. That does not mean to say, however, that attempts and proposals were not made to make a breach in it or to draw from it debatable deductions. A study of these attempts and proposals will enable us to understand more precisely the sense and import of this principle.

2.—THE COUNCILS SYSTEM, OR THE DICTATORSHIP OF THE PROLETARIAT.

The first projects formulated and presented against this principle, and to the realization of which the Independents and the Communists bent every effort, may be characterized in a word: they aimed to give over all political and economic power to Workers Councils, to organize the dictatorship of the proletariat.

These proposals, such as developed particularly by Däumig, theoretician of the Independents, may be summed up as follows:

A parliamentary system—the proof is at hand—is powerless to bring about the triumph of social democracy. The revolution throughout the world, if it is to win quickly—and it must win quickly, for the proletariat can no longer wait—cannot achieve its aims except by other methods. As in

Russia in 1905 and in 1917, so in Germany the necessary change can be only the product of Workers Councils. It is only within the Councils that the union of the proletariat is possible. Only the Councils assure the co-operation of manual and of intellectual workers, which Russia had not been able as yet to realize but which should be and can be accomplished. The system of Councils in its final aspect realizes the most perfect form of democracy, for it gives political and economic equality to all its citizens. While waiting its ultimate triumph, however, it may be necessary to proclaim the dictatorship of the proletariat; but this dictatorship will not be any heavier than that which is borne by the proletariat itself. It will last if necessary till the complete fusion of social classes does away with the class struggle, till the advent of integral socialism.

Therefore, all power to the Councils! No division of influence, no juxtaposition of political assemblies and economic councils! The Councils are an indispensable instrument to substitute permanently a socialist for a capitalist régime. That is to say, they should fulfil two series of functions: political and economic. Politically the Councils system unites in the same organism both parliament and administration, thus rendering possible that constant control of administration which the parliamentary régime is incapable of exercising, and maintaining a permanent supervision of the elected by the electors. Economically the Councils watch over the execution of socialization measures; later they become the regulators of production and consumption.

To this duality of functions there corresponds a double organization. The political system rests on Workers Councils properly so called (Arbeiterräte); the economic system rests on Factory Workers Councils (Betriebsräte).

In each commune, workers, employés, and peasants, organized as much as possible in vocational groups, elect worker councillors, one for every 1,000 electors. These councillors

THE COUNCILS SYSTEM

have as their task, while awaiting the final organization of the system of Councils, the control of municipal administration. Their delegates constitute Local Councils (Kreisarbeiterräte); the delegates of the latter, in turn, make up District Councils (Bezirksräte). In addition, so long as the German Republic is still not united, there will sit in the capital of each state a Central Council (Landeszentralrat). These different organizations are respectively charged with the control of administration of each degree of the hierarchy. At the summit of the edifice, finally, sits the Congress of Councils, which controls all political power, and whose meetings must take place at least every three months. This congress elects a Central Council (Zentralrat) which appoints and controls the Commissars of the People. It is in a word a copy of the Russian system.

Parallel to this political organization, there is created in each factory, shop, etc., a Factory Workers Council (Betriebsrat), elected by the workers and employés in the proportion of one delegate to 100 electors. Small factories and rural enterprises are grouped so as to form electoral units; the same with the professions. The Factory Workers Councils are charged with the defence of the interests of the personnel, and with the control of the enterprises in which they are employed. They co-operate in the application of measures for socialization. But their action, limited to the factory or the shop, cannot pretend to embrace all the problems of production. Germany is divided, therefore, into a certain number of economic districts (Wirtschaftsbezirke). In each of these districts the Factory Workers Councils of each branch of industry and of commerce designate a Council of Groups of this district (Bezirksgrupenrat). All the Councils of Groups in the same district designate delegates whose assembly constitutes the Economic Council of that district (Bezirkswirtschaftsrat). In the same way the district Councils of Groups of each branch of industry elect for the whole Reich a Council of Groups of the Reich (Reichswirtschaftsrat), to which is entrusted the general supervision of economic life, and which, in accord with the Central Council, determines during the transitional period the necessary measures for the maintenance of production and the application of the laws for socialization. The Economic Councils of the districts and the National Council may add to themselves, if they deem fit, experts, economists, etc.

The whole system, so simple theoretically, rests on the elections of workers as councillors in the Workers Councils and in the Factory Workers Councils. The composition of the electoral body therefore takes on a particular importance. The fundamental principle, in which Däumig and his friends would tolerate no diminution, was that no employer as such could take part in the system. *Only employés are eligible as electors.* An exception is made in favour of peasants "who do not permanently employ farm hands." A second axiom stipulates that those elected must remain under the constant control of the electors. The electoral body is therefore free to recall them whenever it seems desirable to it. In any event a worker councillor must not remain such for more than twelve months. He must stay a worker and not become a functionary.

Such is the organization that the Independents and the Communists proposed. In itself lies the proof that it is contrary to the democratic principle; for only part of the nation, manual and intellectual workers, employés, the proletariat would have the right to direct public affairs. And this consideration, without counting all the other criticisms that may be made against the system, such as at least the present incompetence of workers to govern, the necessary establishment of a reign of terror, etc., has grouped against it not only the bourgeois parties but also all the Social Democrats, who depend for the triumph of the socialist idea on democratic and parliamentary means. "I do not wish to dwell long on the study of the question of 'the dictatorship of Workers Councils versus democracy,'" said one of the Social Democratic drafters of the Constitution. "It is sufficient for me to show that this dictatorship is in contradiction to democracy, that we must choose between dictatorship by a minority on the one hand, and democracy or government by the majority on the other. The Committee on the Constitution has declared in favour of democracy, control by the great majority of the people. The idea, therefore, of a dictatorship by the Councils is rejected." (Sinzheimer in the session of July 21, 1919, of the Assembly; see Heilfron, *op. cit.*, vol. vi, p. 4265.) From the side of the Democrats came the criticism, "Those who demand all power for the Councils, who want to place between the hands of the Councils all administration and all legislation are so indefinite as to the means of realizing their demands, that it astonishes one . . . that a programme, so little developed, can be put forward without the least explanation of how it is to be realized. . . . We reject the granting of political right to the Councils. We reject above all the dictatorship of a class that is at the base of these Councils, emphatically and unconditionally. . . . We reject also the Councils as organs of control. The idea of organizing the Councils as a new assembly of control, side by side with each assembly already in existence, seems to us incompatible with democracy." (Erkelenz, session of the National Assembly, July 21, 1919. See Heilfron, *op. cit.*, vol. vi, p. 4236-4328.)

The Councils System was, therefore, rejected by the National Assembly. It must be observed, however, that it did not remain the mere formula of isolated theoreticians. The organizations of the Councils, in line with the plan we have just pointed out, was put forward as the programme of all the Independents and the Communists, and, as we will see, these two parties succeeded in casting 5,337,712 votes in the elections of June 6, 1920, sending 83 deputies to the Reichstag.

3.—THE CHAMBER OF LABOUR OR THE VOCATIONAL PARLIAMENT.

There is another project which was rejected in the name of the democratic principle but whose partisans declared to be compatible with this principle—one which in any event under different modalities has determined champions in almost all the parties. That is the plan for the creation of a Chamber of Labour (Kammer der Arbeit) or Vocational Parliament.

The idea of granting to vocational interests a special representation is not new, but since the Revolution it has been studied in Germany by a group of publicists and students of politics, who have delved perhaps more profoundly than ever before into the project and have given it a new form by introducing new concepts into it.

The supporters of the Chamber of Labour declare that at the present time, in contemporary states, the vital duty of a government is to organize the economic life of the nation. This obligation has particular force in a country whose whole economy had been overturned and ruined by a disastrous war and revolution, and which, unless it decides to enter upon a new road, runs the risk of crashing under the burden of its foreign and domestic debts.

In order to reconstruct Germany economically one cannot depend on a political parliament. A study of the history of the parliamentary system brings the conviction that if a parliament has proved to be an adequate organ of political legislation, it is nevertheless admittedly incapable of solving the economic and social problems it encounters. The parliamentary system, that is to say, the system that consists of the formation of a government with the parties of the majority, is much more a product of classical liberalism than the creator of new social and economic forms. All the ideas current to-day and which constitute the guiding principles of our political life, viz., democracy, national sovereignty, the forming of the popular will, division of powers, belong to an epoch in which the economic activity of the state was combatted with passion. When it has created its political system liberalism remains content with forms that answer only to purely political exigences.

But to-day ideas on the rôle of the state are changing. The state in the last few decades has little by little ceased to limit its activity to the rôle of "watcher of the night," which liberalism assigned to it; and more and more the organs of the state have been forced to exercise an influence on public economy. Modern parliamentarism is insufficient to permit the state to fill its new duties. For the political chambers are divided in parties that group themselves according to changeable ideological conceptions, based on the idea of "what should be," the idea that dominates the parties. But in taking a position in accordance with such articles of faith and political axioms, one does not acquire the necessary technical knowledge to gauge and judge economic questions. In this matter there is only one method of learning, that is to study the facts of economic life. What follows from this is self-evident. We must, if not actually suppress the political parliament, at least put beside it special organs charged with fulfilling the economic duties of the state. (See August Müller, *Socialisierung oder Socialismus?* Berlin, 1919.)

And these organs can be nothing but Councils, Workers Councils, Councils of Producers.

Let us not cry immediately, Bolshevism! It is true that the system of Workers Councils was born in Russia. First appearing under the Revolution of 1905, we see them reappear in 1917, but it was not the Bolsheviks who brought them into being. The Soviets were born because in pre-revolutionary Russia the law did not tolerate unions of workers. As a consequence the only form that an organization could take to combat the tyranny of the Czars was to nominate in every factory, shop, etc., men who could be trusted. In 1917, Russian Workers Councils formed the strongest support of the democracy; they were the firmest adherents of the government formed by Kerensky. But when the Bolsheviks seized power they crushed the democratic Soviets in the sense that they would not any longer permit them to elect their members to office, and they, the Bolsheviks, nominated men to represent these unions. In this fashion they erected their dictatorship, a dictatorship of a small group, with the slogan of, "All power to the Workers Councils!" But the advent of Workers Councils has nothing in common with Bolshevism.[1]

To political representation one must join economic representation, constituted essentially by the Councils. Workers Councils, somewhat like those which Däumig would organize, are retained; to them should be assigned the representation of workers' rights, which have hitherto been defended by the unions.

But by their side should be created Councils of Production (Produktionsräte) charged, as their name indicates, with supervision of production. There will be organized in each locality and for each branch of economic activity a Council of Production. The enterprises of the locality will each be represented by an equal number of delegates of the employers and delegates of employés, for *the principle of parity between employers and employés is absolute.* Above the Councils of Productions of the communes there will be superimposed for each branch Councils of Groups, Councils of the Province, etc., culminating in Central Council of Production (Zentralproduktionsrat). There is thus for the whole territory of the Reich a Central Council of Metallurgical Production, a Central Council of Breweries, a Central Council of Chemical Production, etc.

There is in addition at each stage of the above structure a corresponding economic council or Chamber of Labour,

[1] See Julius Kaliski, *Der Kern des Rätegedankens,* in *Welt-Echo,* ,June, 1919.

THE CHAMBER OF LABOUR 85

formed by a meeting of the delegates of the Councils of Production of that stage.

The union of the delegates of the Councils of Production of each stage constitutes a Chamber of Labour, that is to say, by the side of the political assembly of the commune, of the district, of the province, as well as by the side of the National Assembly, there is room for a communal Chamber of Labour, a Chamber of Labour of the district, a Chamber of Labour of the Province, and a National Chamber of Labour, where all the economic interests of the commune, the district, the province, and of the Reich, are represented. By means of a Chamber of Commerce, the producers, as producers, participate in political life. It is an economic parliament by the side of a political parliament. Whether in the commune, the province, or the Reich, no assembly elected according to merely habitual democratic principles (Volkskammer) can of itself deliver verdicts or decisions of principle. An ordinance of a communal assembly would have to be submitted to the approval of the corresponding Chamber of Labour just as a law passed by the National Assembly would have to be ratified by the National Chamber of Labour, no matter what its subject matter. The Chamber of Labour thus plays the rôle of a second chamber and its veto cannot be broken unless for three years in succession the popular chambers vote the same provisions in the same terms in regard to the matter in conflict. The Chamber of Labour and the popular chamber have equally the right to invoke a referendum. Finally, it belongs in principle to the Chamber of Labour to be the first to examine all projects of an economic character; and it can, when it sees fit, take the initiative in proposing a law.

There are between this programme and that of the Independents profound differences. This programme gives the employers a place; the proletariat is not all-powerful; and if it gives to the organs representing the workers part of the public power, it does not *thereby completely abandon the employers.*

Neither dictation by the proletariat, therefore, nor dictation by the Councils; but a political parliament and another chamber in which employers are allowed to keep the right to existence, collaborating by the same title and to an equal measure with the workers in the direction of public affairs.

From the purely democratic point of view the most serious objections can be made to this system and these were amply expressed.

In the first place, said the democrats, these Chambers of Commerce cannot be made up of men who have the sufficient knowledge and experience with economic questions except by selecting them from among the employers, employés and the workers in the different branches of any given industry. But these men are personally most strongly interested in the problems they are supposed to solve. The danger is great, therefore, that they would decide not according to considerations of general interest but to considerations of the special interests of their particular industry or their own commerce. The decisions of a Council composed of representatives of different enterprises will be dictated by the delegates of the most strongly represented enterprises; and if the interests of all the vocations that have voice in the Councils can agree on something at the expense of the interests not there represented, one can be certain that this solution will be chosen. The proof of this is already here; councils of producers grow always at the expense of the consumers.

The champions of the Chamber of Labour, continue the democrats, are guilty of a fundamental error. They believe that in economic questions there are only such problems as can be studied by the technicians, and that these can give such problems the only and obvious solutions. Actually, however, even in purely economic questions, we ask always not what is, but what should be, what we want of them and what we can effect. A technical knowledge of circumstances, of causes, and consequences is naturally necessary for a serious decision. But, even after the most scientific examination, one arrives almost always, and above all in important questions, at diverse conclusions, only because different aims have been followed. *These conclusions are always dictated by political conceptions.* Technicians can decide the best system for cleaning the streets; though even here it may be a political question to know if such a system, which is the best but also the most costly, can or should be employed. But when it comes to questions of Sunday rest, if woman labour should be countenanced, if and how the land should be distributed, how the relations between capital and labour should be organized in the great modern enterprises, and perhaps above all, who should pay the taxes—all these questions and an infinity of others raise up problems not of knowledge but of will. They are the questions in which the concern is not with economy but with the situation of man, his rights, his liberty, and his dignity within the economy. It is a question of the power of deciding for the collectivity on a subject of collective interests. It is not for the technician to decide, but for the man political.

A last and decisive objection, conclude the democrats, against the system of a vocational parliament is that it replaces or annihilates the democratic Chamber elected by the equal suffrage of all, that is to say, by democracy itself, and substitutes for it a professional chamber elected by a plural vote of privileged persons. Let the proposal be remembered which the Prussian conservatives submitted two months before the Revolution of 1918 to effect, as they claimed, the equality of the right to suffrage. Each elector was to have one vote within his professional vocational group; but the representation contemplated by this proposition was that the group of farmers were to have one seat for every 12,295 electors, whereas their labourers would not get more than one seat for every 110,530, a landed proprietor having electoral power ten times as strong as that of an agricultural labourer, six times as strong as that of a factory worker and one-and-a-half times as strong as that of a civil servant. It is true that the division of mandates in a Chamber of Labour would not result in as anti-democratic consequences as these; but the project of this chamber is based on the essential principle of parity between employers and workers; the two are supposed to be rigorously equal in numbers. That would be self-evident and understandable fully if the two groups had to settle questions in which their reciprocal interests were opposed, or if it were a question purely technical, where the number of delegates does not enter into consideration. But it is absolutely impossible to admit that an assembly thus constituted should take decisions or vote resolutions; for, *a numerically equal representation both of employers and employés would correspond obviously to a proportion of electors much greater for one class than for the other.* In any industry, for example, an employer represents considerably fewer electors than a worker, and to give his voice in the direction of public affairs an influence equal to that of a worker, would be, from the point of view of democracy, an absurdity. One thing or the other. Either the seats in the Vocational Parliament are apportioned among the professions according to the number of electors in each, the representatives being elected in each vocation by the equal suffrage of all without distinction between employer and employé—in which case there would result a duplication of the political parliament of which the least one can say is that there is no apparent utility in it. Or, the number of seats attributed to each profession must be measured by the economic or social importance of that profession, basing representation in each profession on the principle of parity—in which case there would result a parliament of the privileged, condemned by the democratic ideal. An assembly thus composed could very well draw up reports and give advice on questions in which it possesses special competence. But it cannot be a parliament having rights equal to those of a political parliament.

Such are the objections put forward by democrats against the institution of a Chamber of Labour, and their force cannot be denied. But the champions of an economic parliament reply with vigour.

These objections, say they, all take the point of view of *formal democracy*, that is to say, the point of view that considers only the external forms of democracy, which contents itself with a purely theoretical equality of right and equality between citizens corresponding not at all to the facts of reality, which reduce this equality to nothing. To this form of democracy, to-day condemned by reality, there must be opposed *real democracy*, in which one takes into account the special rôle which certain elements in the life of a nation play. Formal democracy has been fully realized by giving all men and women the right to vote. That is not enough. In a modern democracy public economy must be given its proper place, which is in the forefront. Producers, as such, must play the preponderant rôle in the state, for the other members of the community live only as parasites on their labour, and the state does not exist except by the labor of the producers. No decision can be taken in a state if it is not accepted by the producers; the latter must be the touchstone of all decisions.

It is not because of their technical competence that producers are proposed as the constituents of a special chamber. *It is because they judge things from the point of view of production,* which in a modern democracy should count more than any other. It is not a question of abolishing the political parliament, but of placing in juxtaposition to it an economic parliament through which the voice of the producers can be heard and by which the ideology of the politicians can be corrected by the realism of men of affairs.

No division of competence between the two parliaments

in such a way that only social and economic questions shall be submitted to the Chamber of Labour can be admitted. This distinction between political affairs and economic affairs is a pure impossibility, for economy, politics and general culture form a unity which must be respected. It is on production, on "creation" that the existence of the people and all its material and intellectual life rests. The two parliaments therefore should have equal power to study these questions. They must also have equal rights. To give the economic chamber only the right to draw up reports and give advice, and even to oppose its veto only, would be entirely insufficient and would not correspond to the primary rôle which the producers play in the life of a nation.

It is superfluous, continue the partisans of a Vocational Parliament, to present arguments of which history constantly furnishes corroboration. In the countries which practise the system of two chambers, one of the two chambers takes on always a greater importance than the other and plays the preponderant rôle. It is the one which translates best the will of the nation and best satisfies its needs. The other chamber may be able to resist for some time but in the end it is always forced to surrender. Up to now this preponderant rôle has been held by the lower houses, which being the product of universal suffrage, are always nearer the people, have more of their confidence and reflect more exactly their aspirations. Let us create now by the side of the former lower chamber, a Chamber of Labour and let us leave to it the care of determining its own future. It will either become a parliament of the privileged, making decisions that will not correspond to the true needs of the nation; in which case it will be promptly annihilated by the more popular chamber. Or, on the other hand, it will show itself to be the more practical and the more useful chamber to the people. In the inevitable conflicts that will arise between the two chambers, the economic chamber will have behind it the support of the people.

In case of referendum it will be in favour of the Chamber of Labour that the national sovereignty will decide; in which case the traditional rôle of a lower house will pass into the hands of a Chamber of Labour. The proponents of the Vocational Parliament are convinced that it will be this last alternative that will be realized.

The German Constituent Assembly has followed their suggestion only to a very slight measure; sufficiently perhaps to attempt the experiment recommended by the advocates of the Vocational Parliament. The Assembly has created an Economic Council, which will be judged by its work, although it is deprived, according to the Constitution, of any real political authority. It is sufficient for the moment to say that in principle it is the classic point of view of formal democracy that guides it.

4.—THE POLITICAL ACTIVITY OF THE UNIONS.

Meanwhile, however, several things occurred that seemed to support the arguments of the partisans of a Chamber of Labour, when they claim that the natural evolution of events must lead shortly to the advent of this chamber.

We know that on March 13, 1920, counter-revolutionary troops led by the Infantry General von Lüttwitz seized Berlin, that the regular government abandoned the capital and that the Director-General of Agriculture, Kapp, was proclaimed at the same time Chancellor of the Empire and Premier of Prussia. It was a *coup de main* of officers and former reactionary functionaries, all of whose acts aimed at the re-establishment of the old régime. On the 14th the unions of workers and clerks sent an ultimatum to the new masters of Berlin demanding that they immediately withdraw. As this ultimatum was not obeyed, a general strike was proclaimed on March 15.

The counter-revolutionary government lasted four days; then, conquered by the general strike, it disappeared.

But before giving the workers and employés the order to return to work the chiefs of the unions wanted to obtain guarantees against the return of a new *coup d'état*. They called therefore on March 18 the representatives of the parties of the majority to a conference, where they presented to them the following new ultimatum. These representatives were to accept in the name of their groups—which would therefore be bound—the claims which would be submitted to them; otherwise the general strike would be continued in an aggravated form. The unions would not hesitate, if necessary, to prevent the return to Berlin of the Government and the National Assembly. They would even accept the responsibility of a civil war. The representatives of the Democrats and of the Centre refused to pledge their parties. They promised only to do what they could to get them to accept the claims of the unions.

As for the claims themselves, they were presented by the union leaders, and, after a long discussion and some modifications, they were accepted by the representatives of the political parties. These claims formed the celebrated agreement known in Germany as the "Eight Points." They gave particularly to the unions the right to exercise a veritable veto over the nomination of Ministers and the formation of the Ministry.[1]

[1] This is the exact text: "1. For the immediate formation of the cabinets in the Empire and in Prussia, the questions of individual appointments will be decided by the political parties in agreement with the organizations of workers, salaried employés and civil servants taking part in the general strike, and a decisive influence will be accorded to these organizations in the new policies of economic and social legislation, all with the view of safeguarding the rights of popular representation. 2. Immediate disarmament and punishment of all those guilty of participating in the *pronunciamento* or the overthrow of the constitutional government, as well as of all civil servants who placed themselves at the disposal of the illegal governments. 3. All public and industrial administrations must be radically purged of counter-revolutionary personalities, in particular of those who participate in the management, and these personalities must be replaced by trusted elements. Re-employment of all the representatives of organizations in public services who were made the victims of disciplinary measures.

This agreement concluded, the regular government came back to Berlin. But then came its turn to negotiate with the trade unions and to attempt to satisfy their new claims.[1] These new engagements secured, the union leaders ordered the end of the general strike and the resumption of work.

Meanwhile in accordance with the "Eight Points" the cabinet of Bauer was formed. The crisis seemed ended on March 24 by the simple replacement of some ministers; but the unions raised difficulties over the new composition of the cabinet. They no longer wanted as Minister of Finance, Kuno, director-general of the Hamburg-American Line; and demanded the resignations of two former ministers, Schlicke and Schiffer, whom they accused of having treated with Kapp and Lüttwitz. After long negotiations, the unions withdrew their opposition to the retention of Schlicke in the Ministry,

---

4. The earliest possible realization of administrative reform on a democratic basis, with the co-operation of the economic organizations of wage-workers, salaried employés and civil servants. 5. The immediate execution of all existing laws and the enactment of new social laws that will accord to wage-workers, salaried employes and civil servants complete social and economic equality; and the immediate enactment of liberal legislation in behalf of civil servants. 6. The immediate socialization of the branches of industry ripe for socialization on the basis of the decisions of the Committee on Socialization, in which representatives of vocational organizations shall take part. The immediate convocation of the Committee on Socialization. The transfer to the Empire of the coal and potash corporations. 7. More effective appropriation and, if need be, the expropriation of available necessities of life; more vigorous war against usurers and profiteers in the country districts and in the cities; guarantees that obligations of deliveries will be executed, insured by the organization of societies for delivery of goods, and the establishment of definite fines and punishments for all violations of these obligations due to ill-will. 8. The dissolution of all counter-revolutionary military organizations that did not remain faithful to the Constitution, and their replacement with organizations recruited from the masses of tried republican population, in particular workers, salaried employés and organized civil servants, without favour to any class whatever. In this reorganization the rights of all troops and organizations that have remained faithful shall remain intact."

[1] Retreat of the Berlin troops to the line of the Spree; the lifting of the state of siege; no attack on armed workers, particularly in the Ruhr; negotiations with labour organizations with the view of recruiting of workers in the troops of Prussian safety police.

but kept up their objection against Kuno and Schiffer. These two, therefore, gave up their attempt to enter or to remain in the ministry; but the Democrats took the part of Schiffer and the whole cabinet was compelled to resign. It was replaced with the consent of the unions by the ministry organized by Hermann Müller.

Meanwhile work far from being resumed, a new kind of civil war developed in the Ruhr. On the one hand armed workers, who had first organized to fight against Kapp and Lüttwitz, remained united and under arms for fear that even after the conclusion of the *coup d'état* of Kapp and Lüttwitz, there would remain under another mantle a disguised military dictatorship. On the other hand, troops of the Reichswehr, some of whom were accused by the workers of having the support of the counter-revolutionary government and whose powers seemed to be unlimited, alarmed the labouring population. On March 21, there was held at Bielefeld a conference in which met members of the constitutional government, delegates of the parties of the majority, and representatives of the Independents and of Labour organizations. An "armistice" was at first concluded, then an accord was achieved—known in Germany as the "Bielefeld Agreement"—in which to the "Eight Points" of Berlin was added a "Ninth." This would, at least it was so hoped, bring about the dissolution of the revolutionary organizations and the re-establishment of the regular administrative authorities.[1]

In spite of this agreement, however, fighting continued and on April 6 the unions, to whom the two socialist parties rallied, addressed another ultimatum to the government. But

[1] The principal of the new "Nine Points" are: 1. The troops of *Reichswehr* remain in their position and must not advance on the industrial area except with the express authorization of the Cabinet. 2. The red army dissolves and gives up its arms. 3. Adequate police is assured by the constitutional authorities, supported by "committees on public order" and of "local armies" composed of workers, salaried employés and civil servants of all parties. 4. The "committees of action" and the "executive committees" are dissolved.

POLITICAL ACTIVITY OF THE UNIONS

it was precisely the moment at which Franco-Belgian troops occupied German cities on the right bank of the Rhine and attention was thereafter diverted entirely to foreign politics.

Such are the facts. The parties of the coalition have attempted to justify them and to prove that the imperative injunctions addressed by the unions to a government which had to yield almost at every point did not constitute a violation of the constitutional principle of national sovereignty. They pointed out that the first of the "Eight Points" recognizes expressly the rights of national representation; that the decisive influence accorded to the unions in matters of social and economic legislation had to be exercised through the intermediacy of representatives speaking for the unions in the ministries charged with the preparation of law; and that the last word belonged, therefore, always to the popular representation; that, although it is true that the unions protested against the nomination or the retention of Kuno and Schiffer in the ministry, yet in reality the cabinet of Hermann Müller had been constituted according to the customary forms after an accord with the parties of the majority.

Other members of the governmental parties, on the contrary, pleaded extenuating circumstances. The Minister of Post and Telegraph, Giesbert, after having participated in the "Bielefeld Agreement," declared that he did not want to examine whether this accord was contrary to or in conformity with the Constitution; for, "extraordinary epochs and extraordinary circumstances compel extraordinary measures. The conviction of those who participated in the conference (of Bielefeld) is that this agreement was the only possibility of avoiding chaos and devastation in the territory of the Ruhr."[1]

But the opposition parties unanimously insisted that the Government's attitude was really contrary to the principle of national sovereignty. In a democracy only the parliament elected by the whole people should decide; only it could ap-

[1] *Deutsche Allgemeine Zeitung,* March 28, 1920.

point the Government and it was responsible for its decisions and nominations only to the people of the nation themselves. As for vocational associations, their function is to defend only the corporate interests of their members and they had no right to encroach on the political domain. In the events of March-April, 1920, the unions, leaving their vocational domain, revealed themselves the real masters of Parliament and of the Cabinet, which had to submit to their injunctions. The Independents congratulated themselves and proclaimed that thereafter the Government was placed under a certain surveillance of the organized proletariat. The parties of the Right indignantly refused to acknowledge a "side government" (Nebenregierung) over the regular government. "Henceforth," said one of the opposition journals, "workingmen's organizations can say that their orders are always carried out. It is true that the Democrats seem troubled by the state of affairs. But what difference does that make? There are only three parties that govern Germany—workingmen, employés, and civil servants."[1]

These statements are undoubtedly exaggerations in two respects. One fact meanwhile must be noted of importance here. While the government was discussing with the unions the formation of the ministry the newspapers printed vehement protests from vocational associations and from other labour unions and groups of clerks and civil servants, which demanded that they, too, be allowed to participate in the negotiations. For they did not understand why the labour unions should alone have the privilege of participating, for example, in the choice of Ministers—and it is impossible from the democratic point of view to deny the force of their position.

Without deducing from these facts any premature conclusions one may ask if the supporters of an Economic Parliament are not right in saying that formal democracy no longer is able to meet the actual needs of the people.

[1] *Lokal Anzeiger,* April 8, evening.

The events of the months, March-April, 1920, demonstrated, they say, the complete incapacity of political powers to surmount any difficulty as soon as it becomes in the least serious. One of them wrote, "The political party is about to become a superfluous organization; it is being ousted or perhaps absorbed by the vocational association."[1] A new epoch demands new political forms. It is true that it is inadmissable for a certain class of unions to arrogate to itself the right to impose its wishes on a government of the whole people. We must not think, on the other hand, that in the future the unions would renounce the use of means which have hitherto proved to be powerful. There is only one remedy open: to associate the other productive parties of the nation with the political work of the unions; to transform this present irregular and irresponsible political work, such as it is now, into a constitutional collaboration with the government of the state. It is there that the events of the month of March have demonstrated the necessity of changing the present system. These events appear thereby one of the steps which lead from a formal democracy to a real democracy, from a purely political parliamentarism of the past to a politico-economic parliamentarism of the future.

SECTION II

APPLICATIONS

The democratic principle is one of the bases on which the Constitution of August 11 is constructed; more or less immediate applications of it are found in most of the institutions provided for by this Constitution. We shall confine ourselves here to the study of the principal and most direct of these applications.

[1] Lensch, *Erwünschte Nachwirkungen,* in *Der Tag,* No. 83.

1.—THE REPUBLIC.

The normal form of a government in a democracy is the republic. It is logical that if the people is sovereign and if all power comes from the people the chief of the state, like its other organs, should be elected by the people and hold his authority by virtue of it. It is true that there may be and that there are democratic monarchies, such as, for example, England. But this juxtaposition of monarchy and democracy, is, from the point of view of theory, difficult to justify and in practice can be maintained only by reducing the effective power of the monarch to almost nothing. Democratic Germany therefore, must be republican. In reality the National Assembly arrived at a republic much less by logical compulsion than through actual necessity; like the French Assembly of 1875, it adopted the republican form because it was difficult for it, if not impossible, to do otherwise. It seems that the great modern democracies do not become republican until monarchy has been demonstrated as impossible. The republic is at the outset only a last resort; and this must be realized and borne in mind.

Before the Revolution nothing in Germany was republican. Almost totally deprived of political spirit and personal judgment the German people had let themselves be convinced that it was only in the hands of the monarchy, the army, and the bureaucracy that the affairs of the nation were best and most safely conducted; and they naturally came to think that the prosperity in Germany in economic and in technical matters, as well as its development in social matters, was undeniable proof of the excellence of the monarchical system. No political party dreamed of incorporating in its program the establishment of a republic. Not even the Social Democrats themselves really believed that the republican form was a thing which the time had come to demand. They even held that the economic and social interests of the working class could be more solidly assured by a powerful monarchy than by a republic and a democracy of "capitalists."

After the Revolution the situation changed entirely. The sudden and complete bankruptcy of monarchy demonstrated overnight, with all the convincing force of fact, that this monarchy, in spite of its apparent force, was incapable of fulfilling the duties whose accomplishment alone could justify its existence. The powerful monarchy had not had any clear and co-ordinated foreign policy; it had turned against Germany all the active forces of the world; it had shown itself unable to utilize to its full limit the military and economic capacity of the German people for waging a desperate war to an acceptable conclusion; it had not been able to realize indispensable internal reforms. After November 9, one can say that there were no more royalists in Germany; monarchy had become really impossible and the Reich could not continue except as a republic.[1]

Later the monarchist flag reappeared, rallying about it all the deceptions and discontents. During the discussion of the draft of the Constitution the German Nationalists, among them the former Minister Delbrück, declared loudly that they preferred a constitutional, parliamentary monarchy to a republican government; but the other parties did not follow them. In Article 1 of the Constitution it was decided that "The German Reich is a Republic"; and in Article 17 that "each state must have a Republican Constitution."

As a symbol of this change in the form of government the Constitution changed the colours of the German flag; abandoning the black-white-red of the old régime and adopting the colours, black, red and gold because of their historical significance; because these colours had always symbolized in the courts of the nineteenth century the tendency toward political liberty and towards German national unity.

However, the Constitution does not give the new German

[1] Preuss, *Deutschlands republikanische Reichsverfassung.*

state the name "Republic" but keeps the name of "Reich." The Independents protested against that; they insisted on the fact that "Reich" will be always translated in French and in English as "Empire" and that this word will always signify to foreign powers all that militarist domination implies, the despotic subordination and the dangerous pan-Germanism that characterized the old Empire. But Preuss, followed by all the other parties, observed that abroad "Reich" could not be translated as "Empire" except in bad faith, for Article 1 specifies that Germany is a republic and that the republican character of the state appears clearly in even the most casual reading of the text of the Constitution. For him the distinctive trait of the Constitution was that it places to the forefront German unity. "After all, our historical development is precisely in the words 'Reich' and 'German Reich' with which are associated the efforts of the German people towards unity and the re-establishment of national unity. I believe that to keep the word 'Reich' is entirely compatible with the marked emphasis on republican character with which the whole of the Constitution is impregnated."[1]

2.—UNIVERSAL SUFFRAGE, THE POLITICAL PARTIES AND THE ELECTORAL LAW.

Democracy being the government of the state by the will of the majority, the next problem, a difficult one, is how to indicate that will.

First of all, does such a will exist? Hegel once said, "The people is that part of the state that knows not what it wants." It seems at first glance that that is true. How many men there are who, when faced by a political problem, seem completely incapable of judging and making a decision. In regard to questions of prime importance in contemporary politics the great mass of individuals, no matter to what class

[1] Session of July 2. (Heilfron, *op. cit.*, vol V, pp. 2960-2961.)

they belong, remain hesitant and uncertain. There is in the last analysis no firm and conscious will in the many. There are unreflected and obscure impulses which govern men in political matters. And if such are the isolated volitions of individuals, what can one expect of the sum total of these volitions? Is it possible to derive from the sum of these negations anything positive and to extract from these fugitive volitions anything that resembles a collective will?

The individual wills are not only too feeble and too little conscious; they are also too dissimilar and contradictory to permit being constructed into an ensemble. It is a chaos of infinitely diversified indications; making it an absurd project to try by means of an election to secure a parliament that will constitute a faithful mirror of these chaotic indications.

Yet popular will should not be, cannot be, a myth, for in every chapter of modern history it is encountered and its power felt. At the birth of constitutional states and at every epoch of their increase in strength its action is noted; whether in the victorious thrust of the principle of nationalities or in the development of the socialist idea. All these movements—and how many others!—have denoted that there is in the great masses an active and powerful will. In war, too, is it not the popular will that leads masses to consent to sacrifices such as would not have been believed possible? There is such a thing as popular will, and no arguments given against its existence are valid.

It must be examined, therefore, in concrete fashion how what is rightly considered as the popular will is expressed in practice in modern political democracies. If all the processes of this formation are reduced to their essential elements, discarding all complications that may introduce error, there is revealed this: the fact that between the individual and the people as a whole there interposes itself a third element, the political party. What matter if in some respects one may think that, even under the most favorable circumstances, it is only a necessary evil? The political party is a political means not only indispensable but fecund and perfectly rational. Its essential function is *to transform isolated volitions into a collective will of the ensemble.* Therein, too, the apparent contradiction between the fact that the crowd has no conscious will and the postulate of a popular will is reconciled. The tendencies of individuals, chaotic as they may be, change completely in nature when they are joined to equal or similar tendencies of many other individuals. From the contact of these vague and troubled impulses there springs forth the conscious and clear collective will. Certain impulsive forces particularly powerful disengage from others and unite with adjacent currents to create and to strengthen a movement that can attract the masses. It is only when chaos is thus organized and when impulses are thus transformed into forces that these forces acquire a political significance and can be compared and confronted in a parliament.

Such being the primary function of the political party in a democracy, positive legislation must be such as to permit it to fulfil this function in order that the powerful popular will shall be most clearly and easily clarified and formulated by it. We must examine how this has been embodied in German law.

In conformity with the democratic principle the Constitution in Article 22 provides: "The delegates are elected by universal, equal, direct and secret suffrage by all men and women over twenty years of age, in accordance with the principles of proportional representation. The day for elections must be a Sunday or a public holiday. The details will be regulated by the national election law."

This law is dated April 27, 1920, and was itself followed by an ordinance on May 1, 1920, which specifies each application.

I.—GENERAL PRINCIPLES.

The system according to which the delegates to the National Assembly were elected has not given complete satisfaction.

The principal objection made against it was directed above all against the law of November 30, which permits parties to unite their lists of candidates, a privilege from which the parties that lent themselves to neither alliance nor compromise naturally suffered. Such lists have been criticized as corrupting political morality and obscuring the results of elections.

But it has been also estimated that the division of representation in accordance with the Hondt system permits the stifling of small groups and that after the apportionment of seats in the different districts there are votes which secure no representation to the detriment of the small parties.

It is found also that the division of the territory of the Reich into electoral districts has been badly done, some districts being in a general way much too extensive. There are, as a rule, an average of eleven members per district in the National Assembly, and experience has shown that this number is too large for the members to be able to know well the needs of their districts and to maintain close contact with their electors.

It has been decided to abandon, therefore, the system of Hondt and to adopt an automatic system which was inscribed in Article 24 in the Constitution of Baden, and which is more customarily known as the *Baden System*. It is thus defined in the above-mentioned article: "Each party or group of electors is allowed one member for every ten thousand votes cast for its list of candidates. In each district the votes remaining unused are added up for the whole country and are apportioned representation according to the principle described above. Every fraction of more than 7,500 votes is permitted a seat."

The originality of the system consists in this: First, the number of members, instead of being fixed according to the number of the population or of the electors, depends on the number of those actually voting, in such a way that not until after the elections can one count the number of members that will make up the assembly. The latter, therefore, will be more numerous if the electors are more numerous. There is also a superimposition of the tickets. The votes not utilized in the tickets of the first degree are reassembled on a list of the second degree where a new division of seats is made.

This mechanism represents obvious advantages. It insures to each party exactly as many members as it should receive according to the number of votes cast for it throughout the whole state. It realizes the greatest possible use of remnants of votes, and consequently satisfies as completely as possible the exigencies of proportional representation. All attempts by the government or by a majority at a cunning and dishonest division of the country into artificial electoral districts are thus eliminated. In addition this system permits the possibility on the part of parties to give seats to candidates who have exceptional parliamentary experience and who play political rôles of the first order, but who despise mixing in local political struggles, such as may be considered among the principal influences in the lowering of the personal character of parliament. The ticket of the Reich permits each elector to vote at the same time for the man in whom the locality has confidence, who knows the needs of his districts and of his electors, as well as for the leaders who direct his party.

The system of Baden can be in turn applied in different modes. To give the public a chance to discuss these modes and to pronounce on this matter, the government of the Reich in January, 1920, published three advance projects of electoral law, each project defining and regulating a particular modality.

Project A introduced the Baden system in its purest form. It provided for electoral districts in which the number of voters was generally sufficient to elect six members; the unutilized votes in each district would be immediately summed up in a ticket for the Reich, where representation would be apportioned in the same manner as within the district

Project B provided for electoral districts of four members each. But between the district tickets and the ticket for the Reich there would be a third: several adjoining electoral districts being united in "a group of districts," in which lists called "tickets of the groups of districts" would have to be presented. The unutilized votes in the electoral districts would be first added up within the "union of districts" and credited to the ticket of this union. The ticket for the Reich would then receive only the unutilized fractions of each group.

Project C provided for electoral districts of the same extent and for groups of districts of the same nature as Project B. But parties would be free to present or not tickets in the groups of districts, the understanding being, that if they decided to present for election a list of candidates in each group of districts, they could not present lists within the districts of the group. This provision was designed to answer the following need. Groups of electors, not numerous enough to obtain in the first instance one or more seats in this or that district, could unite in groups of the same party for adjoining districts to present a ticket in common (a ticket of the group of districts) which would apply for the whole group or for only some of the districts entering into this group. While the big parties, to avoid the inconveniences of cumbersome tickets, would present in general a list of candidates by districts, the little parties would be able to present but one ticket for several districts, which would enable them to secure seats they could not otherwise win.

The project of the electoral law which was presented by the Cabinet to the Reichsrat on March 2, 1920, adopted the mechanism of project C.

The Cabinet justified its choice as follows: It is only in small districts that the indispensable contact between electors and their deputies can be maintained and, that long lists of candidates, which always lead to unpleasant surprises, can be avoided. If the electoral districts are reduced to no more than four deputies each, as project C would have it, the first candidate on each list would have in general the best chance of being elected; which would in most cases assure representation to the most intelligent electors in the district. The criticism which can be made against the ticket for the Reich that a certain number of members can be sent to Parliament elected not directly by the people but by the executive committees of the parties, is reduced to a minimum in project C as compared to project A, by the introduction of the tickets for the groups of districts. The number of deputies to be elected on the ticket for the Reich is thereby reduced and the influence of executive committees of the parties is diminished in favour of the influence of local organizations.

On the other hand, project B could not be supported. The establishment, the examination, and the publication of each of the lists of candidates for each of the three degrees to which the division of seats would be made, must offer serious difficulties, given the brief time to which would be reduced the preparations of elections. According to Article 63 of the Constitution, elections must be held at the latest on the sixtieth day after the expiration of the legislature or the dissolution of the Reichstag. Electoral authorities could not, except with hasty and desperate work, assure in such a short space of time the preparation of elections of the three degrees. In addition, system B has the inconvenience of requiring a considerable number of candidates before it is possible to foretell, even approximately, how many candidates of each of the two first degrees would be elected. It is true, however, that it had the advantage of reducing to a minimum the number of candidates elected on the ticket for the Reich.

Finally, project C, in giving to groups of electors the choice of either presenting district tickets or joining groups of neighbouring districts in presenting a common ticket, answered best the need of parties to dispose their forces most effectively within the different districts. It permitted them, so to speak, to group their districts according to their fancy, following their particular needs.

This was in outline the system which the Government designed and submitted to the Reichsrat. But before this assembly finished its scrutiny of it the events of March, 1920, transpired, completely changing the political situation and rendering general elections imperative for the following June. Instead of examining thoroughly, as it had been their intention, the project submitted by the Government, the National Assembly, in considering this project on March 27, was compelled to pass to a vote as quickly as possible. Neither did the Government defend its project with any particular consistency. Minister of the Interior Koch explained that the Government adhered above all to the principle of the automatic system and to the grouping of fractions into a ticket for the Reich. As for the division of German territory into new electoral districts, smaller and more equal in extent than those which had served in the election of the National Assembly, but districts that could be united into "groups of districts," that was an interesting innovation. But if this was to be effected it would be necessary to adopt in their ensemble the projects admitted to the Assembly. Meanwhile the question presented itself whether the party organizations would be able to accomodate themselves to so radical a change in the division of districts, given the brief delay which would be accorded them until the elections. The Minister referred the question to the deputies themselves to answer, as being in closer contact with the organizations of their parties. The Assembly decided to retain in principle the electoral districts that had served in their own election; the only modifications to be made were those necessitated by very grave imperfections of the distribution.

Having rejected a new distribution of districts, the Assembly had also logically to reject the institution of "tickets of groups of districts" as a substitute for district tickets; it thus came back to the system of Project A—fixed districts for all parties and the assigning of fractions to a ticket for the Reich.

This ticket for the Reich, therefore, would have been presented if there had not been brought forward some modifications of the principle because of grave inconveniences. Foremost of these was the following objection: In trying to apportion the votes cast by the electors for the National Assembly according to the mechanism provided by Project A, it was seen that 18 per cent of the members of the Reichstag, that is nearly one-fifth, would be elected on the ticket for the Reich and it was estimated that such a result in the elections of future Reichstags would be but little compatible with the constitutional principle of the direct vote. It was decided in rejecting "group-of-districts tickets" to create, nevertheless, groups of districts. Political parties could declare in advance that they would "unite" within these groups the whole or parts of their district tickets, in such manner that the votes cast for these tickets and remaining unutilized would be assigned to the district tickets receiving the largest number of votes. It would not be until this second redistribution that the fractions would be transferred to the ticket for the Reich. The object was to avoid the possibility that by assigning fractions to "joined" tickets and to the ticket for the Reich, the big political parties would be thereby risking loss to the advantage of small groups of electors which could not assemble within any district an appreciable number of votes.

For this reason the following double distribution was adopted. No party will be entitled to a seat by "joining" its district tickets unless one of its tickets has obtained at

THE ELECTORATE AND ELIGIBILITY

least 30,000 votes (half of the number necessary to elect a member). No party will be assigned on the ticket for the Reich a larger number of members of the Reichstag than had been elected for that party in the districts on the district tickets.

II.—THE ELECTORATE AND ELIGIBILITY.

In principle every German twenty years old is an elector, without distinction of sex.

Causes for the deprivation of the electoral right of individuals are reduced to a minimum. The only ones denied this right are those who are placed under guardianship and those who have been deprived of their civic rights by a court decision. Bankrupts and paupers preserved their electoral rights, in contrast to their situation before the war. Soldiers who had taken part in the elections for the National Assembly were again disenfranchised so long as they remained under colours. Finally certain other conditions, which did not involve the loss of electoral rights, still prevented their exercise: detention in institutions for mental ailments and imprisonment, including preventive imprisonment. The laws specified, however, that individuals imprisoned for political reasons could demand that measures be taken to permit them to exercise the right to vote.

To be able to vote, when one is an elector, one has to be entered on an electoral list or on an electoral roll, or be furnished with an "electoral certificate." These last two institutions are unknown in France and must be explained.

Germany ignores the principle known as permanence of electoral lists. Before the Revolution electoral lists were in principle revised for each election to the Reichstag. But the granting to women of the right to vote, which doubled the number of electors, and the fact that thereafter the electors of the Reich would have to vote not only every four years for the Reichstag, but also in the election of the President, and in cases of referendum, initiative, and plebiscites provided by the Constitution, have increased the difficulty of retaining the former system pure and simple.

There were in addition different proposals made to abolish it completely and to replace it by a procedure which would do away entirely with electoral lists. There would be given to each elector an "electoral passport" or a "citizenship card"[1] which would be sufficient to enable him to vote. But these propositions were rejected because of the considerable cost of the passports or of the cards, and because of the technical difficulties of furnishing adequate photographs of all the electors, necessitated by this scheme; and in addition because for certain votes, such as plebiscites and initiatives, it is necessary that the number of individuals having the right to vote be known, which would be difficult according to the systems proposed.

Another proposal achieved more success; that of electoral cards. This system consists in this, that electoral lists, instead of being made up by the administrative authorities, are made up by the electors themselves. To this end there are given by the communes to their electors cards which consist of several coupons. The elector fills out his card and returns it to the municipality, which verifies and completes it. The cards are then sent to the seat of the electoral district and are numbered. Then the coupons are detached. Coupons Number 1 make up the electoral lists; coupons Number 2 make up a duplicate; coupons Number 3 are sent back to the electors. This last coupon is for the elector a proof that he is entered on the electoral rolls and establishes his identity and the number he bears on the roll, before the election board. It is his voting card.

This system is a simplification, in the sense that it dispenses with the making of an alphabetical list and puts part of the

[1] There are differences of detail between these two modes, but of no importance.

THE ELECTORATE AND ELIGIBILITY

work on the elector. But in spite of these advantages it has not been completely adopted. The electoral law *provides, that, the different districts before each election must prepare lists of its electors; and it leaves to them the choice of preparing this list either according to customary rule for electoral lists, or according to the procedure of electoral cards.*

The elector is entered on the list of the district in which he lives, and it is there theoretically that he is supposed to vote. But there is an exception to this rule; if he is away from home on the day of election, either because of business reasons that compel his travelling at the time of election, or because of a necessary absence at some health resort, or because he has had to change his residence before election, he can demand an electoral certificate [1] which will permit him to vote in any electoral district of the Reich.

This innovation has appeared to present little danger, for in the new electoral system a political party is never interested in getting more votes in one district than in another.

Every elector is eligible as candidate for the Reichstag on the double condition that on the day of election he is twenty-five years old, and that he has been a naturalized German for at least a year. In addition to this he must be **regularly placed on the list** of candidates.

It will be recalled that for the National Assembly every elector was eligible; one could thus be elected member at the age of twenty. Actually, however, the youngest elected was twenty-seven years old. The new law returned to the rule followed for the former Reichstag in fixing the minimum age at twenty-five.

It must be noted that those who, without being permanently deprived of the right to vote, are only prevented from voting

---

[1] The origin of this provision goes back to the "certificate" that was given in the elections for the National Assembly to soldiers and sailors returning from the front and to troops assigned to service for the preservation of order in polling places.

by certain special circumstances, because of being under colours, or imprisonment, or because by mistake they have been left off electoral lists, are eligible for election. In the same way civil servants are also eligible. German law does not know relative ineligibilities, which French public law admits.

III.—PREPARATION OF ELECTIONS.

In a country of sixty million inhabitants of whom more than half are electors and vote, above all, where the system of proportional representation has been adopted, preparation of the elections takes on special importance. An organization must be provided which permits to each elector the exercise of his right, and, as far as possible, facilitates it.

German law provides to this end a rather complex machinery. First, it provides for a table of thirty-five electoral districts into which the territory of the Reich is divided, and for seventeen groups of districts, into which districts are joined.

Then it institutes a whole series of organisms appointed by the administration and charged with the duty of seeing that the electoral procedure was carried out properly. These organisms are:

1. Electoral committees, which have as their function the examination of lists of candidates, the union of such tickets, and the compiling of the election results for each degree of the distribution of seats in the Reichstag. There are electoral committees for each district, for each group of districts, and a committee for the Reich. 2. Superintendents of elections, who preside over electoral committees, whose function for each stage of division of seats is to confer with the representatives of political parties, to receive lists of candidates and the declarations in which the parties "join" their tickets or make up a ticket for the Reich; these superintendents announce the decisions. 3. Chairmen of election boards who supervise the electoral operations in their boards. 4. Election boards

which consist, in addition to the chairman, of three members and six assistants, who supervise the voting and pass on the validity of ballots. 5. Men trusted by political parties who serve as intermediaries between them and the administrative authorities. 6. Distributors of electoral envelopes, etc.

The law specifies very clearly the manner in which lists of candidates must be drawn up and presented. There are or may be for each party district tickets and a ticket for the Reich; there are no tickets for groups of districts. These tickets must include only eligible candidates, the status of eligibility of a candidate being examined by the competent electoral committee. The lists must be signed by 50 or 20 electors, according to whether the ticket is for a district or for the Reich. A candidate may appear on the tickets of different districts but not more than once within the same district.

Each party may "join" its tickets; which is distinguished from "groups" of tickets, such as were allowed in the elections for the National Assembly. The "group" of tickets was a contract between the signatories of two or more tickets of different parties, the intention being to have these tickets considered in the counting of ballots as one and the same tickets as against other tickets. It was, therefore, an electoral alliance between different parties within the same district. These unions of tickets, as we have seen, are now forbidden. The new law, on the other hand, provides that tickets may be "joined," that is to say, that a union may be effected of tickets of the same party within different electoral districts, in order to utilize best the electoral fractions. In order to be valid this combination must take place within the same group of districts and between lists belonging to the same party, that is to say, joined on the same ticket for the Reich.

IV.—DISTRIBUTION OF SEATS.

Seats are distributed among the tickets.

Each district ticket receives one seat for every **60,000** votes cast for it in that district; the number of those elected, therefore, depends no longer on the vote of electors or of inhabitants but on the number of those voting.

The votes which cannot enter into this count because their number is less than 60,000 remain unutilized if the ticket has not been joined to another in the same group of districts; or if it has not been combined in a ticket for the Reich. But if, as is the case usually, the situation is otherwise, the votes are treated differently, according as one of two of the following conditions is encountered:

(a) If district tickets of the same party are joined together within a group of districts, the votes constituting the fractions described above are added together and the party receives as many seats as there are groups of 60,000 in the total. These seats are assigned to the ticket that receives the largest fraction, on the condition that this district ticket has already received at least 30,000 votes. The design is to avoid the possibility that small groups, in joining their lists, may obtain a seat at a time when they have not received in any district half the number of votes necessary to elect a member of the Reichstag. If this condition is not fulfilled the vote fractions are not utilized.

(b) If the district tickets are not united, all these vote fragments are immediately transferred to the Reich ticket. Here, too, are assigned the vote fragments that remain after the operation provided in the above provision. (c) The ticket for the Reich receives a member for every 60,000 votes thereon. Beyond that every fraction in excess of 30,000 is considered equal to 60,000. But the ticket for the Reich can never obtain more seats than the total won by the district tickets whose excess fractions have been united therein; for here, too, the design is to avoid the possibility that small groups may secure more seats by means of the ticket of the Reich than they have received by direct votes in the districts themselves.

THE ACTUAL WORKING OF THE LAW

The distribution of seats among the candidates of the same ticket is, because of the system which excludes "splitting" and the joining of tickets, extremely simple. Those elected are designated according to the order in which their names appear on the tickets, so that the wish of the electors has no part in this matter.

V.—THE ACTUAL WORKING OF THE LAW.

The electoral system which we have described was applied for the first time in the elections to the first Reichstag of the German Republic on June 6, 1920. From the purely technical point of view it seems to have worked satisfactorily. It is interesting above all to inquire how the two principal innovations in these elections have worked out: woman suffrage and the automatic distribution of seats.

I.—Women already voted in January, 1919, at the elections for the National Assembly. They voted in considerable numbers. Of the women eligible to vote 83 per cent did so. The percentage among the men was 82.4, which is approximately the same as the women. But this equality disappears when we consider the proportion according to the ages of those voting. Among the male electors twenty years old only 59.6 per cent voted; whereas among the women of the same age 80.5 per cent voted. Thus the young women seemed twice as zealous to use the new privileges that had been accorded to both. Of the electors from twenty-one to twenty-five years old, 70 per cent of the men and 80.9 per cent of the women voted. But the statistics change when we come to the older groups. Past the age of twenty-five it was 84.8 per cent of men that voted, and only 82.6 per cent of women.

At the elections of June, 1921, fewer women seemed to have voted than the year before, and this time it was the men who proportionally voted in larger numbers.

But in 1920 there was tried an experiment in several districts which had not been done in 1919. The men and women of these districts voted in separate polling places, in order to determine their respective strength in the various parties. We will cite, among other facts, two instances obtained in cities of differing political complexion.

In Cologne 119,263 men and 110,364 women voted in the sections in which this experiment was carried out. The vote was distributed as follows:

Centre	32,964 men	49,154 women
Social Democrats	36,295 "	24,134 "
People's Party	17,768 "	15,944 "
Independents	18,245 "	8,973 "
Democrats	6,554 "	4,677 "
German Nationals	3,190 "	3,422 "

In Spandau 23,294 men voted and 23,359 women. Out of every 100 men and 100 women the different parties receive the following proportion:

Independents	35.4 men	32.6 women
Social Democrats	21.3 "	19.3 "
German Nationals	12.8 "	16.7 "
People's Party	12.5 "	14.5 "
Democrats	8.3 "	7.5 "
Communists	6.3 "	4.2 "
Centre	3.2 "	5.0 "
Other parties	.2 "	.2 "

Thus in the two districts women voted more for the Centre and the parties of the Right.

Of the total vote cast for the Independent Socialist Party 33 per cent were women. In the Social Democratic party the proportion rose to 40 per cent. For the parties of the Right the percentage was 52. Whereas of the Centre women comprised 60 per cent.

The newspapers of the Left noted bitterly this irony of history, that it is precisely the parties that have always been against woman suffrage that are most strongly supported by women.

THE ACTUAL WORKING OF THE LAW 117

II.—The application of the automatic system has had several interesting results.

Throughout Germany there were cast 26,017,590 votes. This gave the Reichstag 466 members. The votes and the seats were distributed as follows:

Parties	Votes	Seats
Social Democrats	5,614,456	112
Centre	3,540,830	68
Democrats	2,202,394	45
German Nationals	3,736,778	66
People's Party	3,606,316	62
Independents	4,895,317	81
Communists	441,995	2
Bavarian Peasants' Union	218,884	4
Guelphs	319,100	5
Christian Federalists	1,171,722	21

One may wonder that the Communists with 441,995 votes received only two seats. This is explained by the fact, although they had put up tickets in all the districts they did not receive more than 60,000 votes, that is one seat, in any district other than Chemnitz. The votes that had been cast for them in the other districts and the excess of 60,000 received in Chemnitz were transferred to their ticket for the Reich. But there they could not receive more than one seat according to the provision that no ticket for the Reich may receive more seats than the number which the party in question has won in the districts directly.

Of the members elected 329 were elected directly in the electoral districts; 44 were elected in the district groups; 51 on the tickets of the Reich; 42 other members were sent by territories in which plebiscites had been ordered. These districts had not participated in the elections, and retained until the new system the representation they had received in the election for the National Assembly.

It must be noted finally, what could have been foreseen and

what was aimed at by the law, that the number of votes not utilized is extremely small. The smallest fragment discarded was that of the People's Party with 8,851 votes; then came the Independents with 9,872 votes; the Social Democrats with 11,457 votes, etc.

The cases in which a fragment of more than 30,000 votes became equivalent to 60,000 and therefore won seats were as follows: Democrats, German Nationals, Christian Federalists.

3.—DIRECT GOVERNMENT.

Universal suffrage is the means by which the sovereign people manifests its will in a democracy. Once the election is over it leaves to the representatives it has elected the freedom of directing in its name the affairs of the state. This is the system of representative government. At the same time the people give their representatives only limited powers, and they reserve the right themselves to decide on certain particularly important affairs. In such a case there is direct government. This system constitutes obviously an immediate application of the democratic idea; and it may be said that that Constitution is most democratic which avails itself most of direct government.

The National Assembly has admitted without any difficulty the principle of direct government into the Constitution. According to the expression of Preuss, direct government to-day is a "postulate of democracy"; to this the Social Democrat Quarck has added that direct government is "an essential element of democracy for which to-day there have been found positive, practical, and scientific forms, according to established principles of public law."[1]

But in this form of government there is found not only a logical consequence of the principle of national sovereignty; there are also in it certain considerable advantages.

[1] Session of July 7, 1919. (Heilfron, *op cit.,* vol. V, p. 3314.)

First, there is the educational value in the fact that the people participate directly in the conduct of public affairs. It is true it sometimes happens, in countries which have already applied this form of government that a decision of the people, far from constituting progress, actually marks if not retrogression, at least an arrest in the development of social legislation, or even in some matter of general policy. Nevertheless the very efforts that are made to convince the people and to bring them back to primary considerations, constitutes the best kind of civic teaching and gives them a political experience, the value of which in a democracy cannot be exaggerated. The collaboration of great strata of the population in the creation of laws and in political life profoundly educates the masses in the principles of their Constitution; and an institution which has been established in a country after bitter struggles, perhaps after several defeats, becomes thereafter almost impregnable, or cannot be discarded except with extreme difficulty.

In addition direct government constitutes the best system of democratic control over the organs of the state. Care must be taken in a democracy to institute control over control; for democratic government is essentially the reign of trust. The destinies of a nation should not, therefore, depend exclusively on the parliament. While one may be for parliamentary government, one may still fear that a powerful majority may establish a veritable dictatorship and oppress minorities; or that a majority formed by chance combinations may show itself incapable of action and retard indefinitely the adoptions of measures impatiently awaited by the people.

There is, then, place in Germany for direct government; but to what extent? At first this place seems quite limited. Preuss, who in his draft of the Constitution made only limited use of it, presented direct government as convenient above all for small states; but he doubted that one could apply it in any considerable number of ways in a big country like Germany. In spite of this opinion direct government gained ground little by little and in the final text occupies considerable place. One finds in the Constitution not only the classic forms of constitutional and legislative initiative and referendum such as, for example, have been traditionally employed in Swiss and American democracies; but also we find there new applications of direct government.

The people express themselves not only on the text of a law. They are also the great political judges, the supreme arbiters to whom must be submitted all difficulties of vital importance to the nation. The people give to the organs chosen by them the right to legislate and to govern; but if a discord arises between these organs or if these organs once nominated do not bend to the people's will, they intervene themselves on the appeal of one of the organs or of their own accord. Direct government expresses itself, therefore, when a conflict arises either between the organs of national representation, or between this representation and the nation itself. In these two cases it is the people who decide the conflict.

First, then, discord may arise between the organs of national representation. Being given a multiplicity of these organs the issues in which the people is thus appealed to for intervention may be of several kinds.

(1) The conflict may arise between two legislative chambers of the Reich. If the Reichstag and the Reichsrat cannot agree on the text of a law, the President of the Reich may or must, according to circumstances, order the text to be submitted to a popular referendum. The conditions under which this referendum is to take place are different according to whether the law in question is a constitutional one or an ordinary law.

If the law in question is to be an amendment of the Con-

DIRECT GOVERNMENT

stitution, the presupposition is, that (Article 76) this change has been passed by the Reichstag and objected to by the Reichsrat. If the Reichstag does not yield to this objection and persists in its first decision, or if it modifies it but in a manner not entirely conforming to the exigencies of the Reichsrat, the latter may demand a referendum and the President must order it.

If, on the other hand, it is an ordinary law that is in question, the presupposition is again that the Reichsrat has objected to a law voted by the Reichstag and that the latter disregards this objection. The President in such a case is allowed to decide whether the situation remains as it is—that is to say, that the projected law fails of enactment; or, that the difficulty between the two Assemblies shall be submitted to a referendum. It must be noted besides that these matters referred for referendum to the people must be limited to the divergencies arising between the two assemblies, and that the people pronounce for either the text of one assembly or that of the other. If, however, the Reichstag has rallied a majority of two-thirds against the objection raised by the Reichsrat the choice on the part of the President is thereby limited. He can only either promulgate or publish the law, or refer it to the people.

(2) The conflict may arise between Parliament and the President; and this may present two quite different aspects.

The two chambers are in accord on the text of a law which the President does not approve; this is the first kind of conflict. In such a case, unless the President wants to promulgate the law adopted, he must submit the text to a referendum (Article 73, par. 2). It is in effect a very strong right of veto given to the President and accorded to him without much difficulty. The Independents, however, in accordance with their thesis of the uselessness of the President, did not want to grant this right to appeal to the people in such a case, except to a responsible minister. Also the members of the

German People's Party opposed the granting of this power as useless, being a duplication of the President's right to dissolve Parliament. The majority of the Assembly, however, disagreed with them.

The German Nationals saw in this measure new opportunity to strengthen the authority of the President and did not let the occasion escape them. The parties of the coalition, on the other hand, felt that in investing the President with these powers they only applied logically their democratic principles. The referendum appeared to them, in addition in this particular case, less of an increase of the President's powers than as a corrective of the fact that he has powers too great. A democracy, according to them, can with less risk give itself a strong executive, if it also includes among them his right to call a referendum in case of conflict, which would thereby enable the people to rule on the conflict. On the other hand, the supporters of the principle of separation of powers supported this use of the referendum, which seemed to them more in conformity with their principles than the power to dissolve the Reichstag.

Another kind of conflict which can arise between the Reichstag and the President is not merely a question of legislation but of general policy. According to the terms of Article 43, par. 2, "the President may be removed by the vote of the people on proposal of the National Assembly." This provision was adopted without discussion and its presence in the German Constitution is quite understandable. The National Assembly wished to create a strong president; in fact, it has given him almost absolute power. He is the man entrusted by the people along with the Reichstag and the Cabinet. If he betrays this trust who other than the people themselves should decide that? But if he has retained the confidence of the people, what is there to fear from his being brought before it as a tribunal? In addition to this Article 43 specifies wisely that the vote, whereby the Reichstag decides to place the question of removal of the President before the public, must be a majority of two-thirds. Finally the same Article logically provides that if the people pronounce against the removal of the President in such an instance, the Reichstag is thereby dissolved, for it is the latter in such a situation that has ceased to be in contact with the people.

(3) A conflict can also arise within the Reichstag itself. The hypothesis is provided by Article 73, par. 2, thus: "A law whose promulgation is deferred at the demand of at least one-third of the National Assembly shall be submitted to the people, if one-twentieth of the qualified voters so petition."

This procedure complicates the work of the legislator. Dr. Heinze, member of the German People's party, has developed the following argument with much force: A project of law has been sent by the Cabinet, with the approval of the National Council, to the Reichstag, which, however, votes a different text for it. This text comes back to the Reichsrat, which raises objection to it. The Reichstag on a reconsideration of the text adopts a compromise, as in the great majority of actual instances. But there is always in the Reichstag a minority opposed to this compromise, one which proposes to postpone the promulgation of the law and to submit it to a referendum. For this proposal to become operative, it is required that one-twentieth of the electors of the Reich support it, which, if obtained, compels a popular referendum on this matter. This procedure is extremely complicated and can often become dangerous. For one-third of the Reichstag, forced by the party or the group that is behind it, can feel itself obliged to propose a referendum to the people even when the Reichstag and the Reichsrat have concluded happily a precise agreement. Into this agreement there becomes injected a referendum with all its hazards.[1]

In spite of this criticism the text was adopted because in Germany cabinets are most often formed by temporary coali-

[1] Session of July 7, 1919. (Heilfron, *op. cit.*, vol. V, pp. 3299-3300.)

tion of parties; and the provision in question has the effect of giving an existing coalition longer life and permitting the solution of disputes, thereby avoiding the break-up of the coalition or a dissolution of the Reichstag.

(4) A conflict, finally, may arise between the government of the Reich and that of a state over the question which is perhaps the most serious one that can arise in a federal state—the territorial constitution of member states. Suppose the question comes up of either changing the territorial boundaries of a state or forming a new state. If one of the states in question refuses to give its consent the population is then consulted and it decides.

There is another kind of conflict, more serious perhaps than those just examined. These are the conflicts that arise between the people and its representatives. Let us suppose that the latter do not carry out the provisions or the orders given them by the people. The latter in such a case take matters into their own hands, with or without the collaboration of the representatives, and impose their will upon them. Such a procedure is popular initiative.

But here, too, several hypothesis must be distinguished:

(1) The people, for example, want a law which its representatives do not give it. Shall the people be given the right themselves to bring that law into being?

The parties of the Right of the Assembly supported the negative to this question with considerable force. They held that to give the people such a right to initiate legislation is to set up a rule of mistrust against the qualified organs of national representation. Once these organs are elected, they bear the responsibility of their decisions in the eyes of the nation, and the latter must give them freedom to act. But to submit representatives to the incessant control on the part of the people is an exaggerated democratization. Further, if the Reichstag does not pass the law demanded by the people, the President, the man in whom trust has been placed by the nation, has only to dissolve the Reichstag. Modern laws, also, are too complicated for the people to be able to give qualified decision on everything they feel like deciding.

The supporters of such initiative replied that a control of this kind over Parliament could not be instituted by leaving it all to the President of the Reich alone. Occasions may arise in which both the President and the Reichstag have lost contact with public opinion; in which case it would be necessary for the people to make its voice heard. It is also a truth born of experience that all great political and social thoughts are at first the product of very small groups, and it is only little by little that these become impressed on the masses. The initiative is only a particular form of this evolution, and it presents also this advantage, that it gives the popular movement the chance to concentrate on a particular and important question, instead of, as in ordinary elections, becoming dissipated among a large number of questions of unequal interest. Finally, the example of Switzerland is very encouraging. The proof is found there that the people often see more clearly than their government, and that the initiative is the most solid bulwark against the impositions of extremists. In the last analysis the possibility of a popular initiative makes the political activity of the government more living, and influences public agencies democratically in a very desirable sense.

Finally legislative initiative by the people has been included in the Constitution (Article 73, par. 3), but under certain conditions. It is required that a detailed bill be submitted, to avoid the possibility that the people may be called to decide merely on a general principle, about which it is very easy to create an artificial disturbance. It provides that one-tenth of the electors of the nation must support this bill. This approval given, the Cabinet is obliged to submit the text to the Reichstag after stating its own attitude on it.

The Assembly then either accepts the bill, thus satisfying the people; or it changes or rejects it; in which case a referendum is then resorted to, in which the people decides as the final resource.

(2) A second hypothesis is that in which a conflict between its people and its representatives, or a part of its representatives, occurs as in the case we have already described, where a third of the members of the Reichstag demand that the promulgation of a law be deferred. It is recalled that in such a case a referendum is obligatory if one-twentieth of the electors of the nation support the demand of these deputies. There is in this a combination of the initiative and the referendum. The action of the deputies of the minority of the Reichstag in order to achieve a referendum must be supported by an already considerable number of the country's electors.

But it must be noted—and this applies equally to the two kinds of initiative we refer to—that according to the terms of Article 73, par. 4, certain laws are not open to popular initiative, and consequently to referendum. These are the laws which because of their financial character offer to electors a very strong temptation to profit by their sovereignty to make their personal interest prevail. Such laws are those on the budgets and taxes and those relating to the salaries of civil servants.

(3) There is finally a last instance in which popular initiative may operate. It is that provided by Article 18, par. 4, whereby a population wishes the government of its state and the government of the Reich to proceed to a change in the territory of the state or to the creation of a new one. If one-third of the inhabitants demand it the Cabinet of the Reich is obliged to order a referendum.

Such are the conditions and the limits within which the Constitution provides for direct government within the Reich. It prescribes that a law shall be enacted regulating the details of the application of the principles it puts forward; but up to the present time this law has not yet been enacted. The Cabinet has, however, proposed a bill concerning it.[1]

In the case of discord between the organs of the state, that is to say, in the case where the people are called in by one of the organs in conflict, the government proposes to apply, *mutatis mutandis*, the procedure prescribed by the electoral law.

For the initiative, the procedure is naturally more complicated, for it consists of two phases. One part of the people takes the initiative and collects support for it. If this support attains the numbers prescribed by the Constitution, a referendum is called. The initiative, therefore, is always followed by a referendum, unless in the interim the authors of the initiative have been satisfied otherwise.

The difficulty is to organize effectively the first phase of this procedure, to launch the initiative properly so-called, in a country comprising on the average thirty million electors who vote. In the Swiss cantons, and in the United States of America, the initiative comes into being by the gathering of signatures to a petition. In Switzerland such signatures of electors often require authentification; but this leads to considerable difficulty, for, frequently the electors have their names signed by others whom they delegate to do so. In certain of the United States the conditions for the exercise of the right of initiative are variable. Often it is sufficient that the individuals who gather the signatures to such petitions give assurance that the signers are qualified electors.

In Germany it is believed that such a system could not be accepted and a procedure has been considered in which the electors would inscribe themselves on lists placed at their disposal by district authorities. In addition the formality of inscription on these lists would be preceded by an examina-

[1] See the analysis of this bill in the *Deutsche Juristen Zeitung*, 1920, p. 385.

tion whose purpose would be to see if the conditions provided by the Constitution for the inauguration of a popular initiative have been complied with. This provision has for its purpose the elimination of initiatives doomed obviously to failure. This would permit the public authorities, once the principle of the initiative is accepted, to announce such a possibility officially in order to give the people a chance to take a position on the matter.

A demand that an initiative be admitted must be made by at least five thousand electors. When the proposal for the inauguration of an initiative has been admitted, all the electors can vote on it within a period, which usually is about thirty days. This voting is done under the auspices of the district authorities, to whom the task of gathering and counting the signatures is thus confided as one of their official duties.

If the signatures thus gathered are sufficient in number, the referendum, if it is decided upon, proceeds according to the provisions indicated above and which are analogous to the electoral procedure.

CHAPTER IV

PARLIAMENTARY GOVERNMENT

A democracy, above all one comprising seventy million inhabitants, no matter to what great extent it makes use of direct government, cannot nevertheless govern itself that way. It must furnish itself with representatives charged with the direction of public affairs. Democracy presupposes by definition a representative government.

But this government may assume different aspects, and the republic—for we have seen that the republic is the normal form of democratic government—may be organized according to three different principles.

There may be noted, according to the type, the *presidential republic*, such as the United States of America, which tends to realize a separation of powers as complete as possible and in which the President elected by the people and his ministers or secretaries nominated by the President are never responsible to the Parliament. Then there is the *collegiate republic*, such as Switzerland and the Hanseatic Cities, in which the President is replaced by a college which is, by the side of the Parliament, an organ of popular sovereignty and which exercises executive powers. This college is elected by the popular representative body and depends on it. Finally there is the *parliamentary republic*, such as exists in France.

We know what makes up parliamentary rule. Here also legislative power and executive power are separated and are to a certain measure independent. But the two cannot exercise their functions except when in co-operation. On the one hand, a certain separation; on the other, a certain co-operation, co-operation of separate and independent powers. The functioning of this system is insured by a very simple mechanism. The president names his ministers but these ministers cannot begin functioning or remain as such until they have obtained the confidence of the national representative body. The day that these ministers lose this confidence they also lose their power. Parliament does not only exercise legislative power therefore; it also controls executive action. The chief of states names his ministers, but he has not the liberty to appoint them. He must take those designated by the majority of the Chamber and reject them when they are discarded by the Chamber.

It is this last system that the German Constitution has chosen. One may express surprise thereat. For has not Germany been the classic ground for pleasantries over "parliamentary cretinism"? However, it has chosen parliamentarism. To use the words of Member of the Reichstag Koch, "The best form of expression of democracy is parliamentarism. We know of no other form superior to it and we have consequently decided to make parliamentarism one of the foundations of the new edifice."[1]

Now, the mechanisms which the Constitution has instituted, and through which the parliamentary system must function, are—either because of the federal form of the State, or because of new ideas which it has introduced in its creation—more numerous and more complicated than in most other countries. There is a Reichstag, a President, a Cabinet, a Reichsrat, and an Economic Council.

This last will be studied in the section of this book devoted to the Economic Constitution. In the present chapter we shall study the other organs, and shall inquire in what measure they are capable of insuring and do insure in fact to Germany the parliamentary government which it has chosen.

[1] Heilfron, *op. cit.*, vol. II, p. 969.

SECTION I

THE REICHSTAG

The Reichstag already existed under the régime of 1871. But its powers have become much more extensive, for it is now the principal representative of the people, from whom sovereignty is derived. It is the principal holder of popular sovereignty. In conformance with the principles of parliamentary government, it enacts laws and controls the Cabinet. The regulations that determine its composition and which specify its powers should, therefore, be such as to permit it to fulfil completely its double rôle.

I.—THE PRIVILEGES AND GUARANTEES ACCORDED TO THE REICHSTAG.

The Reichstag, charged with the expression of the will of the sovereign people, must be able to manifest this will freely. Charged with the control of the Cabinet it must be protected against all possible counterventions of the latter. To this end the Constitution contains a number of provisions which give to the Reichstag as a body, as well as to its members as individuals, a group of guarantees designed to insure for them complete independence of the Cabinet.

(1) The Reichstag considered as a whole possesses a certain number of privileges and guarantees, much more numerous than those which were allowed the former Reichstag and analogous to those which in general the parliaments in other free countries possess. To this end the German Constitution contains several special features.

It is known that the right of political assemblies to pass on the eligibility of their members and the regularity of their elections constitutes one of their traditional prerogatives, one to which they have most strongly adhered. For they have seen in it a weapon against executive power to be used in cases where the latter is tempted to abuse its authority and exercise pressure on elections. Also most of the democratic countries confer upon their Chambers the right to investigate the election of their members and to decide in sovereign fashion on the validity of these elections. Such is the rule particularly in France; such was the rule in Germany up to 1919. But the new Constitution abandons this tradition in the sense that instead of leaving election disputes to the Reichstag itself, it entrusts them to a special tribunal working alongside of the Reichstag: the Electoral Commission (Wahlprüfungsgericht). This device, however, was not inspired by any desire to limit the rights of the Reichstag. It was dictated by political considerations. The former Reichstag, when it verified the election of its members, instead of being inspired solely by legal motives often let itself be guided by political considerations. The verification of elections is in itself an act of adjudication, and a political assembly is ill-prepared to fulfil such a function. That is why the English Parliament has already entrusted the function of judging of elections of its members to a separate tribunal. Without going as far as that, the new German Constitution refers contestants to a mixed tribunal, in which there are both members of the Reichstag, and, in order to insure the impartial applications of legal provisions, judges by profession.

The Electoral Commission includes members of the Reichstag elected to it by the whole legislature, as well as members of the Administrative Tribunal; until the creation of this body these consist of members of the National Judicial Court or Reichsgericht. These are nominated by the President of the Reich on the motion of the President of the Commission. In order to become operative the Electoral Commission must be made up as follows: five judges, of whom three must be members of the Reichstag, and two magistrates. The procedure is presided over by a commissioner named by the

President of the Reich. This commissioner is particularly charged with investigation. It is hoped in Germany that in consequence of the introduction of proportional representation, election contests will be less frequent than formerly and that adjudications of elections by this Commission will have less importance for the parties than in the past.

Once elected and the elections verified, can the Reichstag freely meet and continue just as it pleases? In other words, can it be permanent, that is to say, has it the right itself to fix the date and the duration of its sessions? A double danger is here possible. To create a permanent assembly, would it not give to parliament a dangerous preponderance? But to give to the executive power unlimited right to call, adjourn, and prorogue parliament, would it not be to give a prerogative unacceptable to a democratic country and dangerous to the maintenance of its institutions?

Under the old régime, the Reichstag could not meet or commence its work without having been convoked by the Emperor and expressly opened by him. However, the Constitution provided, that the Reichstag must be convoked at least once every year. But the Emperor had the right to prorogue the assembly; and the latter had not the right to sit and continue its work against the wish of the Emperor. The Emperor's right in this respect had but one limitation: the prorogation of the Reichstag could not extend beyond thirty days without the consent of the Assembly, and it could not be renewed during the same session. On the other hand, the Reichstag could not conclude its sessions without the consent of the Emperor. It could only interrupt its meetings.

The new Constitution gives the Reichstag the right to *convoke itself and to meet of its own accord.* It is the Reichstag which decides as to when it is to meet and how long its session is to continue. It is neither convoked nor adjourned by the President of the Reich. According to the Constitution of Weimar the Reichstag meets for the first time no later than the thirtieth day after elections. In addition it is required to meet every year on the first Wednesday in November at the seat of the government. The Reichstag also decides for itself the conclusion of its sessions and the day of its reassembling. However, the President is bound in two cases to convoke the Reichstag at a time prior to the annual date fixed by the Constitution, or to the date fixed by the Reichstag for its reassembling. Such situations are (a) when the President of the Reich, (b) when at least a third of the Members of the Reichstag, demand it.

Independent as it is of the Cabinet, the Reichstag must be assured the power freely to deliberate without fear of riots and insurrections. Most governments have no special legislation in regard to this. They leave to the assembly, to which a special guard is assigned, the right to protect itself. Events, however, have demonstrated that in Berlin revolutionaries either of the extreme Left or of the extreme Right become, when they so desire, "masters of the street." More efficacious measures had to be provided than prevail elsewhere. Accordingly a law was passed by the National Assembly, May 8, 1920, "for the protection of the Palace of the Reichstag and of the Landtag (State Assembly)."[1] This law draws about these palaces a perimeter of protection, within the limits of which no armed troops may penetrate, and it also provides different measures to make these palaces an adequate shelter against any *coup de main* such as may come at any time from revolutionists.

2. The Members of the Reichstag as individuals enjoy, like the Reichstag as a whole, privileges and guarantees such as are necessary to insure their independence. The situation accorded them in this respect is very analogous to that which

[1] *Reichsgesetzblatt,* 1920, p. 909.

other democratic countries assure the members of their popular legislatures. They receive compensation.[1] They are "irresponsible and inviolable."

2.—THE RULES OF THE REICHSTAG.

Protected against the Cabinet, against insurrections, and against individuals who have designs on their independence, the deputies of the Reichstag can and must organize themselves in such a way as to assure for their labours maximum efficiency. It is imperative that the majority shall be able to impose its will without thereby sacrificing the rights of the minority. To this effect Article 26 provides, "The National Assembly chooses its President, Vice-President, and its Secretaries. It regulates its own procedure."

The National Assembly adopted the procedure of the old Reichstag and the new Reichstag seems to have continued it also.

Meanwhile a change of considerable importance has been adopted by the National Assembly. Theretofore the members of the Reichstag were divided by lot into bureaus, and these elected the committees. There are no longer any bureaus; and the essential machinery on which the functioning of the Assembly depends is the group or fraction, each of which consists of all the members of the Reichstag belonging to the same party.

According to the procedure of the Reichstag, no party can constitute such a fraction if it does not have at least fifteen

---

[1] Bismarck was always against the granting of salaries to members of the Reichstag. He hoped thereby to prevent making of politics a career. The members of the Reichstag since 1906 have been receiving compensation which, at first fixed at 3,000 marks a year, was increased in 1918 to 5,000. National Assembly members were paid 1,000 marks a month. The new Reichstag in one of its first sessions decided (1) that its members are to receive 1,500 marks a month; (2) that those of its members who, in the intervals of the Reichstag's sitting, worked on committees, should receive 50 marks a day. In addition, members of the Reichstag have the right to travel free on all railroads of the Reich.

members. To-day it is these groups that nominate the various committees of the Assembly on the basis of proportional representation.[1] The group plays a rôle in Germany much more important than, for example, in France, because of the strict party discipline that prevails in these groups. For every new question brought before the Reichstag each group assembles its members, who discuss among themselves the attitude to take and the way in which the group as a whole is to vote. When the question is most important there are held *interfractional meetings*. At these meetings are called together either all the members of certain groups, or only trusted men or the chiefs of these groups. Sometimes two or more related groups deliberate in common; sometimes they are the groups of the majority parties. Thus, either in single groups or in common the various political factions decide in advance their line of actions; and when the matter comes up for deliberation in the Assembly, everything is already decided. The public meetings of the Assembly are only a kind of show, in the course of which a speaker for each party generally mounts the tribune to acquaint public opinion with the motives that have determined his group in taking such and such a stand. A certain amount of dramatic interest is thereby lost, but perhaps the element of surprise is replaced by more thoroughly considered and riper decision.

The vote is then proceeded to. Voting by proxy is not recognized. Only those present can take part in the vote, which is theoretically taken "sitting" and "rising."

In case of doubt all the members are invited to leave the hall and then to reenter, those voting "yes" coming in by one door, those voting "no" by another. There can also be a vote

[1] There were formerly six important permanent committees: on procedure, petitions, commerce and industry, finance and customs, justice, and budget. We shall see that the Constitution has added to this list a committee on foreign affairs, and a committee on the protection of the rights of popular representation when the Reichstag is not meeting. It goes without saying that the Reichstag may name special committees for such and such functions decided upon.

by name, if fifty members demand it and if the Assembly so decides. In this case ballots of different colours are distributed among the members. These ballots bear the names of the deputies and one of the following: "yes," "no," or "I abstain." At the moment of the vote the leaders of the various groups hold up their ballots above their heads, this movement being immediately followed by all the members of their groups. Then the ballots are given by those voting to the Secretaries, who place them in the ballot boxes. A supervision is maintained to prevent those present from voting for absent members. This procedure presents the triple advantage of giving to the abstaining vote its precise significance, of maintaining strict discipline within the groups and of preventing absent members from voting.

3.—THE DURATION OF THE POWERS OF THE REICHSTAG.

The question of the term for which the members of political assemblies should be elected is always a delicate one. It has given rise in Germany to much lively discussion in committee as well as in plenary sessions.

Under the Empire, the Reichstag was at first elected for three years. Since 1888 it has been elected for five years. Should this term be retained?

On the Left the Independents considered that the motive which had prompted the change in 1888, that is, the fear of too frequent elections, did not deserve consideration. They held that it was necessary to give the German people quickly the political education it lacks, and that frequent elections are the best means to employ. They declared that in a true democracy the people should be given the chance to make themselves heard as often as possible.

The Right replied that in all parliaments the first year that follows general elections is, so to say, lost because of the necessary labour of preparation; and because the old and the new members must become accustomed to working together before their efforts achieve appreciable efficiency.

Preuss added that the question to find out was whether parliamentarism was wanted or not. A parliament, said he, is inefficient to the extent that the term for which it is elected is short. In America the House of Representatives is, it is true, elected for two years, but it is not the centre of power and of parliamentary authority. The Senate has more authority than the House, and it is elected for six years. In addition there is no dissolution of parliament possible in America. If a period of two years is fixed and if in addition the right of dissolution admitted, which is in itself already a remedy against too protracted a term, the development of the parliamentary system would be rendered thereby extremely difficult.

Finally on the third reading of a bill the Assembly arrived at a medium term. The duration of power for members of the Reichstag was fixed at four years.

4.—THE POWERS OF THE REICHSTAG.

The Reichstag is the principal holder of popular sovereignty; as such it is the most important organ of the national representation. Its activity is manifested under different forms and, compared to the old Constitution, its limits have been greatly broadened. Although it is above all a legislative organ, it exercises also an unceasing action on the executive power.

I.—POWERS OF THE REICHSTAG AS PRINCIPAL HOLDER OF SOVEREIGNTY.

The Reichstag being the principal representative of the sovereign people, it naturally falls to it to speak whenever it is necessary in the national or international life of the state to translate or express the will of the people. That is the rôle which has devolved upon parliament in all the democratic countries, and it is also the mission confided to the Reichstag by the German Constitution. The situations in which this Assembly acts as spokesman for the people are of three kinds:

1. The granting of amnesty. Amnesty is a measure of a general character whereby the sovereign, with the object of general pacification, declares such and such crimes legally expiated. In the German Constitution amnesty has to be declared in the form of a law. The ordinary procedure for the enactment of law applies here.

2. Declaration of war and the conclusion of peace. These proclamations, in the same way, must be made in the forms of laws.

3. Treaties of alliance and international treaties. Each of these is theoretically concluded by the President of the Reich; but when these treaties touch questions which are regulated or can only be regulated by a law of the Reich, such settlements are not valid except with the consent of the National Assembly. (Article 45.) This hypothesis differs, therefore, from the first two just examined. In those cases there was required a law, that is to say, the Reichsrat had the right of protest, and the President could only prepare and execute the decision of the Reichstag, to the same extent that he is compelled to prepare other laws of the Reich. In the cases of treaties, however, what is required is a meeting of the wills of both the Reichstag and the President. This agreement is required even for the international validity of the treaty, but it is self-sufficient, and the Reichsrat would probably not have the right to protest against such a conclusion.[1]

II.—LEGISLATIVE POWERS.

In contrast to the terms of the Constitution of 1871, which divided the right to legislate between the Bundesrat

[1] There are thus three kinds of treaties: Those made by a law of the Reich, those made by agreement between the President and the Reichstag, and those made by the President alone.

and the Reichstag but gave the preponderance to the former, the new Constitution gives to the Reichstag the principal rôle in legislative work. The right to legislate is expressly placed in its hands. "National laws are enacted by the National Assembly" (Article 68). But this fundamental right of the Reichstag is limited by important powers granted to the Reichsrat, to the President and to the people.

The principal co-operator with the Reichstag, from the point of view of legislation, is the Reichsrat. The Reich being, at least theoretically, a federal state, the Constitution grants to the Reichsrat, which "represents the German states in the legislation and administration of the Reich," the right of important co-operation in legislative matters. But this right is not as extensive as that which the old Bundesrat had.

It consists first of all in this, that no bill can be submitted to the Reichstag unless it has been *previously accepted by the Reichsrat*. However, this provision does not constitute, as formerly, an absolute obstacle. When the Reichsrat disapproves of a bill which the Cabinet has submitted to it, this project may be, without the consent of the Reichsrat, nevertheless sent on to the Reichstag. The Cabinet is in such a case only obliged to set forth to the Reichstag, in presenting this bill, the dissent of the Reichsrat (Article 69).

The co-operation of the Reichsrat is manifested also in its *right of protest* against the laws enacted by the Reichstag. These laws must in theory be enacted with the express or tacit approval of the Reichsrat, but this provision is not absolute. If, in effect, after the protest of the Reichsrat, no accord is reached between this body and the Reichstag, it devolves upon the President of the Reich to decide whether the project of law will be abandoned by him, or whether he will resort to a referendum against the decision taken by the Reichsrat. If this bill gains the support at the Reichstag of a majority of two-thirds the President has then, in spite of the protest of the Reichsrat, the right to promulgate and to publish the law, without any further vote on it by the Reichstag. But he may also, instead of proceeding to this promulgation, order a referendum, if he does not want to take upon himself the responsibility of deciding this conflict of the Reichstag and the Reichsrat.

There are thus two ways of breaking the opposition of the Reichsrat: either the referendum, or else a two-thirds vote for the law on the part of the Reichstag and joined to it the approval of the President.

On the other hand, when this majority of two-thirds cannot be assembled in the Reichstag, there are two ways for the opposition in the Reichsrat to become effective. First, the President may remain passive after the protest of the Reichsrat, that is to say, he may not order the referendum. The co-operation of the Reichsrat and of the President in such case weighs more than the decision of the Reichstag which has not been able to rally a majority of two-thirds in its favour. The other way in which a protest of the Reichsrat can become effective is for the referendum to support the objection of the Reichsrat and reject the project voted by the Reichstag.

The power of the Reichstag to legislate is, in the second place, limited by powers assigned to the President in certain matters. He has the right to veto any law passed by the Reichstag, in the sense that, according to Article 73, he is not obliged to promulgate the laws voted, and may within a month submit it to a referendum. If the President is convinced that a bill voted by the Reichstag with the consent of the Reichsrat is against the welfare of the people; or if there are serious objection lodged against it of another character; or if he believes that the law does not correspond with the conceptions held by the people, his situation as an independent organ of popular sovereignty gives him the right and imposes on him the duty of submitting this project to a referendum. In addition, the Constitution (Article 72) authorizes him to disregard a demand on the part of a third of the Reichstag that the promulgation of a law passed by the Reichstag and approved by the Reichsrat be deferred. He can, therefore, promulgate the law voted and give it operative power when the Reichstag and the Reichsrat declare it to be urgent.

In the third place the legislative power of the Reichstag is limited by the right reserved by the people itself to decide, and in certain cases directly on this or that project of law. Such are the cases we have described as touching the Constitutional provisions for initiative and referendum.

We must finally note, as the fourth legislative factor, the Economic Council, whose powers, it is true, cannot be considered as constituting a limitation of the Reichstag's powers, but which may nevertheless be called in to co-operate with the latter in the preparation of laws.

Such are the organs that participate in the legislative work. We must now see in what manner they function and how a law is passed through this intricate mechanism.

The *initiation* of a law can take place under any of the following conditions:

1. The Government of the Reich, that is to say, the Cabinet, has in the first instance, the initiation of laws. In theory the Cabinet is supposed to proceed with the consent of the Reichsrat; but in case this agreement is refused, the Cabinet may nevertheless submit the bill to the Reichstag together with a statement of its attitude. (Article 69.)

2. Members of the Reichstag may also introduce bills. (Article 68.)

3. The Reichsrat also has the right of initiation. In theory it is supposed to act on a bill in harmony with the Cabinet. But if the latter refuses its consent to a bill, the Reichsrat may still submit it to the Reichstag together with a statement of its point of view on it. (Article 69.)

4. The people themselves may initiate a proposal for a law. (Article 73.)

5. In matters of social and economic policy, finally, the

National Economic Council has also the right to propose bills; but here, too, the agreement with these bills on the part of the Cabinet is required. If, however, the Cabinet refuses its consent to the bill, it must nevertheless present the proposition to the Reichstag at the same time presenting its opinion.

The law being proposed *how is it voted on and accepted?* Here, again, several different kinds of situations must be distinguished:

1. The normal procedure is the vote on the bill by the Reichstag in agreement with the Reichsrat. The bill may be presented by the Cabinet, duly passed on by the Reichsrat in agreement and without change and accepted by the Reichstag as it stands. Or changes by the Reichsrat may be approved by the Reichstag. Or the Reichsrat may accept without a contest the changes voted by the Reichstag. Or, after a protest by the Reichsrat against a bill voted by the Reichstag, an agreement may be reached by the two assemblies after a reconsideration of the bill by the Reichstag.

2. If an agreement cannot be reached between the Reichstag and the Reichsrat, that is to say, if the Reichsrat having raised objection to a bill voted on by the Reichstag, a reconsideration by the latter has not brought about an agreement between the two bodies on the bill, the Cabinet may then follow another course. The President may decide that this agreement on the bill between the Reichstag and the Reichsrat being impossible, matters rest where they are; then the law does not become operative. If this solution does not commend itself to him, he may prescribe a referendum on the question that forms the conflict of opinion between the two assemblies and the law becomes operative when the referendum sanctions the decision of the Reichstag.

3. If, in the proceeding in case of a difference of opinion between the Reichstag and the Reichsrat, the Reichstag persists, after the protest of the Reichsrat, in its first decision and supports it with a majority of at least two-thirds of those

voting, the President has the choice either of passing over the protest of the Reichsrat and promulgating the law, or else he may order a referendum. His decision must be made within three months after the decision of the Reichstag. In this case the law may become operative, either by the vote of the Reichstag together with the President's favorable decision, or by the vote of the Reichstag together with the sanction by the referendum.

4. The President may, in the case of a bill passed by both the Reichstag and the Reichsrat in agreement, use his right of veto; that is to say, he need not promulgate the law but must refer it to a referendum. In that case the law does not become operative unless the referendum supports the vote of the Reichstag. If the referendum pronounces against it the law is definitely rejected. The Constitution does not say whether the President may, in such a case, propose a change in the bill and submit this change to another referendum. We must consequently conclude that he cannot do so.

5. If one-twentieth of the electors demand that a law already passed by the Reichstag shall be submitted to a referendum; and if, at the same time, at the demand of one-third of the Members of the Reichstag the promulgation of that law has been deferred, the latter cannot go into effect except after having been approved by a referendum. If the referendum pronounces against the bill, the latter is rejected. But this possibility does not exist in the case where both the Reichsrat and the Reichstag have declared a law to be urgent. The President may in such a case promulgate the law in spite of the demand for its postponement.

6. There remains finally the exceptional case in which a popular initiative by one-tenth of the electors proposes the project of a law. In such a case the law, if it is accepted by referendum, becomes operative, whether the bill has been passed without change by the Reichstag, or, with changes by it, or even in spite of the Reichstag's rejection.

It is thus seen that a referendum is never resorted to, unless the Reichstag has first taken a vote on the subject. The decisions of the people appear, therefore, as a kind of control over, and check on, the Reichstag's decisions.

The procedure just described is that followed for all ordinary laws.[1]

In theory it holds also for *constitutional laws,* that is, laws which, according to the Constitution, must be enacted in the form of constitutional laws; but there are certain modifications in the procedure in such cases.

Under the old Constitution, changes in it could be brought about by the same means as ordinary laws. The new Constitution places constitutional law under special protection, and demands that a certain fixed majority be obtained for any change in the Constitution. Decisions of the Reichstag tending to such a change are not valid unless two-thirds of the legal number of members are present and of those present at least two-thirds vote for such change. In the same way decisions of the Reichsrat tending to a change of the Constitution must obtain a majority of two-thirds of all the votes cast in their favour.

The Constitution contains a special provision in case a constitutional change is to be realized on the initiative of the people. In such a case, at least one-half of the *electors* must approve of the change. This particular majority was introduced as a condition for the following reason; the situation had to be met in which the Reichstag rejects a constitutional change proposed by popular initiative. Against such a vote on the part of the Reichstag, which may not be in favour of

---

[1] It must be noted that, contrary to the practice in most parliamentary countries, there is no distinction made between ordinary laws and fiscal laws. The latter, particularly the budget, audit laws, loans, are subject to the same regulation as the former. This is explained by the fact that, unlike most other parliamentary countries, Germany does not practice, properly speaking, the two-chamber system.

the constitutional change proposed, the decision of the people in favour of the change, to become operative must be supported by at least half of the people. Where, however, the Reichstag votes in favour of a constitutional change it is enough for the referendum to secure a majority of those *voting*, provided that a majority of the electors have participated in the vote. Consequently if the Reichstag has voted a constitutional amendment by a vote of two-thirds and if this amendment has been submitted by the President to a referendum, it is sufficient to nullify the favourable vote by the Reichstag, if half of the electors of the Reich participate in the vote and the majority of those voting pronounce against the amendment. In other words, to effect a constitutional amendment by means of a referendum a simple majority is sufficient if the Reichstag has voted for such an amendment; but if the Reichstag's approval is to be nullified in such a case a specified majority is required.

Another provision of the Constitution deals with the case where a divergence of opinion arises between the Reichstag and the Reichsrat on a constitutional matter. In general when the Reichstag, over the protest of the Reichsrat, maintains its stand by a majority of two-thirds, the President has the option either of promulgating the law voted by the Reichstag over the protest of the Reichsrat, or of prescribing a referendum. In the matter of a constitutional amendment, to strengthen the position of the Reichsrat, the President's choice is limited. In such a case, if the Reichsrat demands a referendum the President cannot promulgate the law, even though it has been passed by two-thirds of the Reichstag. This demand must take place within two weeks of the passage of the bill by the Reichstag. If within that time, the Reichsrat has not made use of its right just described, the President recovers his right to choose between promulgation and referendum.

III.—POWER OF CONTROL.

In the parliamentary system, the parliament exercises an incessant control over the acts of the Cabinet, such control consisting of the responsibility of the ministers. How is this organized in Germany and in what manner is it actually exercised?

It must be noted first that the Constitution does not give control over the Cabinet to any but the Reichstag. It is to the Reichstag only that the Ministers are politically responsible. The other assemblies that the Constitution has created, in particular, the Reichsrat, have in this respect no power. On the other hand, the confidence of the Reichstag is absolutely indispensable to the Cabinet. If the Reichstag withdraws its confidence in a Ministry or in a Minister, especially if the Reichstag expresses its lack of confidence, the Ministry or the Minister must resign. (Article 54.) To give to the vote of the National Assembly a complete guarantee of execution the Constitution provides that the Reichstag may prosecute the President and the Cabinet before the National Judicial Court and demand that the people pronounce on the removal of the President. (Article 43.)

The means by which the Reichstag exercises its control over the Cabinet are, with some minor differences in procedure, the same in Germany as in most parliamentary governments.

The Reichstag may, first, demand the presence of the Chancellor or the Ministers at its meetings, whether in committee or in full session. The Chancellor, the Ministers, and the Commissioners have the right to be present at all the meetings of the Reichstag and its committees. The representatives of the Cabinet have the right to be heard on their own demand at the deliberations of the Reichstag even contrary to the order of the day. They are subject to the disciplinary power of the President.

The members of the Reichstag may address *questions* to

the Cabinet. The question must be addressed in writing, and if the author of it agrees, the Cabinet may respond to it in writing. On the other hand, it must not be taken up in public session of the Reichstag except on a Tuesday or Friday at the head of the order of business. It is then read by its author. The Minister interrogated or some one commissioned by the Cabinet replies. But no discussion or motion whatsoever may thereupon at once result on this reply. Only the author of the question may take the floor after the Minister, and then only to complete or to rectify his question. There is naturally no vote taken immediately after the question and it is not permitted to transform a question into an interpellation, as it may be done, for instance, in France.

The parliamentary question seems to play a much smaller rôle in Germany than in England or even in France, if one compares the German procedure on the written question with that of the French. During the first six months of its existence, the National Assembly addressed about 280 questions to the Cabinet, most of them in open session. Most of the Tuesday and Friday sessions commence with a series of questions; some of them with as many as fifteen to twenty questions.

The Constitution does not say one word more on interpellations than on questions; but the first form an essential practice of a parliamentary régime. It existed to a lesser extent under the old régime. It was of necessity retained and developed under the new.

The interpellation must be signed by thirteen members. Thus it is no longer an individual who interpellates, but a party and the individual is only the spokesman for the party. When the interpellation is made the Cabinet declares either that it is ready to answer at once, or it fixes the date of its reply in agreement with the President of the Assembly. In theory this reply must be given within a fortnight. It goes without saying that, in contrast to what the Chancellor permitted himself under the Empire, the Chancellor and the Ministers of the Reich to-day do not use the right, still granted to them by the regulations, to refuse to reply to an interpellation or to refuse to name the date on which they would be disposed to reply.

The interpellation is inscribed on the order of business for the day among the other subjects on which the Assembly is to deliberate. The spokesman of the party who interpellates and the representative of the Cabinet having spoken, no discussion ensues unless at least fifty of the members present demand it. In such a case all those present may in turn take the floor. When all the speakers have finished those present declare the discussion closed and the assembly passes automatically and without vote to the next subject on the order of business.

However, the regulations provide that in the course of the discussion and interpellation motions signed at least by thirty members present may be presented demanding that the assembly declare that the position the Cabinet has taken on the affair which has been made the subject of the interpellation does or does not correspond to the opinions of the Reichstag. The vote is then proceeded to—unless at least thirty of the members present demand that the vote be postponed to the next session, such a postponement being their right.

In practice, however, little use is made of the above provision, and interpellations rarely end with a vote; for that would have for its purpose the ousting of a ministry or a minister. Such a change takes place, as we shall see, in circumstances entirely different. The interpellations, therefore, are used only to give the parties a chance to present their points of view on this or that problem raised by the political circumstances of the hour.

From this ensues a twofold consequence. First, interpellations are much fewer than in France. During the first six months of its existence the National Assembly discussed only about ten interpellations. Second, being rarely the direct cause of the ousting of Cabinets, they provoke less excitement in political circles and in public opinion, and the Assembly may therefore discuss the problem embodied in an interpellation perhaps more objectively.

The control by the Reichstag over the Cabinet may be exercised also by means of a *parliamentary investigating committee*. This is a novelty in German public law. In its first draft the project of the Constitution did not permit the institution of investigating committees except in cases where the sincerity or the legality of an act of the Cabinet is questioned. But the National Assembly has gone further than that and, with the exception of a case of actual lack of confidence in the Cabinet on the part of the Reichstag, the latter assumes the right without limitation of appointing investigating committees. These committees may, for example, be created to examine economic and other questions of importance.

The Reichstag must proceed to the appointment of an investigating committee if a fifth of its members demand it. The procedure according to which these committees may operate is not at all prescribed. The Constitution says only that such a committee may take such testimony in open session as it itself or the authors of the proposal of the investigation may consider necessary. But by a majority of two-thirds the committee may decide that the meetings shall not be public. Tribunals and administrative authorities are obliged to comply with the requests of these committees, with the view of developing evidence. The files of these authorities are, on demand, open to these committees.

The Reichstag nominates in addition two *permanent committees*. One of them is that on Foreign Affairs. Its purpose is to submit the foreign policies of the Cabinet to a constant surveillance by the popular representation. It may after the adjournment of the Reichstag, or when the powers of the Reichstag have expired, or after a dissolution of the Reichstag remain in power until the National Assembly has reconvened. Its meetings are theoretically not public. However, a majority of two-thirds may order that they be such. It has the same powers as an investigating committee.

During the deliberations on the project of the Constitution, serious objections were raised against the institution of the Committee on Foreign Affairs. It was claimed that this committee would in advance be an expression of lack of confidence in the Cabinet and as an organ of surveillance would exercise a particularly troublesome influence on foreign policies. To this the reply was, that in the countries in which there have been appointed committees on foreign affairs there has been no evidence of unfavorable results. In addition, this committee would not be in the first instance a committee of surveillance, but an organism which, in matters of foreign policy would bring the influence of politically experienced personalities of the Reichstag to bear on the professional agencies of the diplomatic service.

The second permanent committee provided by the Constitution has as its purpose the control of the activity of the Cabinet of the Reich when the Reichstag is not in session, between the last meeting of one Reichstag and the opening of a new one.

This committee, which is formed on the model of an institution already in existence before the Revolution in the Grand Duchy of Baden, is supposed, during the period which the Reichstag is not assembled, to safeguard the right of popular representation against the Cabinet of the Reich. It must see to it in a permanent fashion that administration is conducted in conformity with laws, with the decisions of the Reichstag, and the will of the people. It may not sit except when the

Reichstag is not in session. It has also the powers of an investigating committee.

When the Constitution was being discussed, prior to its adoption, this committee, too, was the subject of much lively opposition. Some held that the Cabinet, so long as it enjoyed the confidence of the Reichstag, did not require a special organ of surveillance. This committee, its opponents went on, was only an application of the conception that assumed an opposition between the Cabinet and popular representation. . It was incompatible, therefore, with the principle of parliamentarism that rests on a harmony of the Cabinet and the Parliament. But the majority of the National Assembly held, on the contrary, that this committee would correspond fully in character to the Reichstag as an organ of control, and would be consistent with the confidence and the good will on which the Cabinet depends.

SECTION II

THE PRESIDENT OF THE REICH

The parliamentary system assumes, by the side of the Parliament elected by the people, a titular chief of state with executive power who, himself not responsible politically but assisted by ministers who are responsible, co-operates with Parliament in the different functions of the state. Basing itself, therefore, on the principle of parliamentary government, the German Constitution places at the head of the Reich a President whose situation corresponds generally to that of all the chiefs of state in parliamentary countries. The Constitution also attempts to create within the general framework of the parliamentary system, a new type of chief of state. It is important therefore to examine precisely the principal characteristics of these provisions.

THE NEED FOR A STRONG PRESIDENT

1.—THE NEED FOR A STRONG PRESIDENT

The dominant idea, which guided the constituent assembly when they drew up the provisions relative to the President, was this: the German parliamentary republic requires that its President shall be powerful.

There must be a President. The Independents did not want one. "The President will either take his position strictly within the limits of the functions which are his according to the parliamentary principle," said their spokesman, Haase, "in which case it will be his ministers who will exercise his powers. He will thus play a purely ornamental rôle, therefore useless and one for which the German Republic cannot afford to pay. Or he will exceed his legal powers, and the Cabinet will be compelled to develop in the direction of a régime of personal autocracy. It is enough, for the purpose of government of the country, that there should operate a Ministry in harmony with the popular representation."[1]

These ideas had no chance to prevail. In committee Preuss fought them energetically. The President, he held, could be replaced in two ways; either by a directorate elected by the people or by one elected by Parliament. The directorate would itself name its ministers. A Cabinet thus composed would be doomed to inertia and incapable of making any decision would "cry for a Bonaparte." The Ministers who should be responsible to the Parliament would be practically deprived of authority, and the Parliament, with control only over the Ministers, would itself be weakened. The following system could also be considered: Parliament could directly elect a college whose members would themselves administer the various ministerial departments; that is to say, instead of being appointed by the President, Ministers would be elected by Parliament. This is the Swiss system. But such

[1] Heilfron, *op. cit.*, vol. V, p. 3193.

a Cabinet, admissible in a small country, could not exist in Germany, for the distribution of portfolios depends not according to merely logical premises but according to the relative strength among the different parties of the Reichstag. There could be no unity of direction in a Ministry thus composed. Above all what was needed was a personage who should be in the Constitution a firm centre. The more committees there are, and the more elections, the greater also becomes the need of having a fixed point to which may be attached the various strands in the network of the Constitution. There must therefore be a President.

This President must be powerful. A powerful chief of state is necessary above all in Germany, where people like to be governed. This is particularly necessary in such a revolutionary period as the Reich is traversing. There must be a President who will be a worthy representative of the nation and who will adequately personify, with all the authority needed, a state as considerable as the Reich. The President must be powerful in order also to act as a balance to the Parliament, which without it might become omnipotent.

This is why, first of all, the President of the Reich must not resemble the President of the French Republic. The fact that in France the President is elected by the National Assembly engenders a constitutional situation full of inconveniences. The President there is only a purely representative figure, Parliament having acquired absolute omnipotence which is directly contrary to true democracy. The parliamentarism which Germany wants is a parliamentarism whose mechanism is controlled by the people; and not a parliamentarism in which the President is reduced to complete inactivity and has no other care than to remain on the best possible terms with the Chambers. The members of the Constituent Assembly in supporting this condemnation—unanimous in Germany—of the French system quoted Professor Redslob, according to whom parliamentarism in France is completely adulterated.[1]

But neither must the President of the Reich resemble the President of the United States. True, there were many in Germany at the end of 1918 and at the beginning of 1919 who wished for a chief of state a man who could act and represent the Reich with the independence and the authority of a Wilson. But this wish does not seem to have prevailed. The Constituent Assembly, in any event, wanted to inaugurate in Germany a parliamentary régime; whereas in America, the House of Representatives has only legislative power and the executive power rests wholly in the hands of the President. The Assembly resolved to give the Reichstag the right to co-operate in executive action and to exercise a control over the administration. In addition the President in America himself nominates his Cabinet without concern as to whether or not his Secretaries have the confidence of the Chamber, to whom they are not responsible. He is invested with a dangerous omnipotence, incompatible with parliamentary régime. The American system therefore, like the French system, must be rejected.

None of the forms of existing republican governments were entirely suitable for the German Republic; there would have to be created for its use a new type of chief of state. There would have to be created for the first time true parliamentarism, different from the imperfect parliamentarism such as exists in France. French parliamentarism consists of the omnipotence of Parliament which for four years acts free of all control on the part of the people. After each election democracy in France plays no part. In the true parliamenta-

---

[1] See in general the work of Redslob, *Die parlamentarische Regierung in ihrer wahren und in ihrer unechten Form,* Tübingen, 1918. It is curious to note that every argument and all the investigations of Redslob take as their point of departure the criticisms addressed by Professor Duguit against the French system, particularly in his *Traité de Droit Constitutionnel,* 1911, vol. I, pp. 411-412.

rism, however, Parliament is not omnipotent; but is subject to a control exercised by a democratic authority and this authority must be, in Germany, a President.

The problem is therefore to institute in a Republic what now exists only in parliamentary monarchies, that is, a chief of state sufficiently powerful to act as a balance to the Parliament and to control the latter in the name of the people without, however, giving him such a power as, in abusing it, would enable him to dominate or annihilate the rights of the Parliament and to establish an anti-democratic rule. Let us see how the German Constitution has solved this problem.

2.—THE ELECTION OF THE PRESIDENT AND THE LENGTH OF HIS TERM.

To give the President of the Reich the authority and the independence which it deemed necessary, the National Assembly insured him a very strong personal position.

To this end the Constitution declares first of all that he shall be elected by the whole German people (Article 41); that is, the plebiscite. The President is elected by the same electors as Parliament itself. Thus, President and Reichstag issue from the same source, the pure popular will. Thus, there is the certitude that if one of these two organs rejects the direction desired by the people or deviates from the direction desired by the people, the other organ will immediately be able to apply the necessary corrective. The President can be the sought-for counter-balance to the authority of the Reichstag, for he is truly the man entrusted by the people, delegated by them to rule with the Reichstag.

This system is not without danger. We have seen it in Germany itself when in March, 1920, the rumour spread that Marshal Hindenburg would be a candidate for the presidency of the Reich, a candidacy expressly approved by the former Emperor, one which seemed to open the way for a monarchical restoration. The Social Democrats thereupon declared

THE ELECTION OF THE PRESIDENT

that the election of the President by the whole people was an institution republican only in appearance; that it was in reality much more monarchical than republican; that the President elected by the people could arrogate to himself a power which would weigh heavily on the functioning of the governmental machinery; that to institute the election of a President by the people would subject his person to disputes and attacks which would leave his dignity seriously compromised. They, the Social Democrats, foresaw the possibility of supporting again a proposition which they had already made during the discussion on the Constitution, but which they had withdrawn, according to which the President would have to be elected by the Reichstag. The Democrats, alarmed by the prospect of a conflict that could arise between the Reichstag and a President elected by the people, seemed ready to support such a proposition. The Centre abstained from a decision on this matter. But nothing could be done without the Centre, for since this was a matter of constitutional amendment a majority of two-thirds of the National Assembly was indispensable, and it could not be obtained without the Centre. The *coup d'état* of Kapp and Lüttwitz had meanwhile the effect on these discussions now well known. The Democrats concluded from it that thereafter all attempts to establish a military candidacy would be doomed to failure and that the people would never either nominate or support a dictator; and that therefore there was no longer any need to change the Constitution on this point.

Every German is eligible provided he is thirty-five years old. The proposal in committee as well as the text of the Constitution at the second reading declared for an absolute ineligibility of members of families who had ever ruled a state in the German Empire. This provision was done away with on the third reading by a majority consisting of the German Nationalists, the People's Party and the Centre. The motive expressed by the representatives of these parties was that this measure would constitute a law of exception of the most shameful kind, contrary to the principles of the Constitution, that it was a confession of weakness and an avowal of the lack of solidity in the benefits afforded by the victories of the Revolution.

But how shall the President be elected? After long discussion the National Assembly decided that the election of the President should not be regulated by the Constitution but that the matter should be left to an ordinary law. The Assembly was not able to decide either for the proposition of the Cabinet or for that of the Committee on the Constitution. The proposal of the Cabinet provided for a general election. If in the first canvass no candidate received the majority of the votes cast, a second one would have to take place in which only the two candidates who had received the largest number of votes in the first canvass could run. Of these two candidates the one who obtained the majority would be elected.

This proposal aroused serious opposition in the Constitutional Committee. It was held that, given a multiplicity of political parties, it was probable that in the first canvass a great number of candidates would present themselves and consequently at the second ballot neither of the two surviving candidates would rally to his support any important fraction of the whole people. On the other hand, it would be difficult before the first vote to effect any union among neighbouring parties on a common candidacy, because up to that moment the various groups would not know what possibilities there were for the election of their own candidates. In any event the position of the President would be weakened, for a great number of those voting for him would not do so primarily out of sympathy with him, but in order to keep out some other person still less in their confidence. All the criticisms that were made at another time against the balloting under the former electoral law would be applicable here with added force, since it was a matter of the election of the personality who must be vested with the highest dignity in the Reich.

Having condemned this method of election, the committee adopted the proposal that seemed to them most opposed to this: that candidate should be elected who received on the first ballot the largest number of votes (a relative majority). If this system did away with some of the inconveniences of balloting, there nevertheless could be urged against it and with greater force the same objection as filed against the preceding proposition, viz., that, given the division of political parties as it was, a man could be called to the head of the nation who would have behind him a relatively small fraction of the German population.

According to a third proposition, the second balloting could be avoided in the following fashion. The elector would be permitted to indicate on the first ballot a second person to whom he would give his vote should his first candidate not obtain the necessary number of votes. This proposition had as its point of view the idea that neighbouring groups or parties could in this way and in advance effect electoral compromises in the event that none of their candidates alone should survive the first ballot. In this way there would be the advantage that a second ballot would be unnecessary. But this system was not without danger, for first of all it lacked simplicity, and again there was nothing to show that the electors would thereby abide by the agreements concluded by their parties. A well disciplined party, in which the electors held to the agreements made by the chiefs of their party would risk being put at a disadvantage by this system in relation to a party in which there was no discipline whatever. There was the danger in accepting this proposition that the elections would bring about a result that would not truly express the real wish of the people, but which would depend on the tactics and the more or less effective discipline of the parties.

None of these propositions having been accepted only one procedure remained possible. This was to have two ballots, but not to limit the second ballot to two candidates and to declare elected the candidate who has received the largest number of votes. Thus, no group is obliged to deprive itself of a candidate who might be able to win. But when the different candidates have measured their strength on the first ballot, the parties could then freely come to agreement based on precise results. Nor would it be indispensable that this agreement should be based purely and simply on the proportion of votes obtained on the first ballot. Parties could agree on a candidate who on the first ballot had not been presented. It could be hoped that the political situation, being to some degree cleared by the first vote, there would be a considerable decrease in the number of candidates, with the result that the President elected would receive the majority of all the votes; or at least that he would obtain a number of votes much larger than if he were considered elected on the first ballot by a merely relative majority. The vote which a candidate would thus obtain would be given him by the free choice of the population; he would be much more the man trusted by the people than he would be if a majority of the electors had voted for him constrained by a balloting procedure. But the doing away with the second ballot could not be accomplished without at the same time losing the clearness with which the popular will should express itself.

Such is the system which was finally adopted as law on the election of the President, on March 4, 1920. According to the terms of Article 4 of this law, "The one who has obtained more than half of all the valid votes is elected. If no one obtains this majority a second ballot must be proceeded to, after which the candidate obtaining a plurality of the valid votes

THE ELECTION OF THE PRESIDENT 161

shall be considered elected. In case candidates obtain an equal number of votes election shall be decided by lot."[1]

The President is elected for seven years and is eligible for re-election. The choice for so long a term and the possibility of re-election corresponded closely to the prevailing idea according to which the President should constitute a fixed and permanent point in the constitutional mechanism. "Granting," said Preuss, "that the institutions set up by our Constitution should be as profoundly as possible stamped with democratic character, it is best, for the solidity of the whole edifice, that there should be in some part of it a durable and firm framework." The Social Democrats observed that the longer the term of the President's powers the more difficult it would be to effect a change in the person, and consequently the greater was the danger of seeing a life President installed. They proposed to fix five years as the term for which the President could remain in power and to make re-election more than once impossible. But this proposal was rejected.

Having fixed the term of the presidential power the Constitution had to provide for the situation in which a President ceased to function before the normal expiration of his powers or found himself prevented from exercising them. It was not desired, as in the United States, to institute a Vice-President who, as permanent representative and possible successor of the President, would have the status, in the words of Preuss, of a "republican crown-prince." The provisions which were thereupon adopted are much more supple.

In case the President ceases his functions before their normal expiration, that is to say, in case of death, resignation, or impeachment, a new election is immediately held.

In case he is prevented from filling his duties, there must be made a distinction according to whether this inability

[1] This law has never been applied. President Ebert, now in office, was, it will be remembered, elected by the National Assembly.

seems apparently of short or long duration. In the first case, that is, in case of slight illness or because of a short voyage abroad, or during the first days of a disability which seems likely to be prolonged, or in the interval between the death of a President and the election of his successor, the place of the President is filled by the Chancellor. In the second case, that is, in case of serious illness or insanity, or when a motion has been passed by the Reichstag to impeach the President, or there is inaugurated a penal prosecution of the President before the National Judicial Court, the Constitution decides that an ordinary law shall determine expressly by whom his place shall be filled. This law may according to circumstances either install a temporary Vice-President, or confer temporarily the functions of the President on the Chancellor until the President is able to resume office, or finishes his term.

3.—THE POWERS OF THE PRESIDENT.

The powers vested in the President of the Reich by the Constitution are in general analogous to those possessed by every chief of state in a parliamentary country. Just as the Reichstag exercises in addition to its purely legislative powers a control over the Cabinet and its administration, just so, if the principles of the parliamentary system are to be applied, the President must be invested, in addition to his strictly executive authority, with powers that permit him to co-operate in legislative work and to exercise a control over the Reichstag itself.

It is precisely this, in effect, that the Constitution provides for. The President of the Reich has executive powers. He nominates ministers, he represents the Reich in foreign relations, he appoints all the civil and military servants, he is supreme chief of the forces of the Reich by land and sea, he exercises the right of pardon and he may make regulations.[1]

---

[1] The President of the Reich has not, what is called in France, *le pouvoir réglementaire*, that is to say, the right to issue general ordi-

THE POWERS OF THE PRESIDENT

He has also powers of a legislative character. He alone has authority to promulgate and publish enacted laws. He exercises a kind of right of veto over these laws; and he may, according to circumstances, in the complicated conditions we have already examined, either retard the entrance of these laws into operation, or submit them to the people by means of a referendum. Finally, he exercises a certain control over the Reichstag. He may order the President of the Reichstag to convoke that Assembly earlier than the normal date of its meeting. He nominates the judicial members of the electoral commission for disputed elections to the Reichstag. He may dissolve the Reichstag, etc.

It goes without saying that in none of these cases can the President take action without securing the support and the countersignature of a Minister. That is the essential condition of a parliamentary régime.

But to strengthen the action of a President and to give his position a place of real pre-eminence, which is desired for him, the Constitution entrusts him with a certain number of powers, which we must note particularly, for they are perhaps peculiar to the German Presidency, and give it a special character.

The President exercises an extremely powerful control over the legislative work of the Reichstag. When a law has been enacted he may, before promulgating it, submit it to a referendum. He may, when the Reichstag and the Reichsrat have declared urgent a law which they have enacted, promulgate it immediately even if a third of the Reichstag has demanded that its promulgation be deferred (Article 72). The aim of such a demand for postponement is to give the opponents of the law the chance to prepare a referendum and to proceed to

---

nances obligatory on all citizens. He cannot make regulations of this kind except in cases where the Constitution or an ordinary law gives him special power to do so. In such a case either he issues the regulation, naturally with the countersignature of a Minister (Articles 48, 49, 51, 59 of the Constitution, for example), or he must first obtain the consent of the Reichstag.

it. The fact that the President has the right not to act on such a postponement and to give the law immediate operative power by promulgating it, offers him the chance to prevent such a referendum. It is also in his right when there is no agreement between the Reichstag and the Reichsrat on the text of a bill, either to decide that the law is not in effect and shall not enter into operation, or to decide for a referendum. He is free, finally, when a law has been passed in the Reichstag by a two-thirds majority against the protest of the Reichsrat, either to promulgate this law, or, if he does not wish to take the responsibility of that, to submit to a referendum the question on which the Reichstag and the Reichsrat disagree.

The President commands all the armed forces of the Reich. He is from this point of view the direct successor of the Emperor. He has, therefore, the power called *Reichsexecution;* that is to say, that when a state does not carry out the obligations imposed upon it by the Constitution or by a law of the Reich, he has the right to compel it to do so with the aid of armed force. But, above all, he has the right to *declare a state of siege.*

This is a peculiar point in the German Constitution. Whereas in France, the state of siege cannot be declared except by a law, in Germany it is sufficient to declare it by means of a simple order of the President. Article 48 gives him the right, when security and public order are seriously affected or menaced, to take necessary measures for the reestablishment of security and public order and at need to use, therefore, armed force to that end. But in order that he may be able to resort to these exceptional measures, tranquillity and public safety must be seriously affected or menaced. But he alone has the power to decide if and when this condition is fulfilled. In the same way he alone decides what measures are necessary for the re-establishment of order. He may particularly—the Constitution expressly gives him this right

THE POWERS OF THE PRESIDENT

but only in a general way—suspend individual liberties. As to details in this matter the Constitution provided for the passing of an ordinary law which should prescribe particulars more completely; but this law has not yet been enacted. It is agreed to recognize that until such a law has been passed the *authority of the President in this respect remains unlimited.* He may therefore not only order all measures which seem to him necessary for this or that emergency, but he may also by an ordinance prescribe general and permanent measures. He may institute penalties or increase those provided by the penal code. He may also establish special tribunals. It is in effect a dictatorship.

This extraordinary power which has been given him, the President uses to a very large extent. Germany, it is true, is traversing a particularly troubled period and it is probable that this is responsible for the great number of ordinances issued by the President creating states of siege. There are regions that are almost constantly in a state of siege, particularly the Ruhr. In 1920 Berlin remained in a state of siege from January 13th to May 28th.

The modes of applying these high executive powers are extremely variable and, according to circumstances, the measures prescribed constitute a menace more or less grave to the rights of the individual. In serious situations all the authority goes to the Minister of War, who may exercise them himself or transmit them to his subordinates, and who is assisted in civil administration by a Commissioner of the Cabinet. Penalties are enacted; arson, the illegal use of explosives, flooding, damage done to railways, and resistance to legal officers in the course of a riot are punishable by death. Extraordinary court-martials are created and invested with broad authority. The military powers may even institute court-martials appointed by the commanders of the troops charged with suppressing the disorders and presided over by an officer of these troops.[1] In less serious situations the authority in the territory involved is given over to a commissioner of the civil government, nominated by the Minister of the Interior. The liberty of individuals is suspended, but certain guarantees are retained. Prison sentences and fines are instituted. Between these two extreme types of state of siege there is a whole gamut of provisions more or less severe; and almost daily new ordinances appear establishing the state of siege in this region, sharpening it in another, relaxing here and abolishing it there. There are territories declared in a state of siege in which this abnormal situation is not manifested by a single practical restriction; it is there only a measure of precaution on the part of the government. But there are others where repressions of a terribly brutal nature take place.

The only limit that the Constitution has provided to this omnipotence of the executive power consists in the obligation it places on the President to acquaint the Reichstag with all the measures he has taken by virtue of Article 48; and in the right that is given by the Constitution to the Reichstag to demand that he withdraw these measures. It is because of such a demand that the Cabinet was compelled on May 28, 1920, to abolish the then state of siege throughout the whole Reich, except in the Ruhr, to permit the elections of June 6 to be held under normal conditions.

The parties of the Right, for whom the authority given the President seems never strong enough, wanted to give him still another power, the right to prescribe a referendum or to dissolve the Reichstag without a countersignature of a Minister. The President, they held, would never be able to secure the countersignature of a Minister to a dissolution of the Reichstag, or to appeal to the people against the Reichstag, because ministers depend for their official lives on the confidence the

[1] See particularly the decree of March 19, 1920, *Reichsgesetzblatt*, 1920, p. 467.

THE POWERS OF THE PRESIDENT

Reichstag reposes in them. It will be necessary in such a case, therefore, for the President to form a new ministry to countersign his ordinance. But if the electors of the nation decide against a President, he will have to call back to office the former Ministry. Of what use is this roundabout method?

But Preuss vigorously defended the necessity of the countersignature, dictated by principles of a republican democracy and of parliamentarism.

He began by reviewing the hypothesis of a referendum. In such a situation, he said, one of two possibilities occurs. Either the President and the Minister are in agreement to prescribe a referendum; in which case would the Minister refuse his countersignature? That would be contrary to the normal relations which must exist between the President and his Ministry; especially, too, as a referendum is subject to certain conditions imposed by the Constitution, and these conditions have to be observed and some one must take the responsibility in case they are violated. Or in the other case, the more important, the Ministry are against the referendum; they are determined not to permit such a politically important act to be committed against their best judgment. In such a situation the Ministry will immediately resign and the President, not being able to remain without a Ministry, would have to form a new one. Whether or not, therefore, the countersignature of a Minister to such decrees is required, the situation culminates in a change of Ministry. But it is more natural that if the President wants to bring about an act against the political convictions of his Ministry, he will seek a Cabinet that will accept the responsibility for this act.

The situation is quite analogous in reference to the dissolution of a Reichstag. If the President dissolves the Reichstag and wants to prevail over its majority he can no longer retain the Ministry supported by this majority. Dissolution results from the fact that the President seeks, by a new election, to change the majority to a minority and the minority to a majority. He must therefore ask himself this question. What political combination can I use? Such a calculation must be faced if it is not permitted the President to prescribe a dissolution of the Reichstag except with the countersignature of a Minister. The President is not absolutely subject to the majority; he may attempt, in appealing to the people, to make another majority of the minority, but in that case he must take into this minority statesmen who will accept the responsibility for such an attempt.

The President may, therefore, order the referendum and dissolve the Reichstag; but these two decisions, like all the others, must be countersigned by a Minister.

In addition to the powers we have just examined, all of which are expressly provided by the Constitution, there are others which the President possesses because they logically follow from even the practice of a parliamentary régime. Certainly he has the right to demand reports from Ministers and any information from them on the course of affairs. He has the right also to be present at sessions of the Cabinet; and while it is true that he has not the right to vote there, he may come there whenever he pleases and take the chair.[1]

4.—THE RESPONSIBILITY OF THE PRESIDENT.

Responsibility engenders authority and there is no authority without responsibility. Whatever powers a Constitution may give its chief of state, they will rest a dead letter if he cannot personally assume the responsibility for the exercise of these powers. The President of the United States, who is thus held responsible, really governs. In a parliamentary régime the chief of state is not responsible; thence comes its weakness. But the German Constitution desires at once a

[1] At the meeting of the Committee on the Constitution on April 4, 1919, Preuss, then Minister of the Interior, declared that such was already the practice in Germany and that President Ebert presided over the most important meetings of the Council of Ministers.

parliamentary régime and a strong presidency. It must therefore seek a ground for the combination of the two.

(1) *Politically* the President of the Reich is in theory not responsible. That is to say, that he cannot be overthrown by vote of lack of confidence on the part of the Reichstag. All his acts must be countersigned by a Minister, and it is the latter who takes the responsibility for them and who alone suffers the consequences.

There is, however, a limit to this political irresponsibility of the President. If the conflict between the President and the Reichstag is really irreconcilable he may submit the conflict to the people, who decide. It is recalled to this effect that, according to Article 42, the Reichstag by a decision taken by a majority of two-thirds may demand of the people a vote on the impeachment of the President. If the people approve, the President ceases his functions; therein operates a kind of political responsibility of the President.

(2) The President of the Reich is criminally responsible. Two hypotheses must be considered:

(*a*) The President may have committed some crime for which the ordinary penal law prescribes punishment. Can he be prosecuted before ordinary tribunals as an ordinary individual? This question was vigorously debated before the Committee on the Constitution. It was not desired that the President should be absolved from all criminal responsibility. But, on the other hand, it was equally undesirable that he should be placed in the same status as ordinary citizens, because this would give him a position less favorable than that which the Constitution grants members of the Reichstag. It was decided finally that, like the latter, he cannot be criminally prosecuted during the term of his powers, except with the authorization of the Reichstag.

(*b*) Or the President may be guilty of a violation of the Constitution or a law of the Reich. In this case Article 59 provides that he may be prosecuted by the Reichstag in the

Supreme Judicial Court. The proposal to bring an impeachment must be signed by at least one hundred members and supported by a two-thirds majority. But it must be specified here that this is a matter of legal procedure and that therefore this prosecution can be based only on the violation of a definite provision of the Constitution or of a law. In the case of a simple political divergence of opinion between the Reichstag and the President, only the political responsibility for the matter can be called into the question, and the one way open to the Reichstag is that of an impeachment approved by the people.

What penalty can the Supreme Judicial Court pronounce against the President in case of a verdict of guilty? The Constituent Assembly at first adopted a provision according to which the Court could simply declare the President removed, or to declare him incapable of exercising any public function whatever. Finally, however, it was decided to leave this question to the law organizing the Court of Justice.

But the situation may arise in which an act committed by the President constitutes both an infraction of the penal law as well as a violation of the Constitution. Which shall pass first upon this, the ordinary tribunal or the Supreme Judicial Court? After long hesitation, the Constituent Assembly decided to leave this question also to the future law dealing with the Supreme Judicial Court.

(3) The President is finally *civilly* responsible for any acts of damage he may commit. Although he is not really a civil servant, in the actual sense of the word, he is on this point subject to the same regulations as the civil servants of the Reich. (The law on the responsibilities of civil servants, March 22, 1910.)

SECTION III

THE CABINET OF THE REICH

The Cabinet in a parliamentary government constitutes a bond of union between the parliament and the chief of state.

In Germany it must play a still more important rôle, since both the Reichstag and the President are directly elected by the people and have theoretically the same equal powers. It is therefore indispensable that an organism of co-operation and equilibrium exist between them.

But this mechanism is extremely delicate. The rôle of the Ministry, always very complex, depends above all on the traditions and the circumstances of the men in question. What relations should subsist between the President and the Prime Minister; between the Prime Minister and the other members of the Cabinet; and in what measure should one be subordinated to the others? What is the exact position of the Cabinet in regard to the Chamber? Is it its guide, or must it be limited to the execution of the Chamber's decisions? These are questions of degree that require or may require different solutions in each country for each Ministry.

It is difficult, if not impossible, to decide on these in advance in a complete and detailed manner. In England there is no written provision on the manner in which the mechanism of the Cabinet must function. In France there are a few vague and insufficient provisions in the Constitution. But the German Constitution has attempted to formulate the general rules according to which the government of the Cabinet should operate.

The project by Preuss contained not a single detail on this point; it confined itself to stating the principle of parliamentary government. Against this reserve criticisms were raised in committee as well as in plenary sessions of the Assembly. Former Minister von Delbrück criticized Preuss' project for its lack of a sufficient guarantee that the organism of the government would develop in a specific manner and in the direction desired for it. He held that the evolution of an organism as important as the Ministry should not be left to chance, and that there must be fixed at least the general lines according to which it should develop. He then indicated some of these directing principles and they were incorporated in the Constitution.

The National Assembly has certainly made therein an important attempt and we shall study the regulations which it has thus established. We shall then examine how these regulations work out in practice.

1.—THE CHANCELLOR AND THE MINISTERS ACCORDING TO THE CONSTITUTION.

In the terminology of Weimar, the Ministry is called the "National Cabinet." Article 52 says, "The National Cabinet consists of the National Chancellor and the National Ministers." There is thus stated a difference—fundamental in the German system—between the Chancellor and the Ministers.

It will be recalled how the Cabinet of the old Empire was organized. The Chancellor, properly speaking, was the only Minister; and the Secretaries of State, by whom he was assisted or represented, were simply high civil servants absolutely subordinate to the Chancellor. These Secretaries of State never met together to deliberate on public affairs; each of them freely decided on the affairs of his department and executed them. But the Secretaries of State had to refer to the Chancellor every time that a difference of opinion arose between their departments over any contemplated law or any administrative measure whatever. Such a discussion was often prolonged for months, because the Chancellor was not in a situation to express an opinion, nor to pronounce on the very complex problem. This was the *bureaucratic* system.

For this system, with its obvious inconveniences, von Delbrück proposed to substitute a *collegiate* one. The Ministers form a Cabinet, to which all questions concerning general policy or involving the province of their several departments are submitted. The Prime Minister is only the first among them, *primus inter pares;* the decision is made by the

THE CHANCELLOR AND THE MINISTERS 173

whole Cabinet, which naturally assumes the whole burden of responsibility.

The Constituent Assembly supported an intermediate solution, which partook both of the bureaucratic system and the collegiate. It adopted a sort of *limited collegiate* system. The Chancellor is not as formerly the only Minister of the Reich; he is Minister by the same title as the other members of the Cabinet, but he has a character distinct from those of the other Ministers. Without being a hierarchic superior over these he is on another plane and enjoys certain rights in comparison to the others.

This distinction established by the Constituent Assembly between the two elements of the government, the Chancellor on the one hand and the Ministers on the other, is manifested in the three respects in the nomination of the ministers, their prerogatives and their responsibility.

(1) They are nominated in a different manner. The Chancellor is nominated by the President of the Reich who naturally must be guided therein by the political situation. According to circumstances, the President is obliged to nominate some party leader of the group forming the majority of the Reichstag; or his choice may be exercised among several political figures according to the combination possible among the parties of the majority. It is true that the Ministers are also appointed by the President of the Reich, but *on the nomination by the Chancellor*, and it seems that in practice the President is always bound by this consideration. The Chancellor may not be recalled; his functions cease only through resignation or because he is unseated by the majority of the Reichstag. The Ministers, on the other hand, may be recalled and the decision may be taken here, too, by the President of the Reich on the proposal by the Chancellor.

(2) In regard to powers there exists a still more profound difference between the Chancellor and the Ministers. The

principle is this: the Chancellor determines and alone determines the general course of the Cabinet's policy. The other Ministers direct the affairs of their respective departments along the lines fixed by the Chancellor in his general policy. (Article 56.) In other words, it seems that the German Constitution, without expressly saying so, wants to establish the classic distinction between "governing" and "administering." The Chancellor governs, the other members of the Cabinet administer. This essential distinction recurs more or less clearly enunciated in all the provisions relative to the powers of the Ministers.

The latter have as their most important function the exercise of those powers of which the President of the Reich is the chief holder. They prepare and countersign the ordinances of the President. But do they all indiscriminately countersign all decrees and may each Minister countersign any of the decisions of the President? Not in the least. The Chancellor countersigns all decisions touching the general policy of the Cabinet, but he is also authorized to sign other decrees. The Ministers countersign only the decrees that effect their respective departments. From this results the following: When a decree of the President is countersigned by a Minister it may be considered that the Cabinet holds it to be a purely administrative matter. Every decision presenting a certain political importance is either countersigned by the Chancellor only or by both the Chancellor and the Minister whose department is affected. The Ministers have in the second place their own powers. They make general or individual decisions which they sign themselves. These decisions are of two kinds: some of them must be deliberated on and decreed in the Council of Ministers; other decisions are taken by the Ministers individually.

There are above all powers which the Ministers exercise in the Council of Ministers, and it is here that the mixed character of the regulations provided by the Constitution is

THE CHANCELLOR AND THE MINISTERS 175

revealed still more clearly. The predominant position accorded the Chancellor comes from the fact that he presides over the Council of Ministers—when the President of the Reich is not present; and the fact that in case of a tie he decides. It may be asked if the Chancellor can be put in the minority and what would result from such a situation. Theoretically, according to the *collegiate principle,* a decision adopted by the majority must always be executed. But it seems that the Ministry cannot go against the opinion of the Chancellor, who alone has the right to fix the general lines of policy and who in addition can always exercise the threat of resigning, which would thereby involve the fall of the whole Ministry. The Council of Ministers has its own order of procedure which must be approved by the President.

On the other hand, the collegiate system is found to be very widely applied in the ensemble of the provisions vesting in the Council of Ministers some of the most important powers that properly belong to Ministers. The Chancellor fixes the general course of the policy to be pursued by the government; but the Ministers must see to it that in their various departments the policies practised conform to this general course, as well as that their individual policies do not conflict with the interests or the policies of other departments. Also the Constitution itself enumerates a certain number of matters which cannot be dealt with except in the Council of Ministers; and it provides that ordinary laws may extend the number and character of these matters. They are as follows:

(1) All projects of law. In contrast to what occurs in France, it is not the chief of state who has the initiative in laws but the Council of Ministers. All projects of laws emanating from the Cabinet must be discussed and drawn up in the Council before being sent to the Reichstag.

(2) All matters that touch the domains of the authority of the various Ministers, and on which the latter cannot privately come to an agreement.

(3) The power to issue ordinances. In Germany there is no organ that has general authority to make all ordinances. A particular organ can only prescribe ordinances within its own limits and to the end assigned to it by the Constitution or ordinary laws. We have seen that such is the case for the President; and such is also the case for the Cabinet. The Cabinet of the Reich may prescribe regulations of three kinds:

(*a*) Sometimes the Cabinet of the Reich has authority to prescribe *only* a regulation. This is particularly the case when it has to prescribe administrative measures of the general character necessary for the execution of a law. (Article 77.)

(*b*) Sometimes the Cabinet cannot prescribe a regulation except with the *approval of the Reichsrat*. This is particularly the case in the circumstances aimed at in Articles 88, 91, 77, par. 2 of the Constitution.

(*c*) Finally, the law of April 17, 1919, "On a simplified form of legislation relative to economy during the period of transition," gives to the Cabinet of the Reich the power under certain conditions to enact by means of decrees what amount to veritable laws. According to this law, the Cabinet may prescribe regulations having the force of law, and consequently may even modify laws previously made on condition that it has the *consent of the Reichsrat and of a committee of twenty-eight members named by the National Assembly*. The Ministers finally have powers which they exercise individually. They are in theory purely administrative powers.

III.—The distinction established by the Constitution between the Chancellor and the Ministers recurs in the matter of their political responsibility. Their rôles being different, it is logical that their responsibility operate under different conditions.

The Chancellor and the Ministers are equally responsible before the Reichstag. They "require for the administration of their offices the confidence of the National Assembly. Each of them must resign if the National Assembly by formal resolution withdraws its confidence," says Article 54. To follow the letter of this article it may be believed that there is not a collective responsibility and that only those Ministers must resign against whom a vote of want of confidence is passed. However, that does not seem to be the real meaning of Article 54. This becomes more clear when one compares it with Article 56. These two articles together indicate the following. The Chancellor and the Ministers are responsible to the Reichstag in the same way, but the provinces of their responsibilities are different. The Chancellor is responsible for the general course of policies, that is to say, for principles and plans of great scope, to the exclusion of administrative measures. On the other hand, the Ministers are responsible not for the general course of policies but for the manner in which they direct their departments. In addition the political responsibility of all the Ministers is involved in decisions taken by them in the Council.

As for criminal and civil responsibility the Chancellor and the Minister are placed on the same footing, and are answerable for criminal and civil offences under the same conditions as the President of the Reich.

2.—THE WORKING OF CONSTITUTIONAL RULES; HOW A MINISTRY IS FORMED, WORKS, AND IS DISSOLVED.

It is observed that the Constitution has attempted a kind of codification of rules for a parliamentary régime, such as its authors have conceived it. It attempts to give thus a guarantee that this régime, new in Germany, will develop along the fixed course it has traced for it. It is interesting to inquire how up to now German statesmen have observed these rules. To this end it seems that the best thing to do is to describe how a Ministry actually is formed, works and is dissolved.

(1) Normally, and it must be so according to the German Constitution, when it is a matter of forming a new Ministry, the chief of state charges some political leader with the task of constituting a Cabinet and assuming the direction of its affairs. This man chooses collaborators with whom he agrees or can come to an agreement to the effect that they work in common for the realization of a specific programme. The Ministry thus formed is submitted to the Parliament and presents to it its programme. If the Parliament accepts, the Ministry goes to work. Otherwise it is withdrawn. In any event a ministerial crisis resolves itself in a few days.

In Germany the formation of a Ministry is always an extremely complicated affair. Instead of only two great parties—which seems the ideal condition or at any rate the traditional situation in the normal functioning of a parliamentary régime—there are in Germany five or six parties, none of which consists of a sufficient number of members to have in itself a majority. In addition the Cabinet's difficulties are almost inextricable and the party that accepts a part in the ruling power realizes the risk it immediately incurs in exercising it. Likewise the different parties do not always lend themselves with good grace to this risk and often prefer the egoistic attitude and the convenient rôle of an opposition rather than the heavy and perilous task of governing. Whereas any political party worthy of the name should have an excellent programme in which it believes and should want nothing better than to come into power in order to realize such a programme, the political parties in Germany, little sure of their programmes, prefer, before attempting to apply them, to wait until the insufficiency of the programmes of the other parties has been previously demonstrated.

When a ministerial crisis opens there commences at the same time a period of difficult negotiations. Each political group meets and discusses the position it will take, deciding whether or not it will accept participation in the Cabinet.

WORKING OF CONSTITUTIONAL RULES 179

The answer to this latter question depends most often upon whether certain other groups will participate themselves in power. Then the trusted men or the leaders of the different parties meet together to find a basis for agreement. The President of the Reich naturally keeps in touch with these negotiations; sometimes they are held in his presence. The programme of the future Cabinet is discussed and above all the choice of future Ministers. When an agreement is reached the President of the Reich makes his nominations. There was one occasion, however, when the task of forming the Cabinet was extremely difficult. It was after the elections of June 6, 1920, which gave to the various parties such a distribution of numerical strength that no majority was practically possible no matter what combination was tried. The various groups met and quarrelled but were not able to come to agreement. Then the President charged a member of the Centre, not to make up a Cabinet, but to serve as an intermediary between the various parties and to bring them to an agreement. It is from this preparation that there issued the Ministry of Fehrenbach. *Thus the Cabinet is constituted not by an act, a free decision of the President, but by an agreement reached by the parties.*

From this ensue two consequences:

First, these crises are very long. The one in which the Fehrenbach Cabinet was formed lasted nineteen days. In a country whose situation is as difficult in every respect as that of Germany, such a lapse of time without a Cabinet, entirely taken up in deliberations and discussions between politicians, is obviously a deplorable state of affairs.

Another consequence is, that not only the Ministries are not homogeneous, which is the necessary consequence of the fact that no party has a majority in the Reichstag, but also they are heterogeneous in a fixed and invariable manner. To constitute a Cabinet there must be observed a triple rule. First, Ministers must be taken from the various political parties that enter the Cabinet; those individuals who are not members of the Reichstag being chosen from among the members of the party represented in the National Assembly. *Secondly, each party has the right to a number of Ministers proportional to the number of its members in the Reichstag.* The only exception to this rule is that the number of members in a Cabinet belonging to the same party must remain the same as in the just discarded Ministry; and if a Minister is withdrawn, the party to which he belongs designates his successor. If because of special circumstances another political group is called upon to fill the vacancy, this group in return as compensation to the other group cedes one of the ministerial seats held by it. Thirdly, the composition of a Ministry must remain unchanged for the whole session of the legislature.

The first Ministry constituted after the meeting of the Constituent Assembly in February, 1919, consisted of Scheidemann, its President, eleven members as department chiefs and three Ministers without portfolio. The parties that assumed government in coalition were, the Social Democrats, who had 163 members in the Assembly, the Democrats with 74 members, and the Centre with 89. The Social Democrats had exactly as many as the other two groups combined. In the Cabinet of fourteen members, therefore, they had seven seats, among them that of the President. The other seats were distributed, four to the Democrats and three to the Centre. During the entire period of the Constituent Assembly—with the exception of three months of the Summer of 1919, when the Democrats, who did not want to sign the treaty of peace, remained voluntarily aloof—the Ministry and the Ministers could change, but the composition of the Ministry rested practically identical. The last Cabinet formed under this Assembly, that of Hermann Müller, comprised at the time of its constitution, March, 1920, eleven Ministers, of whom one was without portfolio. And it was understood that it would later be completed by the addition of three other Ministers then

WORKING OF CONSTITUTIONAL RULES 181

not yet designated. Among the eleven members at first, there were five Social Democrats, three Democrats and three members of the Centre. As for the first Ministry constituted after the elections of 1920, that consisted of five members of the Centre, among them Fehrenbach, three members of the People's Party and two Democrats; which corresponded approximately to the respective strengths of the groups in the Reichstag, viz., 68, 62, 45 members.[1]

Generally the number of Ministers is variable. Instead of having a fixed number of departments corresponding to a rational distribution of affairs, there are created or abolished Ministries according to the needs that have to be met to satisfy the demands of this or that political group. The Scheidemann Ministry had a Minister of Finance. But the Bauer, Hermann Müller, and the Fehrenbach Ministries had, in addition to a Minister of Finance, also a Minister of the Treasury. On the other hand, there was in the Scheidemann Cabinet a Minister of Economy, Wissel, and a Minister of Food Supply, Robert Schmidt. These two Ministers kept their portfolios in Bauer's Cabinet formed in June, 1919. Then dissensions arising between Wissel and the other members of the Cabinet, Wissel resigned. But he was not replaced and the two Cabinet posts were made one. They were again made two, however, and provided with distinct titles in the Cabinets of Hermann Müller and Fehrenbach. A similar situation exists in the case of Ministers without portfolio, whose number, when there are any, is variable.

Sometimes in spite of all possible negotiations and combinations the various groups necessary for a coalition commanding a majority cannot arrive at an agreement. As a government must nevertheless be finally constituted, this or that group, which has refused to enter into the combination,

[1] It includes in addition two members that do not belong to any party—the Minister of Foreign Affairs and the Minister of Transport.

promises nevertheless either its support or its neutrality to those who have had the imprudence to participate in the Cabinet. When the Fehrenbach Cabinet was constituted it could only count on the vote of the groups represented in it and, therefore, commanded only 200 votes in an Assembly of 466 members. But the Social Democrats promised not to overthrow the Ministry until the new elections. The consequence of this is that a Cabinet so placed is really not its own master, and this one had to yield to a certain degree to the injunctions of the Social Democrats. But on the other hand the latter, although they had refused to enter the combination, were indirectly responsible for the acts of the Ministry so long as they tolerated them in power.

When the necessary agreements are concluded, the Ministry appears before the Reichstag. It reads its declaration and programme and a grand political discussion commences. But the programme having been in advance submitted to the groups, sometimes even corrected and redrawn at inter-group meetings, the Ministry is sure of a majority and the discourses are only manifestos by which each party explains why it is for or against the Ministry.

(2) Parliamentary government, in practice, may take one of two different forms: government by the Cabinet or government by the Assembly. In a government by a Cabinet, it is the Council of Ministers that governs and it is they who give the direction of general policy. It is the guide and the superior of the Assembly whose confidence supports it. On the other hand, one calls it government by the Assembly when the Ministry is limited to executing the decisions of the Parliament and to following the initiative of the latter.

In Germany, while it cannot be said that the Reichstag exercises considerable authority over them, it seems that the Ministers take little initiative and that they content them-

WORKING OF CONSTITUTIONAL RULES

selves most often with following the direction given them by the Assembly. It is the agreement that prevailed at the formation of the Cabinet that continues as a policy. The Ministers are either the presidents of the respective political groups, or else have been nominated by these groups. How, therefore, can they be completely independent? There are here some factors analogous to what one called in France "the bloc of the Left" under Minister Combes. All the important measures are first discussed between the government and the groups and the Ministry does not act except in agreement with the groups of the majority. Instead of placing itself at the head of the majority and assuming the responsibility for the measures which it feels necessary to take, the Cabinet comes to an understanding with it. Perhaps it cannot be said that it follows the directions given it by the majority. But it does not act, in any event, unless it is first assured of the majority's support. Perhaps, also, in the critical circumstances which Germany is traversing and given the manner in which its groups are organized, it is impossible to do otherwise. The head of a Cabinet appointed by the chief of the executive power on a programme given him for the realization of this programme, may act with independence, if this programme creates its own majority. Even if it cannot command a stable majority, it can lean on some of the minority groups and, according to circumstances, may create different majorities. There are acts which no one can criticize and there are successes which nullify opposition. But such is not the case in Germany, where the Ministry has to abide by the contract which prevailed at its organization.

(3) The preceding remarks suffice to explain the following fact: since the establishment of the parliamentary régime in Germany *no Ministry has ever been overturned* by the Reichstag. How can it be, if it conforms to the condition of its agreement and if, before each hazardous decision, it assures

itself the approval of the majority? On the other hand, if it cannot obtain this approval, or if it does not want to accept the policy desired by the majority groups, why should it go before the Assembly and engage in a battle lost in advance? It resigns.

The Ministry, therefore, is never overthrown; it retreats, or more correctly, it does not retreat, but changes. The number of men available for a Ministry is very limited and the groups present almost always the same men. There is in advance a certain knowledge as to who the men are who will enter a Cabinet as soon as one knows what groups will participate in the formation. Further, the possibilities of combinations within a given Chamber are limited enough. From the beginning of February, 1919, only four groups have participated in power, of these the People's Party participated only after June, 1920. It is inevitable, therefore, that in each new combination there remain at least two groups which already belonged to the preceding one. Quite naturally these groups leave, without exception, the same men in power. Why change? An important part of the preceding Ministry, therefore, is maintained in each new Ministry.

In June, 1919, Scheidemann's Cabinet, which consisted of Social Democrats, Democrats and members of the Centre, was replaced by Bauer's Cabinet, in which only the Centre and the Social Democrats entered. The members of these two groups which were in the Scheidemann Cabinet remained in the Bauer Cabinet and it was sufficient to replace with members of these two groups the vacancies left by Scheidemann and the Democrats. In March, 1920, Bauer's Cabinet, into which the Democrats entered in October, 1919, attempted a new change after the *coup d'état* of Kapp. Conferences took place, in which took part the President of the Reich, the Ministers and representatives of parties, in which was discussed the question as to which Ministers should remain and which must go.

WORKING OF CONSTITUTIONAL RULES

The more the discussion was prolonged, the greater grew the number of Ministers to remain. But the unions intervened and demanded the resignation of the whole Cabinet. Bauer acceded. Nevertheless the Cabinet, which was thereupon constituted by Hermann Müller, retained several members of the preceding Cabinet, notably Hermann Müller himself, who from Minister of Foreign Affairs became Chancellor, and Bauer, who from Chancellor became Minister of the Treasury. The same procedure took place in the constitution of the Fehrenbach Cabinet. It was expected that a Ministry coming after elections that expressed a considerable change in the political situation, and after the Social Democrats withdrew from power and the People's Party arrived, would translate this change by a more profound modification than usual of the Cabinet. But out of thirteen members five had been members of the preceding Cabinet.

It does not seem, therefore, that the attempt made by the Constitution to regulate as precisely as it may be done the functioning of the government of the Cabinet has had up to now any appreciable effect on the practice of parliamentarism. Germany begins at a point that other countries, in which parliamentary government has operated for years, have hardly attained, if they have at all attained it. A concentrated Cabinet, a Cabinet of republican defence, a Cabinet of transition, a *bloc* of the Centre—are these accidental deformities of the parliamentary régime, or are they forms toward which it must necessarily tend? We are told in Germany that these practices, obviously little compatible with the conception of parliamentarism or with the regulations provided in their Constitution, are to be explained by the state of revolution in which the country still finds itself; and that they will disappear if some day Germany recovers its equilibrium, and make place for a correct and complete application of constitutional rule.

SECTION IV

THE REICHSRAT

The Reichsrat is placed by the Constitution by the side of the Reichstag, the President and the Cabinet, and has as its rôle the representation, after these, of the States of the Reich in legislative and administrative matters.

1.—GENERAL FEATURES OF THE REICHSRAT.

The Reichsrat constitutes a bond of co-operation between the Reich and the States. Whereas the will of the whole German people taken together is manifested through the Reichstag, the Reichsrat translates the will of the States, such as it is conceived by the governments or cabinets of these States.

The Reichsrat is the representative in the Reich of the federalist principle. It is the federalist organ of the Reich. In this rôle it joins the unitary organs and completes them.

The Reichsrat is the successor of the Commission of States of the Provisional Constitution and of the Bundesrat of the old Constitution. But as the unitary idea made important progress, the Reichstag was endowed with powers considerably less extensive than those of the Bundesrat. The latter, which represented the confederated governments collectively, was the holder of sovereignty under the Empire. The Reichsrat, on the other hand, since the new Constitution placed sovereignty in the German people, is only an organ by which the governments of the states participate in the legislative and administrative powers of the Reich. Instead of being endowed, as compared to the Reichstag, with powers equal or superior to it, as the former Bundesrat was, it has received but very limited rights.

The question whether it would not have been better to organize instead of the Reichsrat a Chamber of States, which would represent, not the various cabinets, but the populations of the states, was vigorously debated. It may be recalled that it was this solution Preuss proposed: a Chamber of States composed of delegates of German republics. These delegates would be elected by the Diets of the republics and would be selected from among the citizens of these republics. In principle, each state would have a delegate for each million inhabitants.

Such an organism would constitute a very characteristic application of the centralist idea. But it was thought that this would create, by the side of the Reichstag, a new popular representation, and that this would not take into account the necessity of organizing a representation of states. What was needed actually was the creation of an organ, within which would be realized an equilibrium between the voices and the needs of the Reich on the one hand and the voices and the needs of the states on the other; if it was not wished to suppress completely the federal structure of the Reich and make of it simply a unitary state. This organism would have to include technical and vocational representatives of the interests of the states, leaving aside the idea of parties and all the programmes of parties. That is to say, there would have to be representatives of the governments of the states, not merely political representatives. The National Assembly decided on a Reichsrat organized on the model of the former Bundesrat, representing the governments of the states and endowed with less extensive powers.

The Reichsrat differs profoundly as to authority from the old Bundesrat. It has lost completely the sovereign character of the Bundesrat. It has not even the right to issue administrative regulations, this right having been taken away from it and given to the Cabinet. It has ceased to be, in comparison with the Reichstag, a legislative organ invested with rights equal to those of the Reichstag; and it has no more than a very limited right to co-operate with it in legislative work.

This institution, therefore, comprehends both historic tradition and the actual situation of the Reich. But it marks at the same time a progress in the sense of a stronger unity of the Reich, and it should in the future facilitate a new development of the unitary idea.

2.—THE COMPOSITION AND THE FUNCTIONING OF THE REICHSRAT.

"In the National Council each State has at least one vote. In the case of the larger States one vote is accorded for every million inhabitants. Any excess equal at least to the population of the smallest State is reckoned as equivalent to a full million. No State shall be accredited with more than two-fifths of all votes." (Article 61.)

The original proposal provided that three years after the Constitution had entered into effect, small States having less than a million inhabitants would lose their right to be represented in the Reichsrat. The obvious purpose of this provision was to compel, by indirect means, the small States to join together, as well as to prevent the unnecessary parcelling out of territories with the view of creating new States. This measure, however, was not accepted by the committee. We know that in its place the committee and the National Assembly accepted a resolution inviting the government to interpose in the hope of realizing a union of small States.[1]

[1] Article 64 provided also that after the reunion of Austria with the German Reich the latter would have the right to be represented in the Reichstag numerically in proportion to the size of its population. Until such union the representatives of German Austria would have only a consultative voice. This provision, contrary both in letter and spirit to Article 80 of the Peace Treaty, brought a protest from the Supreme Council of the Allied Powers and their associates. The first note on September 2, 1919, demanded the abolition of the offending provision by constitutional amendment within a fortnight. On September 5, the German government replied that no article of the Constitution could be in contradiction with the Treaty of Peace, for

THE REICHSRAT

An early distribution of seats, after the adoption of the Constitution, on the basis of Article 61, gave to Prussia twenty-five votes out of the total of sixty-three in the Reichsrat. But, as we know, after May, 1920, seven small states of Central Germany formed the State of Thuringia, which had 1,584,324 inhabitants and was entitled to two votes. By this the number of non-Prussian votes in the Reichsrat was reduced by five, which also diminished the number of votes coming from Prussia from its former twenty-five to twenty-two. So long as no new changes in the interior geographic configuration of the Reich are made, the distribution of votes in the Reichsrat will be as follows: Prussia, twenty-two; Bavaria, seven; Saxony, five; Wurtemberg, three; Baden, three; Hesse, two; Thuringia, two; other States, one each. Total, fifty-five.

The States are represented by members of their Cabinets. So it was under the old régime. There is, however, an essential difference, for the Cabinets now depend on the confidence

Article 78, paragraph 2, expressly provides that no constitutional provision may carry any attempt against the treaty. This reply justly seemed to the Allies insufficient. Article 78, paragraph 2, constitutes, it is true, on the part of the drafters of the Constitution an excellent measure of precaution against contradictions between the Constitution and the Treaty not provided for in advance and revealed in practice. But the contradiction pointed out by the note of the Allies of September 2 was too clear and evident to have been accidental. The Allied Powers, therefore, demanded that the German Government send by means of a diplomatic document the interpretation contained in its note of September 5. This is the text, therefore, of a supplementary declaration drawn up by the German Cabinet and ratified by the National Assembly:

"The undersigned, duly authorized in the name of the German Government, recognize and declare that all provisions of the German Constitution of August 11, 1919, that are in contradiction with stipulations of the Treaty of Peace signed at Versailles on June 28, 1919, are without force, and that particularly the admission of the representatives of Austria as members of the Reichstag cannot be effected except if, in conformance with Article 80 of the Treaty of Peace, the League of Nations sanctions a change in the international situation of Austria. The present declaration must be ratified by the competent authorities within a fortnight after the Treaty of Peace becomes operative."

in them of the Diets elected by universal suffrage. It is public opinion that governs in the States now and no longer the will of an autocratic government, independent of this opinion. The government of a state is responsible before the Diet for the manner in which its representatives exercise their mandates in the Reichsrat, whether the members of the Cabinet are themselves present there or whether they are represented by civil servants. The former provisions relating to instructions given by Cabinets of States to their plenipotentiaries in the Reichsrat, as well as measures to insure that the representatives of each state shall join in a common vote, have become useless and have not been incorporated into the Constitution.

The provision according to which the states are all represented by their Cabinets has been changed, however, in one respect. Article 63 specifies that only half of the Prussian votes will be at the disposal of the Prussian Cabinet, the other half being at the disposal of the Prussian provincial administrations. Thus the National Assembly, which has not had the force to effect directly a dismemberment of the Prussian state, and which has deferred for over two years every effort to be made toward this end, has nevertheless attempted to anticipate this reform. It seems in effect that if the Prussian provinces receive progressively more and more autonomy, if the powers granted to them become comparable to the more and more diminishing powers of the states, the assimilation of these provinces to states other than Prussia will be facilitated and hastened by the fact that these provinces, like states, are directly represented in the Reichsrat. Each of them will be able to defend its own particular interest, different, perhaps, from those of other provinces. Each province, above all, will be able to defend its rights and make its interests prevail when in conflict with those of the Prussian State, whose dominant centralization will thus be broken.

This solution is not entirely satisfactory, for the regrouping which must be proceeded to in the Reich must be inspired above all by social and economic considerations. And it must have as its aim the creation of an autonomous body capable of self-development and productivity. Above all in this work, the historic frontiers of the States must be disregarded since these frontiers have been drawn to satisfy dynastic interests or to conclude victorious wars. What is true of the interior of the Reich is also true of Prussia. The Prussian provinces are not natural organisms in whose interests there should be created and developed a political life.

Still, Article 63, for lack of other provision, constitutes progress, which, however, does not seem as yet to be near realization. This Article provides, in effect, that the manner in which Prussian votes at the disposal of the provinces shall be distributed must be regulated by a Prussian State Law; and Article 168 provides that until the adoption of this law but, at the most for only a year, all the Prussian votes in the Reichsrat may be cast by members of the State Cabinet. This law should already have been adopted and applied. This has not been done, however, and the Prussian government has asked and obtained a modification of Article 168, which prolongs the delay accorded to Prussia and gives it till July 1, 1921, to pass this law. In support of this request Prussia claimed that the reduction of its total number of votes in the Reichsrat to twenty-two made the distribution of this number among the provinces more difficult. In reality, however, the Prussian government under the Republic remains true to its traditional tactics, which consist in opposing all development and progress by means of the most obstinate passivity. Until the new state of representation is adopted the twenty-two Prussian votes will be cast by the members of the Prussian Cabinet or by delegates named by it.

The Reichsrat has the right to create its own committees.[1]

[1] The committees thus formed are eleven in number and each consists of nine members. They are, committees on foreign affairs, political economy, interior administration, commerce and audits, taxes and cus-

But the privileges which certain states, particularly Prussia, enjoyed in the committees of the old Bundesrat are suppressed; particularly as no state may hereafter have more than one vote on any committee. (Article 62.) The Reichsrat, in contrast to the Reichstag, has not the right freely to convene. It must be convoked by the Cabinet of the Reich. Nevertheless, it has a right to convoke itself if the demand is made by a third of its members. It is the Cabinet that presides over the Reichsrat and its committees; but the Cabinet has not the right to vote in either of these. The Reichsrat has the right and the power to demand that the members of the Cabinet be present at its meetings or at the meetings of its committees. It may invite there the Chancellor and the Ministers and the latter are obliged to attend. Those invited have the right at all times to be heard in the deliberations. By this means the Reichsrat has the possibility of participating in the policies of the Reich. It is true that no fixed influence is guaranteed to it by the Constitution. What authority it will be able to exercise in the future will depend on the quality of its work and on the personalities by which the states will be represented. The Cabinet of the Reich, like all the members of the Reichsrat, is authorized to propose measures in the Reichsrat. The plenary sessions of the latter, in contrast to those of the Bundesrat, are theoretically public; its committee meetings are not. Decisions are made by a simple majority of those voting.

3.—POWERS OF THE REICHSRAT.

The former Bundesrat was an organ which had in legislative matters the same rights as the Reichstag. It exercised in addition important executive functions; in particular it had the right to promulgate general administrative regulations for executing the laws of the Reich. It was the central

toms, justice, the Constitution and interior regulation, the army, navy, and the execution of the Treaty of Peace.

administrative authority in matters relating to customs and taxes. It decided conflicts of a constitutional character as well as miscarriages of justice. Of all these powers few have descended to the Reichsrat. In order to emphasize the idea of the unity of the Reich and of the sovereignty of the whole German people in the Reich, the new Constitution limits to a considerable extent the powers of the Reichsrat. However, it has left it a certain right to participate in the making of laws and in the exercise of executive power.

In legislative matters, it will be recalled, that all proposals of laws on the part of the Cabinet must be presented at first to the Reichsrat; in theory, must be accepted by it before being submitted to the Reichstag. But as we know this consent is not indispensable and the government may disregard it. It will be recalled also that the Reichsrat has the right to protest against any law voted by the Reichstag; but that it may have its protest disregarded under certain conditions.

Already the Reichsrat has made use of its right of protest. That was done in connection with a bill that raised postal taxes. The National Assembly, acting in the character of the Reichstag, had voted a provision according to the terms of which the sending by mail of official documents would have to be paid for, no longer by him who received them, but by the sender. The representatives of Prussia, Bavaria and of Saxony criticized in the Reichsrat this measure, and found support in the Assembly to the extent of a majority of thirty-eight votes. Whereupon the Reichsrat raised a protest against this measure, April 29, 1920. The bill then returned to the National Assembly; but the conflict ended with a compromise, without recourse to the procedure provided by the Constitution for such a case.

The Reichsrat still possesses some executive powers. On the one hand, the Constitution and the law frequently stipulate that a regulation by the Cabinet of the Reich must be authorized by the Reichsrat. On the other hand, the law of April 17, 1919, "for a simplified form of legislation on economic matters" provides that regulations decreed by the Cabinet in this matter must be approved both by the Reichsrat and by a committee of twenty-eight members of the Assembly. The Reichsrat and the Committee have in this case absolutely equal rights. Finally Article 67 provides that the Reichsrat must be kept informed by the national departments of the conduct of national business.

CHAPTER V

FUNDAMENTAL RIGHTS AND DUTIES OF GERMANS

The second part of the Constitution of Weimar is devoted entirely to the fundamental rights and duties of Germans. It is the Declaration of Rights of the new Germany. Aside from several articles relating exclusively to the economic organization of the Reich, the five sections of this part contain a long enumeration of the rights and duties granted to or imposed on the Germans. To enter into details of this enumeration would be to undertake a study of all of German public and private law. Nevertheless an attempt must be made to outline the principal ideas.

1.—LEGAL AND POLITICAL ASPECTS OF FUNDAMENTAL RIGHTS AND DUTIES.

The articles relative to fundamental rights and duties, during the discussion of the draft of the Constitution, were the subjects of lively differences of opinion. It was questioned whether it was necessary and useful to insert such provisions into the Constitution; moreover, every one of these provisions one after another was debated. The Bismarckian Constitution of 1871 contains no declaration of rights. On the other hand, the drafters of the Constitution of 1849 proposed such a great number of fundamental rights and applied themselves with such complacence to the elaboration of these rights that the Constituent Assembly of that time was unable to make itself heeded, and this defeat contributed largely to the defeat of the whole of the project of such rights.

The first proposal of the Cabinet following the tradition of the proposal of 1849 and also the Declaration of Rights of the French Revolution, as well as of the American, Belgian and Prussian Constitutions, enumerated in a few paragraphs several essential legal principles and enunciated some fundamental dogmas which have been considered for a century and in all civilized countries as self-evident truths. But in the Constitutional Committee the discussion went far beyond these generalities. Desirous of creating an intellectual background in which justice and administration would have to operate, desiring also to furnish in the form of some suggestive maxims a guide for the conduct of some of the most important matters in the legal domain, and to furnish a solid foundation for the juridical culture of the German people, the members of the Constitutional Committee nominated a sub-committee, which prepared a new draft whose provisions were embodied in the draft of the Cabinet, in different bills prepared on private initiative, as well as in the new Constitutions of Baden and Wurtemberg. In the drawing up of this new draft the principal rôle was played by Beyerle, member of the Centre.

In the course of the discussions in sub-committee, in Committee, as well as in plenary session, three currents appeared. Some wanted to suppress drastically all declarations of rights in the Constitution of the Reich; for they saw in these principles no stable system, but only a collection of "declarations and declamations," to which were joined some legal maxims figuring already in other laws. Others wanted to retain the system embodied in the cabinet draft, adding to it, however, several provisions to assure the protection of the rights acquired for religious denominations. A third group, among whom principally was Frederick Naumann, held that the cabinet draft, even thus extended, was retrogression and did not correspond to the actual development of German culture. They demanded that there be substituted for it a declaration of fundamental rights which would constitute a recognition of the principal ideas that characterize the most recent development of this culture.

The Constitutional Committee, and after it the National Assembly itself, adopted a middle course. The propositions by Naumann as a whole were rejected; and it was decided not to inscribe in the Constitution, in political sentences and aphorisms without any legal content, a complete and solemn recognition of the directing ideas of the present and of the future. Nevertheless there would be inserted in the Constitution a certain number of political maxims and of "programme thoughts." This done, the Constituent Assembly wished, in the words of Düringer, to give a foundation to the existing legal culture, and to furnish a mirror to German juridical life, and at the same time afford a programme for future juridical development. In addition the principles voted, since they would figure in the text of the Constitution, would have to be placed under the express guarantee of the Constitution and thus become part of the fundamental law of the Reich. The Assembly hoped, finally, that these articles would exercise a certain educational function. They would constitute the basis of the civic and political education of the people. The fundamental rights would have to be not only "the keystone of the edifice, but must also become the substance whereby the Constitution would live."

This was a magnificent programme; unfortunately it was difficult to carry it out and the most severe criticisms were rightly, it seems, made against the manner in which it was carried out.

When the articles relating to the fundamental rights and duties were being drawn up, the members of the National Assembly of necessity remained party men, and were guided, even when they voted on philosophico-legal questions, by party considerations. Also some of these "fundamental rights" had the appearance of being simply extracts from programmes or brochures of political parties. On the other hand, the members who drew them up naturally put in the foreground the problems which, at the time of the discussions, were the burning questions in both Parliament and in public opinion. The result is that the second part of the Constitution regulates questions of the day rather than of the future, and issues prescriptions for circumstances more than it proclaims fundamental rights.

However, all this would have been admissable, if there had been one big party that could have without constraint and without difficulty incorporated its own principles in the Constitution; or even if there had been two or more parties with fairly similar conceptions, which were able to agree on fundamental rights. There would have been at least a Declaration of Rights that might have corresponded to the conceptions of the majority. But there was no such majority in the National Assembly. To be sure, there was an impressive majority that agreed on a democratic Constitution. But on questions of schools, church, the family, and of economic and agrarian reforms—questions that had to be dealt with in the statement of fundamental rights—there was in the National Assembly and in the parties of the majority such divergence of opinion that it was impossible to construct of it any logical or coherent edifice. Also, in reading each provision of the fundamental rights, one can guess which party has furnished the first part of a phrase and which the second. When, for example, referring to property one reads, "The right of property is guaranteed by the Constitution. Its nature and limits are defined by law"; or, when in Article 152 a phrase declares, "There is an economic liberty in the measure indicated by the law," every one, no matter what may be his personal conceptions, may find himself entirely satisfied, according to whether the first or the last words of each provision are emphasized. This evident compromise between the political parties on political conceptions so widely divergent was emphatically pointed out by Member of the Assembly Koch, who characterized the fundamental rights as "an interfractional political programme."[1]

From the legal point of view, the defects of this programme are no less serious. It is extremely difficult, if not impossible, to know what authority and what meaning should be attached to the fundamental rights. What precisely does such a phrase as one in Article 109 mean? "Privileges or discriminations due to birth or rank and recognized by law are abolished." Does, again, the provision in Article 115, according to which "The house of every German is his sanctuary and is inviolable," prevent a commissioner of buildings from dividing spacious lodgings in order to combat a housing crisis?

What is still more regrettable is that the Constitution never specifies to what extent the fundamental rights have or have not legal force. Do all previously enacted laws that are irreconcilable with fundamental rights in the Constitution cease to operate the moment the Constitution comes into force? Should not this solution be applicable only to laws enacted after the adoption of the Constitution and for such of their provisions as are contrary to the Constitution? Or must it be interpreted that the fundamental rights have no importance other than to constrain legislatures to subject existing legislation to the principles these rights proclaim, and to vote only for laws that conform to these principles? Finally, are not these fundamental rights merely general indications which may be expected to have such moral force as they can impose on the legislature?

It was attempted to bring some clarity into the chaos of the discussions on this head. At first a proposal was made according to which any one had the right to complain before a tribunal of all injurious violations of fundamental rights. This was rejected; for otherwise any one belonging to the middle classes could complain on the basis of the provision of Article

[1] See Koch, *Die Grundrechte in der Verfassung, Deutsche Juristen Zeitung*, 1919, p. 609, et seq.

164, according to which "The independent . . . middle-class shall be fostered," and claim that the provision was a dead letter. There was voted, however, on the first reading a provision according to which the fundamental rights would constitute "a course and a limitation for legislation, administration, and jurisprudence in the Reich and in the States." This phrase would have increased, without any possible ambiguity, the immediate legal efficacy of the fundamental rights. It was, however, done away with at the second reading, for it would not have been applicable except to provisions which have a positive content, and it would have had, aside from this, only the character of an abstract maxim for scholastic manuals. It was decided, therefore, not to specify in any way whatever the legal significance of the articles of the Constitution relating to fundamental rights and duties. It would fall to legislators, judges and public officers to interpret in the future each of these articles separately, and to be guided according to the results of this interpretation. If, however, one may attempt such an interpretation, it would appear that these articles, from the point of view of their legal efficacy, may be divided into three catagories.

(1) Those having the force of law. These create actually and immediately some new law, and consequently abrogate contradictory provisions of antecedent laws. Such, for example, is Article 109, par. 6: "No German may accept a title or order from a foreign Government."

(2) Others limit themselves to *indicating* to legislators of the Reich and of the States the *course which they must in the future follow* and prescribe the laws they must enact. But these provisions do not in themselves constitute laws, and, therefore, cannot abrogate *ipso facto*, contradictory provisions in antecedent laws. Such is the principle in Article 145, according to which "Instruction and school supplies . . . are free." This cannot have for its effect the immediate doing away with payments by pupils in the schools for supplies fur-

nished them. There is no doubt that the principle of gratuity cannot enter into operation except through a special law expressly prescribed.

(3) Other provisions express *general truths*, which are most often *ordinary philosophico-legal commonplaces*, whose exact meaning and bearing in a text such as the Constitution is difficult to grasp. For example, it is hard to see the special significance which a phrase can have in a constitutional document such as the one which declares that marriage is placed under the special protection of the Constitution.

However diverse may be the conceptions that prevailed at the drawing up of the fundamental rights, and whatever uncertainty they may present from the legal point of view, it is possible, nevertheless, when the whole of the second part of the Constitution of Weimar is surveyed, to discover in these articles some common characteristics and to unfold the fundamental ideas that have inspired the majority of the Constituent Assembly.

It is evident that the Assembly conceived the fundamental rights and duties in a manner quite different from that of the authors of preceding Declarations of Rights in America, France, or even in Germany. These declarations were inspired by purely individualistic doctrine. Man is by nature free and independent; he holds rights that are limited only by such other rights as will assure to other men the enjoyment of the same rights as his. From this ensues a two-fold consequence. First, he may act in his own right provided that he confines himself within the limits of the right in question. Within these rights he is truly sovereign, and the state may not encroach on them to impose any obligation whatsoever. On the other hand, conversely, the state does not owe any positive service or pledge to the profit of the individual. It must abstain from all interference and allow him free individual activities. The State owes nothing to the individual, who in turn can claim nothing from it.

This doctrine does not appear in the new German Constitution. The Assembly at Weimar has substituted for it a conception by virtue of which man, while still, it is true, enjoying a certain number of individual prerogatives, nevertheless *must place them at the service of the collectivity.* In whatever concerns liberty properly so-called, property, the means of production, the intellectual development of man, there is found everywhere this dominant idea of the social function of man. Individual liberties are no longer an end in themselves, nor do they constitute any longer an independent good. *They are limited and conditioned by the duty of the individual to co-operate in the well-being and the development of the collectivity.* They have no value and are not protected except in the measure that they serve for the accomplishment of this social duty.

2.—FUNDAMENTAL RIGHTS AND DUTIES OF THE INDIVIDUAL.

The Constitution commences by enumerating as completely as possible individual liberties such as traditionally figure in most declarations of rights. Not a single one of them is left out, and there have been even others added: equality, at least in theory, of men and women; protection of minorities; the right to secrecy in telegraphic and telephonic communication; liberty of opinion extended to manifestations of thought by means of motion picture films, etc.

One may, therefore, apply for the Germans the classic table of individual liberties.

First, the civil equality. The suppression of privileges of birth or of class. Titles of nobility have no other value except as a part of a name. Titles may not be conferred except as they designate an employment or a function. The state may no longer confer orders or honorary insignia and no German may accept a title or order from a foreign government.

Then come the individual liberties properly so-called; not only the right to come and go, but also the right to settle in any part of the Reich, to emigrate to any non-German country, to be protected from surrender to a foreign government for prosecution or punishment; guarantee against arbitrary arrests, imprisonment, and other penalties; the inviolability of domicile and correspondence.

In a third place, the right to freedom of activity; liberty to engage in work, commerce and industry; liberty of creed and conscience; liberty to practise religion; liberty of instruction; liberty to express publicly one's thoughts by words, speeches, printed matter, figures, films and in any other manner; liberty of assembly and association.

In the fourth place the liberty of individual property. This cannot be expropriated except for the common good, by virtue of a legislative provision and must be indemnified.

The enumeration of rights and duties is complete, but the idea that prevailed at its adoption is different from that which inspired the authors of preceding Declarations of Rights. In recognizing the liberties of the individual, the object is no longer to protect him against the State, but to permit him to co-operate in the most effective fashion in the well-being of all.

This leads naturally to the imposition on the liberty of the individual of a certain number of restrictions hitherto unknown. On the other hand, it imposes on the state a certain number of new duties, the discharge of which affords, as corollaries, new rights to the individual.

I.—INDIVIDUAL RIGHTS ARE SUBJECT TO CERTAIN NEW RESTRICTIONS IN THE INTERESTS OF THE COLLECTIVITY.—The individual is no longer merely entitled to work. *It is his duty*. This obligation is provided for by Article 1, par. 1, of the socialization law of March 23, 1919, which has become Article 163, par. 1, of the Constitution. "Every German has, without prejudice to his personal liberty, the moral duty so to use his intellectual and physical powers as is demanded by the welfare of the community."[1]

It is true, therefore, that personal liberty is conditioned. The draft of the socialization law submitted by the Cabinet did not contain these conditions, and the Social Democratic Minister, Wissel, in open session of the National Assembly, expressly rejected the principle of the liberty of the individual. In the same manner the Social Democrats and the Independents proposed amendments according to which the sole liberty guaranteed to the individual was that of choosing his profession; this one right availed of, the liberty of the individual was thereupon used up, and he must thereafter conduct himself exclusively according to the needs of community. But a coalition of all the representatives of the bourgeois parties organizing against the conceptions behind the Socialist proposal, the provision concerning the principle of the liberty of employment was introduced into the law of March 23, 1919, and into the Constitution.

Saving his personal liberty, therefore, every German also has work as his moral duty; that is to say, he should contribute all the economic work that he is capable of according to his physical and intellectual abilities. In addition, this work must correspond to a definite condition; it must be such as is "demanded by the welfare of the community."

In Germany many see in this provision a central point of the law and hold that it constitutes as a real transition from the old world to the new. Formerly every German could, under the protection of the law, so dispose of his work that it served only his selfish ends. Without regard to the interests of his fellow citizens or those of the community, he could, pro-

---

[1] It should be observed that this provision has been decreed by a law; consequently there can be no question in regard to it whether it is a provision having the force of law or only a moral maxim. It is a legislative provision. The fact that it was later inserted into the Constitution has only the effect of preventing its abrogation or its modification other than by constitutional amendment.

vided that he observed the outer forms of the law, so to speak, "walk over dead bodies" without violating a single legal provision. In a general way and aside from insignificant exceptions, there reigned in the century of economic liberalism an unlimited egoism of the individual, protected by the adage *qui jure suo utitur, nemine lædit*. The socialization law radically changed this state of affairs. Hereafter every German is obliged, for the well-being of the whole German people, to furnish all the productive labor of which he is capable, and must abstain from all action liable to hinder this well-being. It is only within these limits that economic egoism may hereafter move.

However, this novel duty to work is as yet only a "moral duty." These words, which were not found in the original draft by the Cabinet, were added by the Constitutional Committee; and the Independents tried, but in vain, to have them omitted. It does not seem, however, that the majority which has adopted them, has ever given them a clear, unequivocal meaning. One thing is clear, however; the law wished to distinguish between a moral duty and a positive legal obligation, whose execution can be expressly compelled. But it is perhaps possible to interpret this provision in such a way that the violation of the duty to work may involve legal consequences, which can have as a result the right on the part of the state to exercise indirect constraint on the individual who does not carry out his duty. The German who does not work, or who lets himself be dominated in his work by purely selfish ends, has no longer the right to demand protection of the laws; he cannot demand that his work shall be protected by the Reich. Perhaps one may even go so far as to appeal to the article of the Civil Code, according to which all legal procedure that violates good morals is null;[1] and hold it applicable to acts and contracts that do not correspond to the moral

---

[1] This principle of civil law has also become now a provision of constitutional law (Article 152).

duty imposed by the socialization law and by the Constitution. In the same way perhaps also Article 826 of the Civil Code may be applied, according to which any one who in a manner contrary to good morals deliberately causes damage to others is obliged to repair this damage; and it may be argued that an act or contract inspired by a selfish end falls under the provision of this law and brings about in such a case an obligation to compensate the community.

Being obliged to work, is the individual at least master of the product of his toil? May he dispose of his property as he wishes? No longer. As with his work, the *individual must place his property at the service of the community.* And the same idea that has resulted in the restriction of his liberty to work now leads to a corresponding restriction of his right over property; "Property rights imply property duties." (Article 153.) These restrictions are several kinds.

First, that of *expropriation.* It is true that this was already admitted in individualist doctrine. But this doctrine hemmed the right of expropriation on the part of the state within narrow limits, inasmuch as it prescribed strictly the cases in which the state could use this right, and provided always the payment of a just and, usually, a previously ascertained indemnity. These two guarantees given to property owners are strikingly diminished in the new German constitutional law. On the one hand, it is true the principle is retained that expropriation must not be resorted to except for the welfare of the community. But this notion of general welfare has been particularly elastic. Thus in Article 155 the State is permitted to expropriate in cases of housing crises, in the interests of settlement and reclamation of land, or in the improvement of agriculture. Thus the Socialization Law and after it the Constitution in Article 156 permit the state to transfer to public ownership private business enterprises adapted for socialization. On the other hand, the principle of a just indemnity seems to have been retained. However, there is but one case in which indemnity is imposed and guaranteed by the Constitution; it is that where the Reich expropriates "the property of the States, municipalities, and associations of public utility." In all other cases the restriction provided in Article 153 applies; expropriation takes place with indemnity "in so far as is not otherwise provided by national law."

In addition to expropriation, the Constitution provides other restrictions on the right of property:

Land owners are under the *obligation to cultivate it and utilize it*. However, there is no provision made in case this duty is not carried out.

The right of inheritance is guaranteed, but the State has the right to take part of the inheritance according to provisions determined by the laws of the Reich, in particular fiscal laws.

An increase in the value of land arising without the application of labour or capital to the property accrues to the benefit of the community as a whole.

Entailments are dissolved. This provision is an obligatory prescription imposed on the legislatures of the States, which obliges them to put an end to entailments, for this matter is given over by the Civil Code to the rights of States. By entailments is understood the legal institution by which a patrimony, particularly holdings of land, because of the limitation of the right to sell and the establishment of a certain succession provided by a testament, creates for the owning family in the person of the holder of the entail an economic position of security and thereby of increased advantage. These entails often go back considerably in time, but they are very frequent in Germany, to such an extent that land holdings subject to this legislation comprise, for example, in Prussia about seven per cent of all the landed properties, with about two and a half million hectares. In certain sections entailed property represents about twenty-two per cent of the whole agricultural service. For a long time now it has been questioned whether this institution, which tends to the concentration of more and more land into fewer and fewer hands, should not be abrogated. It is argued in particular against the entails that the community cannot allow a mere decision taken by the private will of a proprietor to be perpetuated; that entails have an unfavourable effect on the distribution of land and that they finally tend to wipe out the small and the average property. It follows of itself that with the victory of the democratic idea and in an epoch in which the tendency is to divide each piece of land as far as possible, entailments must be dissolved. In leaving to the States the legislation on this dissolution, the Constitution has only applied logically the democratic principles on which it rests.[1]

II.—IN TURN THE STATE IS OBLIGED TO FULFIL A CERTAIN NUMBER OF DUTIES TO THE BENEFIT OF INDIVIDUALS.—The classic individualist doctrine limits the rights of the State but does not impose upon it any positive service, no obligation to the benefit of its citizens. The State must abstain from certain interferences, but the individual may claim no more than that of it. German constitutional law, however, adopts another conception, and while it restrains individual rights for the benefit of a community, it also imposes upon the latter obligations to the profit of the individual. From this there arise to the profit of the latter new rights corresponding to the restrictions to which he is subject.

The individual owes the duty of working, but the State owes him the chance to work, must protect his work and according to circumstances must furnish him with the necessities of life. From this is derived for the individual the right to work, the right to the protection of his work and the right of subsistence.

[1] It must be also noted that up to now the States have not as yet complied with this order of the Constitution. In Prussia in particular it does not seem that measures have yet been enacted against the "fideicommis."

The State must furnish work to the individual. This obligation explains itself very easily. When the individual is left free to use his labour as he pleases, that is to say, when he is free to work exclusively in the interests of purely selfish ends, he must also be left the right to look for such work and to dispose of his labour where and how he pleases. The community disassociates itself from a work in which it is not directly a beneficiary or from which it may even suffer. But if it demands of the individual that he devote himself only to such labour as will benefit the whole of the nation, and if it forbids him, therefore, a certain number of occupations which benefit only the individual, it is indispensable that it take measures to guarantee him sufficient remunerative work. Article 163, par. 2, provides therefore: "Every German shall have the opportunity to earn his living by economic labour."

Of what exactly consists this duty on the part of the State? It is certainly not a legal obligation that gives the individual the right to demand before a tribunal the execution of this promise. It is a promise that the Constitution makes and which it sufficiently fulfils if the Reich institutes a general system to make known all the available possibilities for work. An individual may ask only what kind of work is available and what opportunity there is of securing it. The proposal of the Socialization Law provided that every German shall receive work corresponding to his powers. The final text of this law, like that of the text of the Constitution, limits itself to prescribing that every German must be given the opportunity to earn his living by economic labour, that is to say, by labour that produces goods, utilizing to the utmost the available conditions of work. In addition, the compensation to the individual must be sufficient for a livelihood.

The State in addition protects labour. The Socialization Law declares that the power of labour is the most precious economic good and it imposes on the Reich the legal obligation to protect it. The Constitution of Weimar applies in Article 157 the terms of the law of March 23, with the exception of the words, "the most precious economic good." But the Constitution also extends and organizes in outline the duty of the State in this respect. It amplifies this duty in expressly specifying in its Article 158 that intellectual labour also is under the special protection of the Reich. As to the measures for the protection of labour, some of them come under domestic law, others under international law. Within the Reich itself the Constitution prescribes the creation of uniform labour legislation. In addition it guarantees to every individual and to every vocation the liberty of organization for the defence and the development of the conditions of labour and of economic life, and it accords to each employé and laborer the free time necessary for the exercise of the civil duties and free public functions that may be given to him. Finally, it promises a complete system of social insurance to be established for the maintenance of health and standards in labour. In international relation, the Constitution imposes on the Reich the obligation to protect abroad the products of German science, art and technique, and to strive for the establishment of an international regulation of the legal status of workers.

Finally the State must provide for the needs of individuals out of work; and this obligation logically results from the principle that inspires all of this part of the Constitution. Since the Reich imposes on every German the obligation to work only for the good of the community, it must see to it—apart from any humanitarian or financial considerations—that every German's capacity for labour shall be maintained as long and at as high a standard as possible. That is why, not content with merely protecting this capacity of labour, the Socialization Law and the Constitution provide that every German must receive what is necessary for his livelihood, to the extent that a possibility of adequate employment cannot be assured to him (Article 163).

The draft of the Socialization Law provided as a condition to this duty on the part of the State that the individual shall not have been able to find employment. The final text of the law which the Constitution also uses provides only that such opportunity for employment shall not have been offered.

The burden of the proof is thus reversed from the general rule and an attitude purely passive on the part of the individual in this respect is sufficient to entitle him to public succour. On the other hand, it is not sufficient for the discharge of all such obligations on the part of the State if it merely offers the individual any employment whatsoever. For it does not serve the community in any way, as the most interested party, when an individual is employed in work for which he is not fitted. The community, therefore, must procure work corresponding to the mental and physical powers of the individual and to his capacity. If the State does not succeed in doing so, it is obliged to furnish him a livelihood.

To put into operation the principles thus enunciated by the Constitution, different laws are necessary—a law on the offer of employment, a law protecting labour, a law on the help to be given to the unemployed. Such laws have not yet been enacted. However, a certain number of ordinances have been passed that constitute on the part of the Reich the beginning of the execution of the new obligations imposed upon it.

First, measures have been taken to procure employment for individuals. To this end, aside from the ordinance of December 9, 1918, which imposes on municipalities the obligation of organizing employment bureaus, public and impartial, there is also an ordinance of May 5, 1920,[1] creating for the Reich a bureau devoted to finding employment. This

[1] *Reichsgesetzblatt*, 1920, p. 876.

agency has for its principal function a survey of the labour market and the editing of periodical bulletins on the situation in this market for the purpose of establishing an equilibrium between supply and demand in the different regions and in the different vocations.

Measures have been taken also to protect labour. The first step toward the creation of uniform labour legislation was made by the provisional ordinance of January 24, 1919, which, supplementing the divisions of the Civil Code, regulates labour in agricultural and forestry exploitations.[1] Social insurance legislation, such as is found codified in the law of the Empire of July, 1911, i. e., as sickness, accident, disability and death insurance, has been supplemented by different provisions, particularly by a law of December 29, 1919, relative to the protection of pregnant women.

Finally, regarding the obligation to provide livelihood for unemployed, different ordinances have been issued which were codified by an ordinance of January 26, 1920.[2] According to these ordinances, the duty of organizing a service for the supplying of the needs of unemployed—a service which must not take on the character of charity—falls upon the municipalities, which are assisted financially by the Reich to the extent of six-twelfths of the total expense and by the State with four-twelfths of this expense. The municipalities must refuse this help to those who do not accept the work offered them, even if this work does not fit the vocation of the one refusing and even if it must be done away from home, provided always that this work be adapted to the physical

[1] The question of the length of the working day has not been touched by the Constitution. Up to now it has been regulated exclusively by special decrees based on the eight-hour day. The decrees of November 23, 1918, and of December 17, 1918, introduced the eight-hour day for workers in industries with the exception of industries which must not be interrupted. The decree of November 23, 1918, prescribed the length of the working day in bakeries; that of March 18, 1919, did the same for salaried employés. A general law that provides for an eight-hour day and regulating its application is in preparation.

[2] *Reichsgesetzblatt*, 1920, p. 98.

capacity of the unemployed. The only ground on which one may refuse such work is that the pay is not sufficient, given local conditions, to support the individual and, if married, his family.[1]

In the same way that restrictions on the liberty of labour have created for the State a number of duties relating to the employment of individuals, so the restrictions on the rights of private property have, as a consequence, engendered a number of obligations on the part of the State to assure to every one, if not a minimum of property, at least a minimum of well-being.

The Constitution guarantees individual property, but on the condition that the distribution and the utilization of land do not present abuses. The aim of this is to, *"to insure to every German a healthful dwelling and . . . homestead corresponding to his needs"* (Article 155). To this end colonization must be favoured, the development of agriculture and the utilization of the soil must be promoted; a survey must be made of all the mineral resources and all economically useful forces of nature.

In accordance with their conception of the duties of the State, the Constituent Assembly outlined a vast programme of agrarian and social policy. In addition they themselves passed several laws which form the commencement of the execution of this programme and which are intended to guide future legislation.

In order to insure every German a habitation and a homestead, the Reich first promulgated a decree, July 31, 1919, "On small gardens and little farms," according to which tracts of land, which cannot be used profitably, must be rented out at rates fixed by administrative authorities after expert appraisal, or may be leased, and later sub-leased, for gardens, by the authorities.

---

[1] As yet there has not been organized insurance against non-employment.

Later the law of April 11, 1919, was passed "on colonization." This law obliges the State to create interior colonies and small undertakings. To this end territory belonging to the State must be put on sale to "collective colonization enterprises"; these enterprises may be subsidized by means of expropriations of swamps and uncultivated tracts. They have the right of pre-emption in the sale of tracts of land of less than twenty-five hectares. On the other hand, to develop colonization tracts, there must be organized "associations for the furnishing of tracts" in all districts where more than ten per cent of the cultivatable soil is in the hands of big holders, that is, of more than one hundred hectares per holder. These associations, formed by a union of big landholders, must, on the demand of collective colonization enterprises, put at the disposal of the latter at reasonable prices tracts of land taken from the big properties. Their obligations in this respect cease when they have thus given over to colonization a third of the utilizable surface of the large properties, or when the total area of these properties is not more than ten per cent of the area of the district. The right of pre-emption by the colonization enterprises in respect to large properties is exercised through the associations for the furnishing of tracts. In urgent cases these associations may proceed by means of expropriation.

The Reich, finally, in order to assure a habitation to individuals, must take a whole series of measures in the case of housing crises. Already before the Revolution a decree of September 23, 1918, gave to municipalities the right to make regulations for the prevention of the demolition of buildings or their use for other purposes than dwelling. The municipalities had the right to draw up leases, even against the wish of the owners, through the intermediacy of "offices for the distribution of lodgings," and to appropriate all unusued buildings for the purpose of converting them to dwellings. A later decree of November 7, 1918, provided that associations of municipalities and groups of municipalities could be created to fight against housing crises. After the Revolution, a new decree of January 15, 1919, contained more important provisions for meeting the most urgent needs created by such crises. The State Cabinets were obliged to appoint "housing commissioners," charged with the care of homeless families and the creation of small and average appropriate lodgings. To this end, they received considerable powers. They could expropriate by a summary procedure unoccupied buildings they deemed necessary, or have such buildings erected on grounds which they had authority to lease for terms as long as thirty years. They could dispense with the requirements of legislative provisions, expropriate tile and other building materials necessary for the rapid construction of buildings; they could seize building lumber and forbid unnecessary construction. The service of these Housing Commissioners was under the Minister of Labour for the Reich.

Finally, in order to protect tenants, the ordinances of September 23, 1918, and of June 22, 1919, sanctioned and supplemented by the law of May 11, 1920, *limit considerably the rights of owners to dispose of habitable quarters* and entrust to the "offices for distribution of lodgings," extensive rights relative to the renting out of apartments and the terms of lodgings. In particular, according to the law of 1920, if grave inconveniences result from the lack of lodgings, the states may, with the consent of the Minister of the Reich, authorize or constrain the municipalities to take, or themselves take, measures that constitute encroachments on the liberty of settlement and the inviolability of domicile, on condition that these measures be expressly necessary to meet a housing crisis or to combat it. This law specifies, in addition, that decisions taken in the fight against the shortage of houses may be executed by administrative constraint.

3.—FUNDAMENTAL RIGHTS AND DUTIES OF COMMUNITIES.

The Constituent Assembly did not limit itself to the establishment of a list of rights and duties of the individual. The social conceptions by which it was dominated led it to proclaim, after the rights and duties of the individuals, the rights and duties of certain groups and communities that seemed to it to play a particularly important rôle in society—the family, associations, municipalities, civil service.

I.—THE FAMILY.—For the first time the family, the natural foundation of all ordered national life, finds itself mentioned in the Declaration of Rights of a modern state. The Constitution of Weimar formulates the general principles which should dominate legislation relating to marriage, to the education and the protection of children and to the duties of education devolved upon parents.

Article 119 places marriage under the special protection of the Constitution. Marriage, which forms the basis of family life and on which depends the increase of the population of the nation, is based on the equal rights of both sexes. Marriage and the family are recognized as the basis on which social life reposes and as the primary source from which develop German customs and culture. In consequence Article 119 enunciates a legislative course of considerable social and political importance. It prescribes the care of the purity, the health and the social advancement of the family as a duty of the state and of the municipalities. Families with numerous children have a claim to equalizing assistance. Motherhood has the right to the protection and care of the State.

Proposals were made, during the discussion of the draft of the Constitution, to lighten the lot of illegitimate children. They were aimed to assimilate, from the point of view of family rights, illegitimate and legitimate children. The majority of the National Assembly decided, because of the difficulties of regulating in a constitutional text questions of private rights, to leave this matter to legislation and to later development. The Assembly limited itself to forming guiding principles only. Legislation must assure to illegitimate children the same conditions for physical, moral and social development that legitimate children have. But convinced of the need of legislative reform on this matter, the Assembly passed a resolution that there should be taken, as soon as possible and by legislative means, a new ordering of the legal and social status of illegitimate children.

Concerning education, Article 120 declares only that parents have the right and the duty to educate their children; "The physical, mental, and moral education of their offspring is the highest duty and natural right of parents." But the State must not leave it entirely to parents and intervenes as an organ of surveillance. The political community watches over the execution by the parents of these duties imposed upon them.

In addition the State assumes as an obligation in a general way the protection of youth; the care of children and youth comes under the legislative authority of the Reich. As a guide for the accomplishment of this obligation, Article 122 specifies that youth shall be protected against exploitation as well as against physical and mental neglect.

II.—ASSOCIATION.—The right of assembly and association was already regulated by the law of April 19, 1908; in addition to this the Civil Code contained some provisions on the acquisition of civic rights. The Constitution contents itself with taking as its own the principles that inspired these laws, but it makes certain changes in the existing laws.

As to the liberty of assemblage, Article 123 holds to rules previously adopted, "All Germans have the right of meeting peaceably and unarmed without notice or special permission." The obligation that public meetings be reported in advance to the authorities, which formerly existed, is abolished. Furthermore, while the law of 1908 demanded that public meetings in the open air and manifestations on public ways and squares receive in advance authorization by the police—authorization which must be applied for at least twenty-four hours in advance—the Constitution, on the other hand, declares that *in theory* these meetings are free and do not need to be authorized. It adds, however, that in the interest of security and public order, liberty of assembly may be limited by law, this limitation consisting furthermore not in the need of authorization, but only in the obligation to give the police notice in advance.

As to liberty of association the Constitution still holds to the principle of the regulations of 1908. "All Germans have the right to form associations or societies for purposes not contrary to the criminal law. This right cannot be limited by preventive measures." (Article 124.) Associations may acquire a legal status according to the regulations provided by the Civil Code. Hitherto these regulations gave administrative authorities the right to oppose the acquisition of legal status by associations of a political, social or religious character. This opposition resulted in the associations in question being kept from the register of associations, and thereby prevented them from acquiring legal standing. This restriction is abolished by the Constitution as contrary to the modern principle according to which liberty of association must be kept intact. To this effect it is expressly provided, "Every association has the right of incorporation in accordance with the civil law. No association may be denied this right on the ground that it pursues a political, social-political, or religious object."

III.—MUNICIPALITIES.—Article 127 provides, "Municipalities and unions of municipalities have the right of self-government. . . ." Thus the *principle of decentralization* is found introduced in the list of fundamental rights.

The Constitution declares that this autonomy must be exercised "within the limits of the laws."

IV.—CIVIL SERVANTS.—Finally, the Constitution reaches the question of civil servants, to which it devotes no less than six articles.

Before the Constitution went into effect, the status of civil servants of the Empire was regulated by the law on civil servants, March 31, 1873, as amended by the law of May 18, 1907. The new Constitution left this law intact, but it superimposed a series of general rules, some of which were borrowed from the preceding laws applying to the civil servants of the Empire, and which are destined hereafter to hold good for all German civil servants, as well as those of the states and of public corporations.

The principles that serve as a point of departure are: that civil servants are in the service not at all of the party in power, but of the community; that, therefore, civil servants who remain faithful to the community all their lives have the right to be kept in office for life and to have guaranteed them a financially adequate situation; finally that outside of his office every civil servant is neither more nor less than any other citizen. These principles the Constitution applies in the provisions relative to the free access of all citizens to public functions, to the political liberty of civil servants and finally to their financial responsibility.

(1) "All citizens without distinction are eligible for public office in accordance with the laws and according to their ability and services." (Article 128.) In the future, citizenship in a particular state may no longer be demanded by the laws of the States as a condition for public employment; for the Constitution expressly provides that citizens must be admitted to public employment "without distinction." In addi-

tion, Article 110, par. 2, formally declares, "Every German has the same rights and duties in each State of the Commonwealth as the citizens of that State." On the other hand, Article 16 provides that as a rule officers directly charged with the administration of services that depend directly on the Reich, and who are assigned to a State, shall be citizens of that State. From this it must be concluded that the civil servants of a State may as a rule be recruited from among the citizens of that State without violating the spirit of the Constitution.

Already in preceding laws one finds no legal obstacle to the admission of women to civil service. The Constitution declares, meanwhile: "All discriminations against women in the civil service are abolished." By this—a logical consequence of the provision of Article 109, by which men and women have in principle the same civil rights and duties—all obstacles to the admission of women to the service of the State on the same conditions as men are abolished.

(2) *Civil servants are in principle appointed for life.* However, exceptions are provided for, either in case future legislation on civil servants contains contrary provisions, or if, up to then, the law on civil servants of the Empire and the laws of the states have provided a different rule. A proposal by the Independents, according to which civil servants would have to be chosen by election and therewith lose all guarantees the Constitution and the laws accord them, was rejected by a great majority. The rights acquired by civil servants must be *inviolable*. Claims in money matters must be heard by tribunals. Civil servants may not be temporarily deprived of their function, retired for a time or permanently, or be given new work of a lower nature except under conditions and according to forms provided by law and not by simple arbitrary administrative measures.

Against any disciplinary measure, civil servants may enter protests and commence procedure for damages. Furthermore, the system of secret reports on persons employed is abolished. Every civil servant has the right to consult his record, and no disparaging entry may be introduced in it without the opportunity being given to the employé to explain himself on this matter.

(3) *Civil servants are in the service of the State, of the community and not at all the servants of a party or the party in power.* In consequence of this they retain the liberty of political conviction and of association. A later law of the Reich was provided for organizations in which civil servants are represented and which are supposed to co-operate in the regulation of all questions concerning them. The same idea that led to the recognition of the right of workers and clerks to co-operate in the form of Factory Workers Councils applies to civil servants and gives them the right to co-operate in all matters concerning them.

(4) Finally the Constitution prescribes in a uniform manner for the whole Reich, for the public servants of the states as well as those employed by public corporations, the limits of the *financial responsibility of public servants.*

The responsibility of civil servants is regulated by Section 838 of the Civil Code. "Every employé, who through premeditation or negligence, violates the duty imposed upon him by his function, to the damage of a third party, must recompense this party for the damage thus caused." As to the manner in which this compensation is to be awarded, the Civil Code leaves it to the legislatures of the individual states to determine. Making use of this authorization, most of the States individually have decided that the State shall be responsible instead of the civil servants, and that the public treasury assume the indemnity to the limit for which the civil servant is responsible, the treasury retaining, however, the right to proceed against the civil servant. Prussia adopted this system in the law of April 1, 1909, and the Empire followed it, for the employés of the Empire, in the law of

May 22, 1910. However, there are still member states, Saxony for example, in which this solution has not yet been adopted and where the civil servants are still directly responsible to any individual who suffers damage through them.

The Constitution confirms in Article 131 a state of affairs that exists in most of the States and in the Reich, and declares that if a civil officer in the exercise of the authority conferred on him by the law fails to perform his official duty toward any third person, the responsibility is assumed by the state or public corporation in whose service the officer is. The right of redress against the officer is reserved.

4.—RELIGION AND THE CHURCHES.

Declarations of Rights generally contain, justly so, principles relative to religious liberty and the free exercise of creeds. But the Constitution of Weimar could not limit itself on this point to traditional general maxims. The question of the relations of church and state forms an essential article of the programme of the Centre, and also of the programme of the Social Democrats. Their solutions would seem to be self-contradictory. The Centre wanted to guarantee to the Church a privileged and preponderant situation within the State. The programme of Erfurt, on the other hand, declared religion to be a purely private matter, and refused all subsidies levied on public resources in behalf of ecclesiastical or religious needs. But these two parties entered at that moment into a coalition which, together with the Democrats, governed the Reich. As neither of these two opposed conceptions was able to prevail, the conflict of the two theories was finally settled by a compromise—which before consummation required laborious negotiations.

The Constitution first proclaims the principle of liberty of belief and conscience and the free exercise of religion. These liberties are expressly placed by the Constitution under the protection of the State. They are guaranteed against every invasion no matter from what side it comes. But the general laws of the State remain intact and religious liberty finds itself limited by the general regulations for the maintenance of order and public security. Every abuse in the exercise of religious liberty is punished by ordinary law. Civil rights and duties must not be restrained or conditioned by the exercise of religious liberty. The enjoyment of civil and civic rights as well as the admission to public employ are independent of the religion professed. No one is obliged to divulge his or her religious convictions before any authority whatsoever, and the right of an authority to inquire into the sect to which one belongs may not be exercised except as one's rights and duties depend upon this, as, for example, in the matter of church tithes or in the matter of guardianship or instruction; or where it is necessary for the gathering of statistics ordered by law. No one may be forced to attend any Church ceremony or to take part in any religious exercise. No one may be forced to make use of any religious oath as was formerly prescribed in civil and penal procedure. It is sufficient, in taking an oath, that the one swearing shall declare without a religious formula, "I swear!"

On the other hand, the Constitution contains several provisions regarding the exercise of religion. Sundays and legal holidays remain protected by law as days of rest and spiritual edification.

These principles being admitted, there still remained the difficult problem of the relations of State and Church. The following solution was adopted: There is neither complete separation nor any close union of the Churches and the State. The Churches are emancipated from the State, but they enjoy certain privileges.

The Churches are free. "There is no State Church." The union that formerly existed between the Church and the State, in Prussia, for example, and in the majority of the German

States between them and the evangelical church, has disappeared, and the principle according to which religious affairs depend upon the state is abolished.

This freedom of the Churches is manifested first, in that the creation of religious denominations and sects is free, and that the assembly of religious denominations in associations within the Reich is subject to no limitation whatever. It is also revealed in the complete independence of the Churches in regard to the State. Each religious denomination administers and conducts its affairs freely, provided that it observes the laws that apply to all. It conducts its work without the co-operation of the State or of the municipality. The new system realizes thus the emancipation of ecclesiastical administration from secular control. The State may neither decree regulations affecting faith, nor appoint any one to ecclesiastical service nor demand that its assent be required to the nominations made by ecclesiastical authority.

However, the Constitution does not push the principle of the separation of Church and State to such a point as to allow religious denominations no more than the merely private rights accorded by law to natural persons. Recognizing the social force and the importance in public life exercised by the Churches, the Constitution accords them *privileges similar to those given to public corporations*. Religious denominations existing in Germany at the time of the adoption of the Constitution remain recognized as public corporate bodies. As for other similar organizations, the same rights are accorded them on the motion of the state government if, by their constitution and the sufficient number of their adherents, they offer guarantees of permanence. While recognizing that in theory the smaller religious groups, chapels, and sects may be invested with rights similar to those of the principal churches, the object of the above limitation is to prevent ephemeral organizations from acquiring the standing of public corporate bodies.

The Constitution does not expressly state of what the rights of public corporations consist, for these rights result from provisions made in the legislation of the various states. In a general way, however, public corporations, in addition to the legal standing that private law gives them, are under the special protection of the State. Their organizations are indirectly public agencies, and they have the right to levy taxes. This right, practically the most important of those accorded public corporations, is expressly emphasized and guaranteed in the Constitution.

Religious denominations that are public corporate bodies have the right to *levy taxes* on the bases of the lists established for the collection of civil taxes. The right to levy the taxes granted to public religious denominations is limited, as a rule, to their members. They may, however, in exceptional cases levy on certain other taxables, particularly corporations and joint stock companies, etc., to the same extent as on their co-religionists, if the laws of the particular State authorize this.

If several religious bodies combine into one association, the latter, without being required to secure any special authorization, becomes a public corporation. This provision is important and has been voted out of consideration for the evangelical churches of the States which up to now were territorially separated, and which are seeking to unite in a German ecclesiastical organization, such as had to be formed after the disappearance of the régime in which reigning princes ruled the churches.

The financial situation of religious bodies is regulated by Article 138. The property and other rights of religious bodies and associations for the maintenance of their cultural, educational, and charitable institutions, their foundations and other possessions, are guaranteed. As a consequence of the separation of Church and State, the Constitution provides that the obligations hitherto imposed on the State to participate financially in the expenses of the Churches no longer exists. But on this point the Constitution compromises. Payments due from the State to the Churches because of some law or of legal title to such, must be commuted by state legislation, on bases fixed by the Reich. The States, however, cannot proceed to do this before a law of the Reich has fixed these bases. Till then, these payments continue. (Articles 138 and 179.)

The liquidation must include not only the payments owed because of a law or treaty, but also those due by virtue of some special legal title, particularly those resting on customary law and tradition.

The question whether, in the new legislation relative to the Churches, there subsists still any special right of supervision by the States, cannot be answered uniformally. Properly speaking there is no right of supervision by the States. But the latter may exercise over the Churches the same control as over public corporations for the purpose of maintaining order and public security.

5.—EDUCATION AND SCHOOLS.

After having regulated the question of the relations between Church and State, the Constituent Assembly took up the problem of education. It approached it in the same spirit that inspired the provisions it adopted relative to fundamental rights and duties. Here, too, it exerted itself to give its work a marked social character; and to a very large measure it succeeded.

However, the Articles concerning the schools were the subject of long deliberations and lively discussions in committee and in the full session of the Constitutional Assembly. In the debates on schools, on the relations of Church and State, and on the relations of schools and churches, two conflicting conceptions were manifested. Whereas the Centre and the parties of the Right declared in principle for religious schools, the Social Democrats championed the idea of secular schools, and long negotiations were required to find a compromise between these two apparently irreconcilable doctrines.

The Constitution, in its final text, contains provisions relative to public instruction, and to private instruction as well as provisions applicable to both of these.

I.—Public instruction must form an "organized whole." That is to say, it must not consist of a collection of schools of different kinds without any logical bond between them; but on the contrary it must be systematically organized, in such a manner that each kind of school will be part of a harmonious whole, constructed on a rational plan and answering a definite object. This instruction must be systematized by co-operation of the Reich, the States and the municipalities.

But what principles should guide this organization and what should be its aims? It is here that the social doctrine of the Constituent Assembly reappears. Public instruction whose detailed organization is left to the regulation by ordinary laws to be enacted must present certain characteristics, all arising from the same idea—*guaranteeing to every individual a maximum of development to the end that he may co-operate in the most effective fashion in the well-being of the community.*

(1) At the base of the educational edifice there is the common or elementary school (Grundschule), which gives all children an equal education, from the point of view of length of time and content. *This is the principle of the "uniform" school.* This does not mean, however, that everywhere and in all the states public schools must be organized after an invariable pattern. They are uniform in the sense that they are one in the conception underlying their establishment, in that they are inspired in every respect and exclusively by the same democratic principles, that no difference in instruction is made and that the economic and social position and the

religious beliefs of parents are deliberately disregarded in according to children the right to an education.

(2) Above the common schools are the secondary and higher schools. The Constitution does not say how these are to be organized. It indicates only the idea that is to serve as a guide to legislators when they construct the educational edifice. The State is not to yield to the will and the desires of individuals, but is to be guided before all by the aptitudes and the interests of the children.

(3) All children are naturally not compelled to go through the whole educational curriculum, but there is an *obligatory minimum of instruction*. Educational obligations are notably extended in the Constitution as compared to their former limits. "Attendance at school is obligatory. This obligation is discharged by attendance at the elementary schools for at least eight school years and at the continuation schools until the completion of the eighteenth year." Formerly the obligation to attend school was only for seven years for the public schools. Supplementary instruction, therefore, thus becomes an essential part of public education in all the Reich.

(4) Instruction is free, at least in the elementary and supplementary schools. This is a necessary result of compulsory education. The secondary and higher schools are in theory not free, but "to facilitate the attendance of those in poor circumstances at the secondary and higher schools, public assistance shall be provided by the Commonwealth, States, and municipalities, particularly, assistance to the parents of children regarded as qualified for training in the secondary and higher schools, until the completion of the training."

(5) Instruction in public schools, with some exceptions, remains religious. The most serious disputes arose over this point. Undoubtedly obvious progress has been realized by withdrawing the public school from the local supervision of members of the clergy; and by making hereafter public instruction as a whole subject to the inclusive control of the

State. Municipalities may in addition be summoned to participate in this supervision. This will permit future educational laws of the Reich and administrative laws of the States to give the municipality a share in supervising the instruction —not only over the work of the schools but also over the spirit in which it is carried on. Even parents will be allowed the right to co-operate in it and teachers will be given a voice in the management. The supervision of the schools on the part of the Reich will be hereafter solely by civil servants, who will have this as their principal function and who will be especially appointed for this purpose.

But the principal question was whether the public school, even when supervised by the State, should be neutral or whether it should remain religious in teaching.

Three systems were submitted. One was the system of the secular school, where no religious instruction is given. Another was the mixed school, where children of all religious faiths are admitted without distinction and where the parents indicate whether they wish their children to receive religious instruction, and if so, what. The third was the denominational system, properly so-called, in which the public school is specialized by religious denominations, each denomination having its own school where the child receives the religious instruction of its denomination.

The discussions on this question went through three successive phases. At first there was some agreement on a plan according to which schools would be mixed, in theory, but the denominational school, properly so-called, would not be completely excluded; for the law could admit, on the proposition of parents, the creation of schools in which only the children of a single denomination would be received.

This compromise not completely satisfying the Centre, which used its influence to effect a change, a new plan was therefore accepted. This introduced the denominational school, properly so-called, into the Constitution. According to this plan, the wish of parents would decide whether a school should be secular, mixed or denominational, the free choice by the parents being limited only by the requirements of well-ordered scholarship. The parties of the Left vigorously opposed this. The most serious objection they raised was that it would have as a consequence the necessity on the part of some states, such as Baden and Hesse, which had already introduced mixed schools legally, to renounce them again. A new compromise was thereupon arrived at, which under the new form became the final text. Denominational schools and lay schools would constitute exceptions and could not be established except when demanded by heads of families and conditioned by the requirements of well-ordered scholarship. As for the rest the educational questions must be regulated, the principles by an educational law for the Reich, the details by the legislation of the States.

Thus *in principle the public school is mixed.* The public school is attended by all children no matter to what religion they belong, and religious instruction forms part of the regular school curriculum. (Article 149.) The imparting of religious instruction in the school must take place within the general framework of educational legislation. In other words, it is not the church but the State which gives instruction. It is the State that must take into its hands the organization of religious instruction. It is the State that decides what place religious instruction shall hold in its curriculum. It goes without saying, however, that, as to the content of religious instruction, this must be in agreement with the principles of the religious society concerned. No teacher, according to Article 149, par. 2, can be compelled to give religious instruction or to participate in religious exercises. In the same way no pupils are obliged to take religious instruction or to participate in ecclesiastical ceremonies and festivities. They may only be compelled to do so if the persons who have the right to decide on their religious education express the desire that they do so.

But public secular schools and public denominational schools, properly so-called, also may continue, and their existence is constitutionally guaranteed. These schools, by the same title as the mixed schools, are elementary schools, on which may be based secondary and higher education. But these cannot be established in municipalities except under certain specified conditions. There must first be a formal demand on the part of a sufficient number of heads of families. Then the organization of the school asked for must conform to high educational standards. From all this it may be concluded that the system of the uniform school and the transition from the public school to secondary and higher schools must not be interfered with. In addition, the arrangement of instruction based on the diverse vocational needs, must not be made impossible. Finally, public instruction must not be handicapped by the unnecessary establishment of useless and inefficient schools. The wishes of heads of families, as far as possible and in accordance with the above conditions, must be taken into consideration and their proposals accepted. Questions of detail, such as, what is understood by "head of a family"; how many such are sufficient within a municipality to be able to demand a sectarian or a secular school; how many schools there shall be and of what kind, must be settled by educational laws of the Reich and by laws of the States which must follow those of the Reich.

II.—*Private instruction is permitted.* (Article 142.) However, this liberty is subject to important restrictions (Article 147) in the case of private schools considered as substitutes for public schools.

In general, establishments of private instruction, no matter of what grade, can be created only *by the authorization of the State.* This authorization is subject to the following conditions: the programme and the equipment of private schools must not fall below the programme and equipment of public schools. The scientific training of teachers of private schools must be of as high a standard as that of public school teachers. The economic and legal position of private school teachers must be guaranteed. Finally, private schools cannot become the schools of class or caste.

Elementary private schools are subjected by the Constitution to several special conditions. Their establishment is authorized when in any municipality there does not exist for a minority of heads of families, whose needs must be considered, a public school of their denomination, or one that conforms to their ethical system. Such a school may also be established if educational authorities recognize in the demands of such a group a special pedagogical interest. The Constitutional provisions relating to programmes and free instruction apply also to private elementary schools.

Private preparatory schools are abolished.

Finally, for private schools that are not substitutes for public schools, such as commercial and professional schools, the laws formerly in existence still operate.

III.—The Constitution contains a number of provisions for instruction, both public and private. It provides that vocational instruction and moral and civic education shall be part of the programme of all schools. By means of vocational instruction children must be made to understand the great importance of work, for the individual as well as for society as a whole. Civic instruction must acquaint children with the rights and duties of citizens, with the organization of the German State, and with the public life of Germany. To this end, every scholar on completion of the course in compulsory education shall receive a copy of the Constitution.

Such are the provisions relative to instruction in the schools.

They constitute, as compared to the former state of affairs, a considerable change. But these provisions cannot be effectively put into operation except by a series of laws on the part of the Reich as well as of the States, a process which threatens to be a long one in point of time.

However, in April, 1920, the first law on this matter was passed by the National Assembly. It was the law *on the elementary school.* According to this law, primary schools must be so organized that the first four years may at the same time serve as a preparation for secondary and higher education. Every child who has successfully graduated from the highest class of the elementary school must be sufficiently prepared to enter immediately a secondary or a higher school. Public preparatory schools and public preparatory classes are abolished. As for private preparatory schools, their suppression will take place only after a sufficiently long reprieve; their complete abolition need not take place until the commencement of the school year 1929-1930; since economic difficulties prevent the earlier abolition of these schools, and means must be taken to provide for the teachers who will be deprived thus of their occupations. Private instruction is not allowed except in particular cases and can only in special circumstances be substituted for the elementary school. The law ·does not touch instruction and training in auxilary classes; nor does it concern itself with the instruction of children physically or mentally diseased.

In addition a certain number of interesting innovations have been enacted into legislation. These have as their purpose the participation by parents and pupils in the administration of schools. On the one hand, in the secondary schools there are organized Students' Councils (Schulgemeinden). These Councils are formed by pupils of the three upper classes, who meet periodically in assembly to discuss questions of instruction—educational matters, quarterly reports, discipline, duties, etc. Teachers attend these meetings without the right to vote. Up to now these assemblies have had only the right to propose reforms without power as yet to make them operative. On the other hand, parents elect for each school a Parents' Council, one member for every fifty pupils.[1] This Council concerns itself mostly with classes, examination and discipline. If a pupil has committed a fault involving the possibility of expulsion from the schools, it is before this Council that this question is taken. Teachers are sometimes admitted to these deliberations but have not the right to vote.

[1] The political parties interested themselves in these elections, the platform being "for or against religious instruction." The number of socialists elected was less than that of bourgeois parties.

CHAPTER VI

THE ECONOMIC CONSTITUTION AND SOCIALIZATION

The Constitution imposes on each German the duty of work. It is not sufficient in modern states, especially in one defeated in war, that every one therein merely work, unless this work is directed in a certain spirit, following a given plan and toward a determined end. The fundamental idea that inspired the Constituent Assembly in the last provisions of its work is as follows: The whole German system of economy, public and private, is destroyed or demolished by the war. Germany cannot dream of rising from its ruins unless it realizes immediate and radical reforms. It must completely reconstruct its former economic system. The whole country must become an immense enterprise directed by a conscious will aimed at a definite goal. All the forces of the country solidly organized and scientifically utilized must be so managed that a maximum of production will be assured.

To this end, two series of reforms are contemplated. They are summed up in these words, "councils" and "collective economy." On the one hand, there is projected an Economic Constitution, whose organs are progressively destined to be parallel to those of the political Constitution. On the other hand, the effort is made to realize in the organization of production and distribution an economic system that is intermediate between that of private economy on the one hand, and a purely socialist régime on the other.

Nothing systematic, however, has as yet been achieved. The ground is new. Surprised by the Revolution, the theoreticians of new systems have not yet fixed their schemes nor elaborated complete and coherent plans. On the other hand, the majority of the National Assembly is formed by a coalition of parties whose economic conceptions differ still more than do their political conceptions. This lack of definiteness and these differences endanger all effective realization of a solution. But the necessity of reforms has made itself imperatively felt and economic difficulties are so grave and menacing that they cannot wait indefinitely for solution. Further, there are very many people who are restive and who do not hesitate to resort to general strikes and even to revolts, when governments hesitate too long in effecting a reform from which they hope an amelioration of their lot. That is why one will look in vain for a plan as a whole or a logical order in the provisions we are about to study. Most of them were adopted by an assembly uncertain of the work it should do, one which went about its tasks most hurriedly and obeyed the pressure of external forces more powerful than itself.

SECTION I

THE ECONOMIC CONSTITUTION

The Economic Constitution rests wholly on the idea of the Councils. It is recalled [1] that the system of the Councils, even under the parity principle which the supporters of the Vocational Parliament wished to give it, was left out of the political Constitution but is included in the Economic Constitution, for which it forms the framework.

1.—THE "ANCHORAGE" OF THE COUNCILS IN THE CONSTITUTION.

Before the Revolution, said the Socialists and Trade Unionists, there was in Germany neither political autonomy nor economic autonomy. Just as in their political life the people were governed by a coterie of junkers and bureaucrats, so in

---

[1] See Chapter III.

their economic life the people were under the absolute domination of the entrepreneur. This autocracy of the capitalists expressed itself legally in the fact that the conditions of work were fixed solely by the employers. The omnipotence of the latter was, however, modified by the collective bargains concluded between them and the trade unions. While it is true that these agreements or bargains did not have legal guarantees, nevertheless thanks to the existence of workingmen's organizations there was instituted by means of these agreements a contractual and coequal workingmen's right.

The Revolution of 1918 introduced in Germany political democracy. The republican government in its establishment has even taken several steps along the road of economic democracy. Reforms, such as the granting of complete liberty of organization, the abolition of ordinances on wages and exceptional laws against agricultural labourers, and the protection of workers and salaried employés against arbitrary discharge, certainly mark interesting progress.

But the Socialists, followed on this point by the National Assembly, held that these reforms were only preparatory in character. True economic democracy can not content itself with the mere recognition of workers' organizations and collective bargaining. Economic democracy cannot be established and therefore economic and social transformation cannot be effected, unless the working class can exercise on production the influence that is its due. There must be provided an organization that accords the workers the right to participate actively in the determination of the ends and of the duties of the vocation and the enterprise; which makes of the workers co-operators with the capitalist. There must be in every district, in the states and in the Reich an economic representation created, in which workers and employés will be represented by the side of their employers, and in which, on a footing of equality, they will be called upon to co-operate in the regulation of all economic questions. Such is the thesis;

and all efforts and struggles which we shall observe, centred about the problem of according to the working class the right of codecision (Mitbestimmungsrecht); and about the problem of organizing this right. But so far nothing has been done beyond the statement of some indefinite principles and the roughing out of the first measures of their realization.

These problems were not new. Already before the war the law of 1891 provided for "Committees of Workers" in the factories, who could be consulted on the provisions of factory regulations; but as the formation of these committees depended entirely on the good-will of the employers, the workers looked with little sympathy on this institution. In fact, such committees existed in several thousand factories, but their activity was limited to the administration of the income from fines and the institution of welfare work.

During the war the rôle of the workers increased considerably in importance. The laws for compulsory patriotic service which took away from them the liberty of work owed them compensation. There were established therefore in all enterprises where there were more than fifty employed, "committees of workers," which were elected by all the workers and had definite functions. There were in addition "joint arbitration committees," where conflicts between employers and employés were settled. "Committees on decisions" also existed, charged with ruling on other questions raised by the law for patriotic service. These different organisms at once assumed an important place in the economic life.

On the advent of the Revolution the unions easily obtained some reforms for which they had fought for a long time, and which constituted their immediate claims.

On November 15, the unions concluded an agreement with the employers' associations, which has served as the basis of an important development, begun on that date and known as the "labour board" (Arbeitsgemeinschaft). The *Arbeits-*

THE "ANCHORAGE" OF COUNCILS 239

gemeinschaft appeared several months before the end of the war, but assumed a rôle of prime importance in the new organization of economic Germany.

The *Arbeitsgemeinschaft* has been defined as "the combination of big associations of employers and of workers for the regulation of reciprocal relations between employers and workers and for the solution in common of all economic and social questions touching industry and labour." [1]

The essential principle of the *Arbeitsgemeinschaft* is that of *parity*. In the agreement of November 15, the labour unions are recognized as the vocational representatives of the workers. The most complete liberty of organization is accorded them. The agreement specifies as its practical tasks the feeding of veterans, the distribution of raw material, and the regulation in common of labour disputes. For the settlement of pending questions there was organized a special committee composed one-half of employers and one-half of workers.

Several days later, December 4, 1918, there was drawn up the "statutes of the *Arbeitsgemeinschaft* of the employers and employés of Germany." All German industries were divided into a certain number of groups, which had common organs composed half of employers and half of workers, each elected by their respective organizations. There was in addition a central council, which was the *Arbeitsgemeinschaft* of all the employers and organized workers of all German industries. Its members were elected by the groups from their membership; and these in turn elected a Central Committee, which executed the decisions of the Central Council.

All these organs—and this point must be emphasized—were composed half of employers and half of workers. The parity principle is at the basis of the whole organization of the *Arbeitsgemeinschaften*. Thus all economic and social questions concerning industry and labour were regulated by com-

[1] Max Schippel, *Schicksalstunden der Arbeitsgemeinschaft, Sozialistische Monatshefte*, 1920, p. 328.

mittees in which the employers' associations and the labour unions were each represented by one-half in each committee. The *Arbeitsgemeinschaft* is a treaty of peace.

In addition on December 23, 1918, the Commissars of the People signed a decree "on collective agreements, workers and employers committees, and the arbitration of labour disputes." This decree [1] maintained the committees which were developed during the war by virtue of the law for patriotic service, and increased their powers. Here, too, the whole mechanism rested on the parity principle. According to this decree, committees of workers and employers had to be organized in all industries, in all the administrative bodies and in all offices where there were at least twenty labourers or employés. These had as their mission the protection of the economic interests of labourers and employés against employers in the factories, administrative bodies and offices. The committees had to supervise in co-operation with the bosses the carrying out of the various provisions in the collective contracts. In factories where there was no collective contract the committees were supposed to co-operate in the regulation of wages and other conditions of labour in agreement with the economic representatives of the workers and employés. It was their task, in addition, to maintain good relations among the workers, as well as between the workers and employers.

It would seem that an evolution thus commenced could have continued normally and without difficulty, and that economic and social problems raised by the reorganization of Germany could thereafter be regulated by the *Arbeitsgemeinschaften;* that is to say, by direct agreement between employers associations and labour unions. But the problem was peculiarly complicated by the introduction and rapid diffusion in Germany of Russian revolutionary ideas. The Soviet differs essentially from the committee above described.

[1] It has been changed by a law of May 31, 1920. (*Reichsgesetzblatt*, 1920, p. 1128.)

Whereas in the latter employers and employés are placed on terms of equality and the committee itself becomes a purely economic institution, the Soviet, according to the Russian conception, is a political organization, whose purpose is to eliminate the employers and to establish the dictatorship of the proletariat. The Soviet must have in its hands all the political and economic power of the State.

As to this conception of the political omnipotence of the Council, we have seen that powerful opposition ensued on the morrow of the Revolution and that in January, 1919, the Social Democrats remained in full control of power after having eliminated the Independents. We know that this struggle continued, however, and it will be recalled what organizations the Independents provided for and wished to institute in order to assure to the Workers Councils the political sovereignty they claim. Parallel to the political struggle between the Social Democrats and the Independents, there developed another, on the economic field, between the Trade Unions and the Councils, which found themselves in conflict as much over what reforms should be demanded by the working class as over the rôle these two groupings should respectively retain in the struggle for the recognition of their claims.

The Trade Unions declared themselves satisfied with the agreement they had concluded with the employers, as well as with the decree of December 23, 1918, which Legien, President of the General Confederation of Labour, called "The Great Charter of Labour." They were convinced that thereafter there was nothing more to do but to wait for time to develop logically and peacefully the rôle of the *Arbeitsgemeinschaften* and of the Committees provided for by the decree of 1918. *They did not believe that in this evolution there was any room for Councils.* It was they, the Trades Unions, that had theretofore been the only ones to occupy themselves with economic questions, and they did not propose to permit special groups, operating in isolated factories, to deprive them of their traditional mission. Legien in particular did not want to hear any talk of the Councils. They did not seem to him to be able to "incorporate themselves in the actual hierarchy of the organizations and agencies of the workers." He protested against any concession to the system of Councils, and declared that the only organisms in position to defend the economic interests of the working class, were the Trades Unions.

But an increasingly important part of the working class, attracted by the ardent propaganda of the theoreticians of the Councils system, physically and mentally depressed by misery and unemployment, irritated by the mistakes of the Cabinet and disillusioned by the impotence of the Assembly of Weimar, rallied to the doctrines of the Councils. The Trades Unions were no longer believed by them able to lead the battle which would assure to the workers the preponderant rôle which should be theirs in economic matters. They showed during the war, co-operating with the militarists and the bureaucrats of the Empire, that they were always ready to compromise. They were directed by veritable functionaries, whose whole careers developed within the Trades Union administration and who had no qualification for representing the working class. In order to secure what the working class wants these claims must be taken in hand by organs issuing directly from the workers—militant organizations in position to lead a swift energetic fight—these organs being the Workers Councils. *The Councils must be placed above the unions,* and it is to them that belongs the right to decide on the campaigns that should be waged.

Between these two opposite conceptions there arose an intermediate theory. The trades unionists of the later school and the Christian Trades Unionists, energetically as they rejected all economic dictatorship by the Councils, held, however, that there is something just and legitimate in such theories. Giesbert, who holds an important situation in the

THE "ANCHORAGE" OF COUNCILS

Christian Trades Unions and who was to be Minister of Posts, wrote in April: "We have not sufficiently appreciated and above all we have realized too late the degree of sound truth in the idea of the Councils. The reason for this is that this idea has come to us from Russia as a political conception, and also because it arrived accompanied by all the tragic manifestations of the Russian Revolution. If the system of Councils assures to the workers the right to participate more completely in the organization and development of economic life, then it cannot help but contribute, if this is done in a reasonable manner, to the reawakening of the love of work and the establishment of a close community of interests between employers and employés."[1]

As for the Cabinet, it declared itself from the first against the Councils, and in an official communication on February 26, 1919, Scheidemann, President of the Council of Ministers, declared that the Cabinet never considered the introduction of the Councils System in Germany, and that above all, if any part should be accorded the Councils, it could only be that of an intermediary between the employers and the trade unions.

But it soon became impossible for either the Cabinet or the Trades Unions to remain in this almost completely negative position; for the struggle for the *Mitbestimmungsrecht* ceased to be merely a debate among theoreticians. At the beginning of March the workers in the metallurgical industry declared a general strike in Berlin; and in April the miners of Central Germany did the same.

The Cabinet found itself forced to modify its point of view. Receiving at Weimar a delegation of strikers come to present an ultimatum to him, Scheidemann recanted the communication of February 26, and engaged himself by a written promise to effect the recognition of the principle of Councils in the Constitution.[2] One month later he fulfilled his promise.

[1] *Deutsche Allgemeine Zeitung,* April 29, evening.
[2] In the discussion that arose on this subject an expression used in it

On April 5, a new note made known under what conditions and to what extent the Cabinet envisaged the possibility of organizing and utilizing the Councils. He proposed to inscribe in the Constitution an article proclaiming in general terms the right of workers to participate in common and on equal terms with employers in the regulation of questions of wages and work, as well as in the development of the forces of production in the common economic interest. By the side of special Workers Councils there were to be mixed Councils which would have general economic authority.

On their side the Trades Unions also found themselves obliged to seek a working basis, and they concluded by agreeing to the introduction of Councils in German economic life, on the condition that a very sharp separation be marked between the powers of the Factory Workers Councils and the Economic Councils on the one hand, and those of the Trades Unions themselves on the other. Another condition was that assurance must be given the Trades Unions that the *Workers Councils would fulfil their mission in accord with the Trades Unions*. At the Congress of Nuremberg, July, 1919, the Trades Unions engaged themselves to use their whole influence to secure for the workers and employés the *Mitbestimmungsrecht* in the various industries and to help the Factory Workers Councils to play an effective part.

2.—CONSTITUTIONAL PROVISIONS RELATIVE TO THE COUNCILS.

It was agreed, then, to recognize for wage-earners and salaried employés the right of co-operation in the conduct of industries and that all parties to the productive organization of the nation must co-operate in the regulation of economic questions. This idea is developed and in part realized in the provisions of Article 165, which form the foundation of the future Economic Constitution.

has achieved popularity and is in current use. The strikers demanded and obtained the "anchorage" of the Councils in the Constitution.

PROVISIONS RELATIVE TO COUNCILS

The Constitution sets forth the idea that the economic organization of the country must pursue two different courses and should therefore have two different series of organs—the "Workers Councils" and the "Economic Councils." This double organization is based on considerations that were expressed by Member of the Assembly Sinzheimer at the session of the National Assembly on July 21, as follows: "In economic life there is both a conflict and a community of interests. The conflict that exists in our economic life and which it is impossible not to perceive is the conflict between capital and labour. It is therefore necessary, since the employers are already represented publicly in Chambers of Commerce, etc., that the side of labour should also receive special public representation which should include all wage-earners and salaried employés. The mission of this representation should be to express all the interests of the working class, as such, in an organized manner, through a public organ of representation. This public organ of representation is the Workers Council. This Council is a unilateral representation of interests. It has as its purpose the increase and realization of the economic influence of the working class. But in economic life there is not only a conflict, there is also a community of interest. The latter is based on the common interest in production on the part of both employer and employé. The Economic Councils have as their mission, in contrast to the Workers Councils, to realize these common 'duties of production,' that are equally incumbent upon employers and employés. They must satisfy all the interests of production and bring into co-operation for production all the elements that participate in it, to increase production, diminish its costs and to regulate it as far as possible according to considerations of social good."

Workers Councils are: Factory Workers Councils, for each establishment; District Workers Councils, organized for each economic district; and the National Workers Council, whose authority extends over the whole German territory. These Councils have as their mission the safeguarding of the social and economic interests of the workers.

The Economic Councils are organized according to a geographical division. They consist of District Economic Councils and the National Economic Council. The former consist of the union of District Workers Councils with the corresponding representatives of the employers and other interested classes of the population. The National Economic Council consists of the union of the National Workers Council with the corresponding representatives of the employers and other "interested classes of the population." The Constitution does not state precisely what is to be understood by this last expression. In the Constitutional Committee it was unanimously agreed that the consumers shall be particularly represented in the Economic Councils. The creation of these Councils is obligatory and legislators are bound by the Constitution to enact the necessary laws to this effect.

In addition there may be created "autonomous bodies" (Article 156, par. 2) the administration of which is incumbent upon Economic Councils organized not by regions but by industries. Unlike the regional Economic Councils, the creation of these autonomous bodies is only optional; they must be organized, says the Constitution, "in case of urgent necessity."

The Constitution specifies with a little more detail than for the Workers Councils, the powers of the future Economic Councils. These have for their purpose, in addition to general economic duties, *to co-operate in the execution of socialization laws.* In addition the Economic Councils of the autonomous bodies are charged with the administration of enterprises placed under the economic collectivity, such as coal, potash, etc.[1]

[1] See p. 307.

PROVISIONS RELATIVE TO COUNCILS

Finally, the National Economic Council must have certain political functions, and thereby the Constitution makes concession to the supporters of the institution of an Economic Parliament. The solution adopted constitutes a middle ground between the views held by the latter and those of the partisans of a purely formal democracy. It gives to the National Economic Council a certain political influence, but it does not accord it absolutely any power of execution. It has the right to be heard on all bills of social and economic character before they are presented to the Reichstag by the Cabinet. It has, in addition, the right itself to propose laws on social and economic matters, and the Cabinet is obliged, even if it does not approve of these projects, to take them before the Reichstag. It may only present its own point of view as opposed to that of the Economic Council. Finally, the latter may send a representative from among its members to present its proposal before the Reichstag. The situation of the Economic Council is, on the whole, on the social and economic field very analogous to that of the Reichsrat.

The existence and the activity of free vocational associations, that is to say, the unions of workers and employers, are not affected by the institution of Councils. Article 165, par. 1, expressly recognizes vocational organizations of workers and employers. In theory the spheres in which the Councils and these organizations respectively move are distinct, and the differences between them naturally result from the difference in the aims of the two organizations. After the Constitution, as well as before, these unions of employés and workers had as their function the regulation of the conditions of labour and of wages with the aid of collective agreements; whereas the Workers Councils and the Economic Councils are concerned with questions other than the contractual determination of the conditions of labour and wages. But we shall soon see that in practice this separation is extremely difficult to maintain and that it gives rise to considerable difficulties between the Councils and the unions.

3.—FACTORY WORKERS COUNCILS.

I.—Of the different organisms provided by the Constitution, which shall be created first?

Some wanted to start from above. They wanted, said these, to organize first the National Economic Council, and to charge it immediately with the important functions attributed to it by the Constitution, as in the conditions prevailing in Germany at present these powers should not remain without titular direction. They desired also that the National Economic Council prepare and propose the bills necessary for the organization of inferior councils. In other words, the National Economic Council was asked to be the Constituent Assembly for the future Economic Constitution.

Others wanted to commence from below, so as to erect the edifice progressively, and not to construct an upper story before the one below it was sufficiently built to afford a solid foundation.

It was the latter opinion that prevailed. On August 9, 1919, the Cabinet announced a bill creating the Factory Workers Councils. It was urgent, said the Cabinet, that these Councils be created first, because there already existed in many enterprises Workers Councils; some of them had been created by the provisions of collective contracts, others by the will of the workers which had made itself felt during the Revolution, but both kinds of Workers Councils lacked altogether a legal standing.

The bill expressed the idea that the power, hitherto accorded to the Committees of Salaried Employés and Wage-Earners should be transferred to the Factory Workers Councils, but that these powers should be considerably enlarged. This bill was such as could be expected from a Cabinet in which there co-operated, in addition to the Social Democrats, the Centre and Democrats. It corresponded to the economic and social ideas of the trade unionists of all shades, ideas evolutionary and not revolutionary.

From Right and Left the most strenuous criticisms were directed against this bill.

The employers recognized that it was necessary to institute workers representation in each industry and enterprise, and they accepted the creation of the Councils, in which both employers and workers would be represented, which would discuss questions of work and wage, which would supervise the execution of collective bargains and which would serve as an intermediary between the workers and the bosses. But they energetically rejected all measures that, under more or less roundabout devices, tended to recognize for the workers any right of control whatever over production or the management of enterprises, since merchants and manufacturers must above all have freedom of operation. They protested energetically against all provisions that gave the Councils the right to intervene in the direction of business, in questions of hiring and discharging; just as they rejected the proposals that the workers be allowed to participate in the consideration of new technical methods, and that they, the employers, must submit their balance sheets to the workers, reveal the amounts of their profits or their losses and admit workers as members in the Administrative Council.

The supporters of the pure doctrine of the Councils, on the other hand, criticized the Cabinet's proposal for the opposite reason, because it did not organize the real workers representation, but only Councils in which the employers and the workers have the same right. It is impossible to conciliate labour and capital, said they; for, the co-operation of these two must inevitably end in the domination, by the employers, of the workers. The Councils must be made up exclusively of workers who would have an absolute right to control production. The powers given by the bill to the Councils were illusory; they would be only petty unions. The regulation of production would remain intact as before. These Councils would be allowed to examine once a year the balance sheets of each establishment, but they could not control the direction of its business, its purchases, its selling or its profits. The only real advantage would consist of being able to discuss the questions of hiring and discharging.

Thus attacked and criticized the bill, after the most impassioned discussion,[1] after many important alterations, was finally adopted on January 19, by a vote of 213 to 64. This is the law of February 4, 1920.

II.—The organization of the Factory Workers Councils must be supple enough to permit them to fulfil their mission, whatever the importance or the form of the factory may be. They must be neither too small nor too cumbersome; they must comprise both employers and employés; each of these groups must be in position to defend its particular interests; the electoral right must be wholly democratic and minorities must be insured representation, which imposes the obligation of establishing proportional representation; those delegated must always be guided by their duties as representatives. As a consequence of the last, it must be provided that the assembly of electors be enabled to withdraw its support from its representatives and to recall them. The greater part of these conditions was realized by the law of February 4.

The forms that the Factory Workers Councils may assume are extremely diversified.

There is first of all the "Factory Workers Council," properly so-called, which exists in every industrial or commercial

[1] It will be recalled that in order to obtain increase in authority for the Factory Workers Councils, the Independents organized a great manifestation in Berlin in January, 1920, in the course of which about forty of the participants in the manifestation were killed on the steps of the Reichstag.

CONDITIONS OF WORK

unit and in all the public and private administrations where there are at least twenty workers.

The wage-worker members of the Factory Workers Council constitute a "Workers Council" and the salaried employé members make up an "Employé Council." If the Factory Workers Council has more than nine members it elects according to the principles of proportional representation a "Factory Committee" of five members. If the Factory Workers Council comprises both representatives of workers and of employés, each of these two groups must be represented in the Factory Committee.

A "General Factory Workers Council" must be created for enterprises of the same kind situated in the same locality or in adjoining localities and belonging to the same owners, if the Factory Workers Council in each plant so decide. This organization may either remain in juxtaposition with the Factory Workers Councils of the different plants, or it may replace them. In that case it functions as a common Factory Workers Council.

A "shop chairman" must be elected in the place of a Factory Workers Council in establishments employing less than twenty workers, of whom at least five must be electors.

There is finally a "Factory Assembly" composed of all the regular employés of the factory. It is convened by the president of the Factory Council. He must convoke it if the employer or at least one-quarter of the workers demand it.

III.—The powers of the Factory Workers Councils are two kinds; social and economic. *With one or two exceptions they are both purely deliberative in character.*

SOCIAL POWERS: (A) *Conditions of Work.*

(1) The Factory Workers Council supervises the execution of legal decrees, of collective bargains and of arbitration decisions in favour of the workers. The regulation of the con-

ditions of work by collective bargaining remains the essential purpose of the Vocational Unions. The Factory Workers Councils cannot and must not replace this general trade union agreement by a regulation which would intervene between the workers of any single factory and the management of that factory, for the conditions of labour, particularly wage scales, must be fixed not simply according to the conditions prevailing in any single factory, but according to the general situation of the industry. On the other hand, the Factory Workers Councils must see to it that the conditions of work agreed to between the manufacturer's union and the labour organizations are strictly carried out, and must adjust any difficulties that may arise in their application. Each Council must perform the same function in regard to the execution of arbitration decisions and the carrying out of legislative regulatory provisions relative to the condition of the workers.

(2) The Factory Workers Councils co-operate in the fixing of wages and other conditions of work, when these questions are not settled by collective agreement. But it is understood that, even in such a case, the Factory Workers Councils must act in accord with the Trade Unions concerned.

(3) They co-operate with the employer in the adoption of rules for the factory within the framework of the collective bargains in operation.

(4) They examine the questions of pensions for wounded veterans and compensation for those hurt in course of work.

(5) They establish in agreement with the employers rules concerning the hiring of wage-earners and salaried employés and they have the right to oppose their discharge. In the respect to the former, the law specifies that the rules relative to hiring must contain no provision by virtue of which the hiring of a worker would be affected by his political, military, religious or union activities. When these rules permit it, the right of the Factory Workers Council, in so far as it concerns the hiring of a worker, is waived and it is the boss or his rep-

resentative who thereafter decides in each particular case of hiring. But if the boss or his representative violates the rule of contract, the Council of Workers or the Council of Employes may raise a protest. If an agreement is not thereupon reached between the boss and the council, the difficulty is taken before the competent Arbitration Committee which decides finally. On the other hand, in regard to discharges, the law of February 9 gives to the discharged worker the right to appeal it to the Workers Council, and, if an agreement is not reached by this Council, to appeal to the Arbitration Committee in any of the following circumstances: (a) If the discharge is due to the fact that the worker is active in certain political, military, denominational or trade union matters or that he belongs or does not belong to this or that political, denominational, or labour organization; (b) if the discharge is without cause; (c) if the worker is discharged because he has refused to do any piece of work other than that agreed upon when he was hired; (d) if the discharge appears particularly severe, and justified neither by the attitude of the worker nor by the situation in the industry.

(B) *Differences between Employers and Workers.*

The Factory Workers Councils maintain harmony among the workers as well as between them and the employer, and insure the liberty of organization among the workers. They must help avoid all troubles or disorders that may make difficulties between the employers and the workers, and if such arise, they must abate the trouble as soon as possible.

It is not the part of the Factory Workers Councils to take sides in economic disputes in favour of this or that tendency. It is the organ of all the workers of any industry taken together, and it must permit any labour organization, no matter to what tendency it belongs, to enjoy all the rights and all the control to which it is entitled.

(C) *The Well-Being of the Workers.*

(1) The Factory Workers Councils must combat the dangers of occupational accidents and diseases.

(2) They must co-operate in the creation of pension funds, the building of workers' homes, and other institutions of well-being in the factory.

ECONOMIC POWERS.—(1) The Factory Workers Council aids by its technical advice the employer in giving the factory as high an economic efficiency as possible, and co-operates in introducing in the factory new methods of work. This co-operation on the part of the Factory Workers Council assumes that the employer keeps it in touch with the condition in the industry and with the most important events in it. The Council may therefore demand that the employer supply the Factory Committee, or the Council with all the necessary information on the work and the condition of workers, and that he show the pay-rolls—for the purpose of checking up with the schedules agreed upon by collective contracts—and all other documents necessary for the supervision of the execution of collective agreements. This right of inspection is limited in two respects. On the one hand, the Factory Workers Council can only examine records on the economic aspects of the factory, thus excluding all political, union, militarist, denominational, scientific or other investigations on the part of the Councils. On the other hand, the law specifies that this right of examination must not be exercised in such a way that it jeopardizes secrets of the factory or commerce. The question remains as to what must be understood as a secret of the factory or of commerce; this must be settled by judicial decision. From the first moment commentators on the law of February 4th, held that business contracts, records of profits and loss, the schedules and payrolls, estimates of net cost, and the purchase price of raw material are not questions that the Factory Workers Councils are forbidden to investigate. In addition the employer must at least once every quarter furnish the Factory Workers Council with a report on the situation and the progress in general of the factory, on its output and on its prospective needs in the way of workers. Finally the Factory Council may demand that every year a balance sheet for the factory and a statement of profit and loss for the preceding year shall be submitted to the Factory Committee, or the Council, if there is no Factory Committee.

(2) In the factories that have Administrative Councils,[1] the wage-earners and salaried employés are represented on these councils by one or two delegates. This representation of workers on Administrative Councils has aroused among the employers the liveliest opposition. The Cabinet's project provided that the worker representatives have the same rights and duties as the other members of the Administrative Councils. But the National Assembly has not followed the Cabinet on this point and has limited the power of the workers' representatives in the Administrative Council to the mere statement of the interests and claims of the workers, and to the execution of their votes and wishes concerning the organization of the factory. In addition this representation must be regulated by a special law, and, until such a law is passed, that of February 4 confines itself to prescribing that the representatives of the workers have a seat and voice in all the meetings of the Administrative Council, but that they receive no remuneration other than the pay for the time of attendance at the meetings. They are obliged to keep confidential what they learn at the meetings of the Council. The underlying spirit intended for the workers' representation in

---

[1] These enterprises are: Stock companies, limited joint-stock companies, mutual insurance companies, and eventually limited liability companies.

the Administrative Council is indicated as follows: "The granting of so extensive a power, changing the right of codeliberation generally accorded to the working class into a right of codecision, is proposed in the conviction that nothing is better calculated to increase the love of work, the sentiment of responsibility and the output of industries than the right accorded to workers to co-operate under their own responsibility in the supreme direction of the factories."

One cannot conclude the study of the economic powers of the Factory Workers Councils without saying a word on the question of the co-operation of these Councils in the socialization process. The supporters of the theory of Councils have always forcefully insisted on this co-operation to justify the necessity of giving the maximum power possible to the Factory Workers Council. But the law of February 4 does not grant these councils in economic matters anything but powers of deliberation, hardly even conceding them the right of decision; nor does it give them any privilege other than that of supporting and helping their employers in the achievement of the factory's purposes. Thereby is denied all action on the part of the Factory Workers Councils that might directly influence the socialization of the factory itself. The law of February 4 seems to take the point of view opposed to that of socialization.

Socialization is a work relegated exclusively to the State and legislation. It cannot be included in the mission of the workers' representations in a factory. To socialize is to modify economic organization and the right of property, and this change cannot be made except by law. Further, no particular factory can be socialized of itself, that is to say, be transformed by itself into the property of a community. The work of socialization must be undertaken by whole divisions of industry. To accomplish this work it is not the Factory Workers Councils that are competent, but only the parliamentary representation of the whole people.

However, among the partisans of the Factory Workers Councils, some hope that these Councils will be able to give the workers a socialist education by affording them the chance to participate in economic affairs. They believe that, thanks to the Workers Councils, there will finally be formed a working class ready, under responsibility, to fulfil administrative duties in a socialist commonwealth. The Factory Workers Councils according to them will be a school for socialism.[1]

4.—THE TRADE UNIONS AND THE COUNCILS.

Such, in outline, is the law of February 4, 1920. The first elections of the Factory Workers Councils were held during the month of May that followed. Immediately there broke out disputes and rivalries, more violent than before, between the Trade Unions and the partisans of the Councils systems over the rôle which the Factory Workers Councils should play, and particularly over the relations that should subsist between these Councils and the Trade Unions.

The union leaders wanted to maintain their traditional policy, "the wage policy" of the joint committee and the *Arbeitsgemeinschaft*. They held that economic and social reforms can only be accomplished progressively, given the complexity of economic phenomena, and they were convinced that the necessary evolution will take place naturally, thanks to co-operation of employers' and employés' organizations in the *Arbeitsgemeinschaften*.

The development of these organisms since the revolution seems to support their opinion. On the basis of agreements concluded in December, 1918, the *Arbeitsgemeinschaften* have taken on considerable extension. Little by little the organisms provided by the statute of December 4, 1918, have been created and expanded. Not only have individual *Arbeitsgemeinschaften* been established between employers' and employés'

[1] See Paul Umbreit, *das Betriebsrätegesetz*, Berlin, 1920, pp. 20-21.

organizations, but these have also been formed into larger groups. For example, the *Arbeitsgemeinschaft* of the Ruhr mines, those of the Sarre, of Saxony and of Upper Silesia have united into a central *Arbeitsgemeinschaft*, that represents the interests of the whole coal mining industry of Germany. It is administered by a Central Council composed, of course, of equal numbers of employer and worker delegates. A great number of other industries have organized on the same model and they, too, have added above the local organs a Central Council that represents the general vocational interests. Finally, the Central Committees of the different industries have joined and thus created on December 12, 1919, a central *Arbeitsgemeinschaft*, which constitutes the supreme organization and which is charged with settling by direct agreements between employers and employés and on a parity basis all the problems that touch the life of the industries and trades in Germany. This is sub-divided into fourteen vocational groups: iron, provisions, construction, textile, clothing, paper, leather, transports, glass and ceramics, chemistry, oils and fats, forest and land workers, mines and lumber. The Central Executive Committee (Central Vorstand) is composed of twenty-three members chosen by the employers and twenty-three by the workers. Other Committees are created on which the Central Committee places part of its work. Seven such have already been constituted, on the study of wages, labour legislation, economic policy, raw material, coal and transports, tariffs, the execution of the treaty of peace and the internal regulations of the *Arbeitsgemeinschaft*.

All this movement, say the trade unions, represent undeniable progress. For the hostile interests of employer and employé is substituted the *interest of the vocation as a whole,* which creates in the employers and workers of the same vocation a consciousness of the community of their interests and engenders among the different industries a fruitful rivalry. In uniting the *Arbeitsgemeinschaften* of all the in-

THE TRADE UNIONS AND THE COUNCILS

dustries, conflicting interests are placed in equilibrium and neutralized and there remains only common consciousness of national interests.

What can the Factory Workers Councils do otherwise than enter into the framework of already existing organisms and, directed by the Trades Unions, aid in the development of these organisms? In other words, the Factory Workers Councils —and this is also the formal will of the legislator—should be the *delegates of the Trades Unions in each factory* to supervise there the application of the agreements adopted by the Trades Unions and the employers associations. In addition what could the Factory Workers Councils do if they had not behind them the power of the strong organizations of the Trades Unions? A Factory Workers Council, that could not count on the support of a strong union, could exercise no useful activity whatever. It would be soft wax in the hands of the employers. If they want to do efficacious work, the Factory Workers Councils, even though they are the direct emanation from the workers of the factory, must conduct themselves as organs of the Trade Union, and can only play an important rôle if they march hand in hand with the Trade Union.

This dependence of the Factory Workers Councils on the Trade Union gives rise naturally to two considerations. *The Factory Workers Council is without resources,* whereas the Trade Union is rich; the one cannot undertake anything without the aid of the other. But naturally it will not obtain this aid unless it submits to the guidance given it. On the other hand, in order to discuss adequately with the employer the difficult problems that come within the authority of the Factory Workers Council, there is required a preliminary education which the worker does not possess unless he has had long experience in Trade Union life. He often lacks the knowledge and the experience which cannot be acquired except slowly and in the school of the Trade Unions. For this reason also, the Factory Workers Councils should follow Trade Union direction.

The champions of the system of Councils do not concede this subordination of the Factory Workers Councils to the Trade Unions. There is an essential difference between the two, they declare. The Trade Union has as its exclusive mission the preparation and the direction of struggles for wages and conditions of work *under the régime of capitalist production*. The Factory Workers Council is *warring for a new system of production*. And its mission is to prepare the working class to take into its own hands the direction of production. That is why the *organization of the Factory Workers Council must be independent of the Trades Unions, and must develop outside of the framework of the Trades Unions*.

The task which the Factory Workers Councils must accomplish and which must serve as the basis of all their future activity, is to achieve a unity of front of the whole working class. The Trade Unions have not yet brought themselves to take the initiative in this fundamental reform. At the present time workers are still scattered among approximately fifty Trades Unions, which are divided still further into a number of sections and branches. There is an inextricable network of collective contracts, "tariffs," and wage agreements down to the smallest labour group, representing a great amount of work; but this cannot in the least ameliorate the economic condition of the working class.

One thing must immediately be abolished, the *Arbeitsgemeinschaft*, because it is contrary to the doctrine of the class struggle, and because, under the pretext of co-operation, it insures the domination of the capitalist over the worker.

As for the Trades Unions, the champions of the Factory Workers Council recognize that the latter, although working on a different plan, must remain in intimate contact with the former. But there is an indispensable reform to be realized. Organization by trades must be replaced by organization by industries or factories. In other words, all the vocations functioning at the same time in the same industry must be grouped within the same organization. In still other words, the separation of wage-earners associations from the associations of salaried employés must be done away with. On the contrary, all manual and intellectual workers of the same industry must join together and consecrate all their efforts to a common end.

Finally, declared the partisans of the Councils, the Factory Workers Councils cannot remain isolated in the various separate industries. They can only fulfil their function if they unite in district assemblies and organize in such a way as to create a "Central Organ of the Factory Workers Councils," which will direct the activity of all the Factory Workers Councils of Germany.

These arguments were not without effect on the Trades Union leaders. They still maintained, naturally, the principle that the Factory Workers Councils must enter into the Trade Union organization and that they must remain an organ of the latter. But they declared themselves ready to accept a great part of the reforms demanded by their critics.

Moreover the General Federation of Labour and the General Federation of Salaried Employes organized "A Central Union of the Factory Workers Council," whose purpose is to unite the Factory Workers Councils with the unions of wage-earners and salaried employés, and to incorporate them into the whole Trade Union organization. To this end they undertook a complete local organization of the Factory Workers Councils. First the District Committees of the Trades Unions were to proceed to a redistribution of the Factory Workers Councils into fifteen industrial groups. Each industrial group was to decide independently on the matters that concern the vocations included in this group. The Group Council had to include a member of the Trade Union or of the corresponding union of salaried employés. This organization by groups was to insure the co-operation of Factory Workers Councils on an industry basis, and thus attempt to meet the criticisms of partisans of the Councils. Above the different industrial groups three organs were provided which would represent the Factory Workers Councils as a whole: the General Assembly of all the Factory Workers Councils, the Central Council, and the Central Committee.

The mission of the Trade Union organization of the Factory Workers Councils would be to give the latter a Trade Union direction and development, to unite in the factories all economic and social forces available, and to utilize these forces for the defence of the common interests of all workers. There is thus a division of labour between the traditional mission of the Trade Union branches and that of their local committees, on whom would be still incumbent the duties of specifically Trade Union organization, whereas questions of general, social and economic policy would be given over to the "Central Factory Workers Council." It follows that the two parallel organizations must work hand in hand and must consult each other on all questions, thus doing away with all possibility of conflict.

Such was the plan, duly elaborated by the Trade Unions, which at this time is submitted for discussion in common by the Factory Workers Councils and the Vocational Associations of Germany. Naturally, it is impossible to foretell what will result from these deliberations. All that can be said at present is that the members of the Factory Workers Councils are almost exclusively elected from among the wage-earners and salaried employés *already active in the Trade Unions*, and thus the conception to which the Trade Unions seem to cling above everything else, the incorporation of the Factory Workers Councils into the Trade Union associations, seems destined to be realized of its own accord.

5.—THE PROVISIONAL ECONOMIC COUNCIL.

These discussions, these vacillations, these difficulties, have up to now prevented the government from submitting the necessary projects of laws for the creation and organization of Councils, other than Factory Workers Councils, provided for by the Constitution. In May, 1920, there was an attempt to propose a law on "Local Workers Councils." But the government declared that it had not yet arrived at a clear conception of the relations between the Factory Workers Councils, the future Economic Councils and the employers' organizations, and that it was still pursuing its studies.

In view of the impossibility of continuing the building of the structure from below, it was decided to change the method and, returning to the system rejected the year before, resignedly the attempt was made to continue from above. There was thus created a "Provisional Economic Council."

The organization of this Council, provisional as it must be, has not proceeded without presenting great difficulties, which it is interesting to sum up.

I.—This Council must consist of the representatives of all economic, agricultural, commercial, and industrial interests. The first question that came up was to fix the number of representatives to be allowed to each different interest. Naturally, violent conflicts arose, each interest fighting for the largest representation possible. Instead of establishing a proportion based on the respective importance of the various vocations in German economic life, and of holding to this proportion, the Cabinet increased the total number of members of the Economic Council as fast as this or that interest claimed a stronger representation, with the result that the number of representatives, originally fixed at a hundred, increased to 280 and finally became 326. It is clear that the resulting proportion that came from these successive increases favours agriculture to the detriment of industry and the middle classes.

A place was given to the representatives of consumers; unwisely, according to some critics. For one can understand the adding of the consumers to the assembly of the producers of some one single industrial group, that of coal, for example, which grows always at the expense of the consumers. But in the Economic Council, all industries and vocations are by definition represented; the producers in one industry are the consumers in all the others and it is unnecessary to add to them, in order to represent the interests of consumers, additional representatives, who by hypothesis are only consumers.

The 326 members of the Economic Council are allotted as follows:

68 representatives of agriculture and forestry.
6 representatives of market industries and fisheries.
68 representatives of general industry.
44 representatives of commerce, banks and insurance.
34 representatives of transport enterprises.
36 representatives of small business and small industries.
30 representatives of consumers (municipalities, consumers' associations and organizations of women).
16 representatives of civil servants and the professions.
24 other persons named by the government.

II.—There then followed the question of how the delegates of each group are to be appointed. The discussion reverted to the question whether these delegates should be appointed by vocation or region. Where employers and workers were grouped, the principle of parity was naturally adhered to. Agriculture, for example, which is entitled to 44 delegates, was represented by 22 land owners and 22 agricultural workers. On the other hand, the mode of nomination in all groups representing workers offered but few problems, for—at least until the Factory Workers Councils have united and become organized geographically over the whole Reich—the only labour organizations are those of the Trade Unions; that is to say, organizations almost exclusively vocational, and the labour delegates to the Economic Council cannot be elected except by means of these organizations. But the problem became much more complex in the case of the election of representatives of employers and property owners. These had, in addition to their industrial associations, organs of regional representation, such as chambers of commerce, chambers of agriculture, boards of trade, etc. Should their delegates throughout be elected by regional organs or by associations? The Reichsrat replied, by chambers of commerce; and the National Assembly declared for associations.

The partisans of representation by chambers of commerce pointed out that these chambers are, according to existing legislation, the only representatives of industry and of commerce in public law; that they embrace all the industrial and commercial circles, considered vocationally as well as regionally, and that they constitute an electoral body more complete than the organizations on a purely professional basis; and that, in contrast to the associations, the chambers of commerce are elected by all the manufacturers and merchants inscribed on the register of commerce.

The supporters of the associations replied that, great as was the service rendered by the Chambers of Commerce as local and regional corporations, they play almost no rôle whatever in the public economy of Germany. Their influence on economic management is practically nil; and they are limited in the matter of projects for new laws, to the voting of resolutions that have no outcome whatever. The special business associations, however, although without official standing in public law, are acquiring more and more importance in the public economy of Germany. What is most important is to make up the Economic Council of "heads"—of the most eminent men from each industry, whether of the North or the South, the West or the East.

The solution adopted does not seem to have been a particularly happy one. Of the sixty-eight industrial delegates, forty-eight represent vocational divisions and twenty represent regional groups. Of the first, forty-two are designated by the *Arbeitsgemeinshaft* of the employers and industrial workers of Germany (twenty-one employers and twenty-one workers); six others represent the Council of Coal and the Council of Potash. Of the regional representatives, twenty employers are named by the Chambers of Commerce and of Agriculture but twenty workers are named by the labour element of the Central *Arbeitsgemeinschaft*.

III.—The authority of the Provisional Economic Council is not quite the same as that of the final Economic Council, provided by the Constitution.

It must, and that was its essential mission, construct the framework on which the future Economic Council is to be erected, and determine how it shall be elected. This necessitates its organizing in advance Workers Councils, aside from Factory Workers Councils, and Economic Councils for each locality, which, according to the Constitution, must contribute to the formation of the National Economic Council.

In addition, the Provisional Economic Council must examine the projects of all important laws, economic and social in nature, that the Cabinet is required to submit to it for advice before placing them before the Parliament. It must be heard on proposals for decrees and important regulations. It has itself the right to present proposals for laws.

These powers are the same as those projected for the final Economic Council. But the two differ in an important respect. Whereas, according to the Constitution, the Economic Council will have the right, when it differs in opinion from the Cabinet, to present its point of view by one of its members before the Reichstag, it has not been considered feasible, for constitutional reasons, to recognize the same right for the Provisional Economic Council.

Generally, however, the Provisional Economic Council is considered as already constituting an Economic Parliament, and at the commencement of its work [1] it was so regarded by the press.

It does not deserve this name, for it has no power of decision. It is purely and simply a technical Council that advises the Cabinet on principal economic questions. It differs from ordinary technical Councils in that instead of being appointed most of its members are elected. One cannot therefore criticize it from the point of view of formal democracy, in the way that any parliament composed according to the parity principle can be criticized, viz., that each employer-member represents much fewer electors than the worker-members. As it is here a matter of a council of experts, the most important thing was to gather the best qualified authorities of the whole country. It is evident, therefore, that in the present state of affairs such authorities are found much more easily among employers than among workers. The relative proportion of these two elements within the Provisional Economic Council matters little since decision lies exclusively with the assembly elected by universal suffrage.

Meanwhile, however, the importance of the services that the Economic Council can be called upon to render must not be underestimated. It is undeniable that, as at present composed, it has gathered together nearly all the men considered in Germany to-day as the most experienced and trained authorities in economic matters. It must not be lost sight of also that a great number of these men, aside from their individual importance, have behind them the support of the whole force of the extremely powerful vocational and economic associations by which they were elected.

[1] It met for the first time on June 30, 1920.

One immediate danger menaces the Economic Council. It is that the men who compose it will let themselves be guided on the technical questions they are to examine by party considerations. It may be divided—as is natural—into groups of employers, groups of workers, groups of agriculturalists, industrialists, and merchants. If it turns out to be an assembly of conservatives, democrats, Catholics and socialists, it is doomed to sterility.

If, however, the Economic Council avoids this danger it will render, first of all, the service of clarifying the political atmosphere itself. The members will defend very legitimately only the interests by which they were charged with representation. In this way economic groups will not need to act indirectly through the intermediate agency of political representatives. They will be able to express their point of view clearly and support their interests directly. The political parties, too, will gain thereby; for they will be freed of all considerations of interest and they will no longer have to complicate technical problems by imposing on them their general political conceptions. As for the authority that will accrue to the Economic Council, it depends entirely on itself whether it will be nullified or preponderant, and its future lies in its own hands.

Former Under-Secretary of State, von Delbrück said before the National Assembly—speaking, it is true, of the Economic Council to be organized by the Constitution, but the Provisional Economic Council is nevertheless its precursor—that the Economic Council is without doubt, by the side of the Reichstag and the Reichsrat, a third legislative assembly. For such an assembly, "called upon to deliberate on the most important questions in the national life, will necessarily have a natural tendency to enlarge its powers. We are undoubtedly on the eve of a period in which the Reichstag and the Reichsrat will be considered as one side of a balance, and the Economic Council as the other. Behold in this a wholly new political evolution. There will come a day when the Economic Council will seek to become the heir of the Reichsrat and to take its place."

Will this prediction be realized? It will if the Economic Council is able to render the government and the people the services they expect of it. It will not if it does not deserve to be heard by them and does not know how to make itself heard.

SECTION II

SOCIALIZATION

In order to reconstruct in Germany the public and private economy destroyed by the war and the revolution, it is not enough to give the producers a special right to co-operate in the regulation of economic questions; nor to recognize particularly for the working class the right of co-deliberation in the determination of these matters. It is hoped that such measures will increase production. But it is also necessary that no part of production be lost and that all of it be utilized to the utmost for the community. One is thus led to inquire whether the system of production and the distribution of wealth, such as prevails under a capitalist régime, is capable even if improved, of attaining such an end; whether it were not better to substitute a new system, socialist or not, giving the utmost guarantee that production will benefit the entire community.

We must inquire what attitude the Constituent Assembly took on this question and what solution it adopted.

1.—THE PROBLEM OF SOCIALIZATION.

On the morrow of the Revolution, power passed entirely into the hands of socialists, that is to say, by definition, men whose programme may be summed up in these words: the abolition of private property and the taking over by the state of all the means of capitalist production.

The Independents undoubtedly would have set about at once the task of realizing this programme. But we have seen that they had but a brief period of power; and the Social Democrats seemed less in a hurry to keep their promises.

For the moment the political revolution was enough to absorb all their activity, and they postponed the economic revolution. They declared that an industry cannot be socialized until it is "ripe" for such a measure. But, they further declared, this maturity cannot be suddenly effected by a vote of Parliament or even by the decision of the majority of the people. It is the product of a slow social development, which may find its expression in the vote of a majority, but which cannot be thereby hastened. To tell the truth, the Social Democrats, whom events had placed with their back to the wall, perceived how difficult it is to put into practice the vague theories with which they had heretofore contented themselves. Not only did they realize that the solution of economic questions raised by socialization is extremely difficult, but they became also convinced that it was necessary first to consolidate some of the elements of German economic life that had survived the war and its unhappy conclusion before proceeding to experiments which might accomplish their ruin. They resolved therefore to study the problems of socialization more deeply before passing to its realization. For this purpose they created, November, 1918, a "Committee on Socialization" which was not to be an official organ but a free scientific committee charged with the drawing up of reports and proposals on the question of socialization. It consisted of eleven members with Kautsky as chairman.

But the impatience of the masses did not give the Socialist Cabinet the respite they required. The people, who for years had been promised the abolition of private capitalist property, and who saw in the realization of the Socialist programme the end of the miserable situation into which the war and the revolution had plunged them, demanded immediate measures. The general strike which broke out in Berlin in March, 1919, and which, as we have seen, prompted the Cabinet to promise the "anchorage" of the Councils in the Constitution, also pushed it to prepare in haste two projects of law— one on socialization, the other on the regulation of the coal industry, the two projects being adopted within a few days by the National Assembly. The two laws carried the date of March 23, 1919. The first is what is called in Germany a "blanket law" or a "skeleton law." It indicates the different forms according to which socialization of private enterprises may become operative, and the conditions in which these enterprises, once socialized, may be exploited. The second makes immediate application of these principles to the coal industry. In addition another law voted several days later, April 29, 1919, regulated according to the same principles the potash industry.

Whereupon the members of the Committee on Socialization, who complained of having their work constantly impeded by the Cabinet, and their recommendations remaining unheeded, handed in their resignations on April 7, 1919.

On the other hand, the Minister of Public Economy, the Social Democrat, Rudolph Wissel, finding the measures for socialization taken or proposed by the Cabinet too timid and insufficient addressed a memorandum to the Council of Ministers on May 7, which had great reverberation throughout Germany as soon as it became known.[1]

The Cabinet, said Wissel, followed a policy inconsistent and without unity. Within the Council of Ministers a decision on fundamental questions was avoided in order not to put the coalition in danger; and the few measures taken were compromises dictated by necessity.

---

[1] This memorandum did not represent the personal opinion of the Minister. The ideas expressed in it were the opinions of a group that included both socialists and bourgeois elements, men like Walter Rathenau, von Möllendorf (under-secretary of State under Wissel), Andreas, a banker, Georg Bernhard, editor of the *Vossiche Zeitung*, and others.

Meanwhile the economic situation of Germany was in an almost desperate state, and a menacing catastrophe could be avoided only by completely transforming the system of production that prevailed in peace times. Wissel declared that he was not speaking of expropriation, for that would do no more than substitute the state for private capitalism, that is to say, one exploiter for another. But what he referred to was the restriction of illegitimate profits, the regulation of prices and the control of the distribution of profits. *Production and consumption must be organized according to a coordinated plan* in such a way that enterprises may be exploited in the interest of all and not to the exclusive profit of some. It was imperative to proceed by some solution as a whole and not by incoherent and isolated attempts.

The principal measures for which Wissel demanded immediate adoption were the following:

(1) The organization of the system of Councils by a special law without waiting for the adoption of the Constitution. They must include organizations of workers and of employers, regional and vocational. These last, which would rest on the parity principle of the *Arbeitsgemeinschaft,* would have for their mission the direction of the economy in the vocation they represented, this direction to follow the principles decreed by the Cabinet. There must be in addition an Economic Council, which will be the supreme organ of the whole German collective economy.

(2) Other branches of production must be regulated on the model of the regulation already in operation for coal and potash. The next to be thus regulated must be electricity and the cereals.

(3) The State must take a more and more important part in the functioning and in the profits of industrial enterprises. By an inheritance tax and by a tax on capital there must be put into the hands of the State a great part of the industrial fortunes. Instead of collecting these taxes in money or in

war loans, the state must become the proprietor of part of the enterprises in the form of shares.

(4) The stocks and bonds of the industrial concerns of the State will be administered not by a Minister, but by a national bank which will conduct its business according to purely economic rules to the exclusion of all political considerations.

By these last two measures will be realized what the supporters of this system call a "progressive mediatization of capital."

(5) There will be created funds of several billions of marks which will be administered by an office acting in close relation with the vocational economic organization and designed to procure employment for German workers.

(6) The cost of necessities which Germany must import exceeds greatly the cost of domestic commodities. This circumstance compels the increase of wages, which in turn causes the cost of living to rise and lowers the value of money. To counteract this part of all wages must be distributed hereafter in provisions, clothes, etc. Credits will be opened by financiers and by the State.

(7) Temporarily the right to strike in certain industries vital to the German economy will be restricted. The right to stop work will have to be voted by nine-tenths of those employed in that industry.

(8) To realize this programme the number of Ministers who will occupy themselves with economic questions will be reduced to three. They will constitute within the Cabinet an "Economic Committee," whose directions will have to be followed absolutely by the political Ministers.

On the whole this project aimed at the realization of a state intermediate between capitalism and socialism.

Defended only among the socialists by a small group of doctrinaires, this project had against it at the same time the Independents, the bourgeois parties and the Social Democrats. The Independents opposed it because it permitted capital to survive. The bourgeois parties opposed it because the supervised economy prevented the free play of economic factors and paralyzed initiative. The Social Democrats opposed it for fear of dissatisfying the Centre and the Democrats, of whom they had need to maintain themselves in power. Particularly opposed to Wissel's project were the Trade Union conceptions supported in the Cabinet by the Minister of Food Supply, Robert Schmidt. He presented a counter-project which embodied the argument which the Socialists of the government opposed to the theoreticians of socialism. The work of socialization, said they, must be undertaken but slowly and the socialization of an industry must wait until that industry is sufficiently matured. This last conception prevailed and in July, 1919, Wissel resigned. Thereupon the offices of the Minister of Public Economy and that of Food Supply were merged and Robert Schmidt given the unified post.

It was to be expected, therefore, that the process of socialization would be considerably slowed up. In fact, the Constitution of the month of August confined itself to specifying and enlarging in several respects the principles of the law of socialization of March 23; and for several months there was only one law enacted along these lines, that of December 31, 1919, on the socialization of electricity.

But once more the people intervened. It may be recalled that one of the "Eight Points" of the agreement imposed on the Cabinet by the Trade Unions after the *coup d'état* by Kapp, provided that the Committee on Socialization be at once reconvened, that representatives of vocational associations be added to it, that new industries be socialized and that the socialization of industries already decreed be enforced.

In conformity with these engagements, the Cabinet in the beginning of May, 1920, submitted to the Reichstag a project of law that provided for the municipalization of a certain number of industrial enterprises, and reconvened the Committee on Socialization. The members of this committee, who were authorized to add to their number new colleagues on the condition that the total number of the members should not exceed thirty, were given a double mission. First they were to study and clarify the fundamental principles of socialism, for the purpose of determining the general lines along which the capitalist system should be transformed. Then they were to submit concrete and immediate proposals, which, inspired by the laws of collective economy, would permit the commonwealth to utilize directly the natural resources and the sources of power. The committee had also to study how the industries already socialized were functioning, what results had been attained and to propose, if necessary, all needful changes.

2.—THE COLLECTIVE ECONOMY.

All these labours, all these investigations, all these discussions of the problem of socialization had one result. They have shown how confused, even among the socialists, is the concept of socialism; that behind the same word may hide two economic systems extremely different, and that a whole series of almost imperceptible gradations may exist between the capitalist system and complete socialism.

The Constitution raises the following principle: Economic organization must cease to be dominated by considerations of private interests in order that hereafter it may be inspired exclusively by considerations of public interests. Private interests must be subordinated to collective interests. The present economic régime, based on private ownership, must be substituted by a new régime based on collective ownership (Gemeinwirtschaft). What is understood by this?

In its largest sense the expression "collective economy" may be defined as an organization, following a certain predetermined plan, of the economic system of a country for the purpose, on the one hand, of obtaining as large an increase as possible in production by the union of all forces affecting economy; and, on the other hand, for the purpose of devoting a proper part of the product to the community or to its productive members.[1] Thus a system of collective economy is any system that increases public influence in private enterprise, on the condition that it results in a more just administration and distribution, particularly in the cases of monopolized industries already organized into trusts or cartels.

In practice, the principle of collective economy may be applied under three different forms:

(1) The State may take over immediately and entirely the ownership of the industries it wishes to subject to the new régime, and direct by itself and alone, with the aid of its civil servants, the industries which it has seized. *This is complete socialization.*

(2) The State may content itself with participating in the ownership of certain private enterprises. It owns, for example, a certain number of shares in a corporation. In such a case, it does not manage the enterprise wholly, but it has the right of codecision in the general direction of affairs. *This is partial socialization.*

(3) Finally, the State may leave in the hands of individuals the ownership of enterprises which it wishes to subject to the principles of collective economy; but it unites, if necessary by constraint, all those that belong in one industry or in the same category of industries, such as chemistry, coal, metallurgy, etc. Thus united the enterprises are administered by means of organs in which are represented all the categories of the population interested in it, such as owners, workers, trade unionists, consumers, etc. These organs must be guided, in the direction they give to this management, above all by a concern for the general interests of the commonwealth. This is *collective economy* properly so-called or *nationalization.*

This last form of collective economy is particularly interesting, be it said. For, on the one hand, it avoids the just criticisms of bureaucracy and exaction generally directed

[1] Reier, *Sozialisierungsgesetze*, Berlin, 1920, p. 14.

against socialism properly so-called. On the other hand, it takes into account the principal demands of the working class at the present time in recognizing for the workers the right to participate in the direction of business enterprises.[1]

The Constitution does not clearly choose between these three different methods of applying the principles of collective economy in the large sense of the word. It declares all three possible and leaves to the ordinary legislature, whenever it is desirable to regulate an industry in the general interest, the task of choosing the bearing it wishes to give such regulations and the régime to which it wishes to subject the industry in question.

(1) In effect, according to the terms of Article 156 of the Constitution, the Reich may transfer private business enterprises to public ownership, that is to say, take over the property for the Reich, the States, or for the municipalities.

(2) The Reich may participate itself or have the States or the municipalities participate in the administration of these enterprises, or may secure for itself in some other manner a decisive influence in these enterprises.

(3) Or, finally, without taking to itself all or part of these enterprises the Reich may regulate, on the basis of autonomy

[1] Wissel, then Minister of Public Economy, on March 7, 1919, before the National Assembly thus defined collective economy properly so-called: "Collective economy means the organization and management of private economic enterprises in the interests of the Reich, the subordination of private interests to collective interests. The application of this general principle to particular cases must be adapted to the special conditions of the different branches of the economy. Nothing can be worse than to want to make the economy rigidly uniform. Every economic group is a different organism that demands forms appropriate to it. This seems to be indicated in the exterior forms of union, such as capitalist economy practiced in its associations and cartels. But the spirit that prevails in these organizations must be raised above purely private considerations up to a sense of responsibility toward the people as a whole, up to the conception of a collective economy. *Collective economy does not mean state economy, but autonomy.* The State is not the master of economy. It can and should exercise supreme supervision and hold in equilibrium the opposing interests with justice and wisdom."

and according to the principles of collective economy, the production and the distribution of wealth.

In this last case the Constitution specifies that the business enterprises which are made subject to a nationalization measure, shall form "an autonomous body" (Selbstverwaltungskörper). This is a new form in public law. The "autonomous body" is somewhat analogous to ordinary public corporations. It administers itself with the organs necessary for it. It enjoys great independence, but it is nevertheless subject to supervision by the State. Article 156, par. 2, of the Constitution specifies that when legislation subjects a given industry to the system of nationalization and organizes the autonomous body it must constitute the administrative organs of this body in such a way that there shall be insured the co-operation of all the producing elements of the people, and that the salaried employes and wage-earners participate in administration and that the production and distribution satisfy first of all the interests of the commonwealth.

These organs form the Industrial Economic Councils which we have already examined. An example will illustrate this hypothesis. Legislature decides, for instance, to subject the chemical industry to the régime of the collective economy. It combines, therefore, all the manufactories of chemical products into a sort of obligatory *cartel*, the bond uniting the different manufactories being more or less close according to circumstances. The system of administration by "autonomous bodies" will consist of the institution of one or more organisms, such as Economic Councils of the Chemical Industry, in which will be represented all the individuals, associations and Councils interested, and which will manage together the German chemical industry. The chemical industry will thus form an autonomous body, that is to say, a sort of public corporation under the supervision of the State. Further than this, however, it is not possible at the present time to specify the distinctive traits of this new legal category. We must wait until legislation has organized a number of autonomous bodies before we can state precisely their general characteristics and give them a place in the collective institutions of public law. Still less possible, naturally, is it to forecast the economic consequences to which they may give rise.

However, the Constitution has not felt that it should give the ordinary legislator absolute freedom to proceed according to his fancy to the enactment of measures for socialization more or less complete. It has therefore provided certain limits on the exercise of the rights it confers on the legislature.

(1) Only the legislature of the Reich may enact socialization measures.

(2) No industry may be socialized except when it is "ripe for this socialization." This is the so-called *maturity clause*.

(3) Enterprises which the legislator wishes to organize as "autonomous bodies" may not be so proceeded against except "in case of urgent necessity."

These last two restrictions may seem very important. In reality, however, they constitute a purely fictitious restraint; for the legislature is the sole judge, at any time that it wishes to socialize an industry, as to whether that industry is "ripe" or not, and whether or not the case is one of urgent necessity.

(4) There remains finally the question of indemnity. As may well be imagined, during the discussion of the project of the socialization law as well as during the deliberations on the project of the Constitution, this question was very vigorously discussed. The Socialist parties wanted no allusion made to this question in the text of the law or that of the Constitution. The bourgeois parties demanded that at least in the case of complete socialization the state should be absolutely obliged to accord an indemnity. It was impossible to arrive at agreement. So that although the principle of indemnity was incorporated, it was left to the legislature, whenever it enacts a

special law decreeing a socialization measure, to decide whether or not indemnity shall be accorded and to what extent.

In accordance with the above provisions a certain number of industries have been placed under the régime of collective ownership, where they are about to be transformed.

For the coal, potash and iron industries the laws of March 23, of April 29, 1919, and the regulation of April 1, 1920, have chosen the system of collective ownership, properly so-called. That is to say, the industries of coal, potash and metallurgy, although to a very limited extent, have been organized into autonomous bodies, self-administering under the supervision of the Reich.

As to electricity, the law of December 31, 1919, provides that electrical plants that have acquired a certain importance will become the property of the Reich, the latter, however, providing a suitable indemnity.

The project of the law relative to municipalization, finally, provides that municipalities may, with the authorization of the Reich, transfer to the régime of collective ownership private industries that serve principally common local needs. Full authority is given the municipalities over all that concerns transportation, water, gas, cinematographs, theatres, burial, baths, etc. These enterprises may be either taken over entirely as the property of the municipalities, or be organized into autonomous bodies. In principle the municipality is required to indemnify in all such cases.

It is impossible to examine here in full detail these or later laws. It is interesting, however, to devote several pages in describing in a very general way, in view of the great importance of the coal industry at the present time, the system into which it has been transformed.

3.—THE REGULATION OF THE COAL INDUSTRY.

The crisis in coal which to-day exists in almost every country in the world has led the different governments to take

REGULATION OF THE COAL INDUSTRY

various measures either to avert it or to diminish it. In general, coal mining has remained in the domain of private economy. Distribution, however, has passed more or less completely into the domain of collective economy. The systems of distribution to which the different countries have resorted are various. According to the given circumstances they adopt one or another of three possible modes of public economy. In France, the distribution of mined or imported coal is carried on by the state itself. In Germany it is done by a group of organisms in which are represented the various interested elements of the population, but in which provisionally the mine owners predominate.

It is advisable to study first the existing system in the coal industry in order to understand better the changes we are examining.

I.—As regulated by the law of March 23, 1919, and the decree of August 21, of the same year, the mechanism of the coal industry consists of three organs: the Colliers Association, the National Association, and the National Coal Council.

The German Reich is divided into a certain number of coal mining districts. In each district all the mine owners associations must form a Colliers Association. If this cannot be accomplished voluntarily the Minister of Public Economy promulgates the organization by means of a decree. Each Colliers Association must have a Council of Administration, in which it is obligatory that the workers be allowed representation. In addition, in the Councils of Administration of the five biggest associations there must be admitted a representative of the salaried employés. The Council of Administration has the authority commonly accorded to the councils of administration of stock companies by the Commercial Code; it appoints its own president. In the same way all the owners of gasworks that produce coke are united for the whole territory of the Reich into an Association of Coal-gas Manufacturers, formed on the same model as the Colliers' Associations.

The Colliers Associations, the association of Coal-gas Manufacturers and the German states that belong, by virtue of ownership of mines, in the Colliers Associations, are united into a *National Coal Association*. This has a Council of Administration in which must be included three wage-earners and salaried employés and one representative of the consumers.

The National Coal Council is composed of sixty members —representatives of the states, of mine owners organizations, wage-earners, office workers, consumers, etc.[1] It is convened as often as conditions demand and at least once every six

[1] These sixty members are divided as follows:
  3 representatives of states;
  15 representatives of colliers' organizations;
  15 representatives of mine workers;
  1 employer and 1 worker in gasworks;
  2 salaried employés of the technical service of the mines;
  1 salaried employé of the commercial service of the mines;
  5 coal merchants;
  1 employé in the wholesale coal trade;
  2 employers and 2 workers in industries using coal;
  2 representatives of consumers' societies;
  1 user of coal in the cities, 1 in the country;
  2 representatives of small industries using coal;
  1 user of coal for railroads;
  1 user of coal for maritime navigation;
  1 user of coal for river navigation;
  3 mine and boiler experts.

The representatives of the states are named by the Reichsrat from among the municipal administrations and consumers of coal. The representatives of employers and employés in the mining industries as well as the twelve representatives of the colliers' associations are elected by the mine groups of the *Arbeitsgemeinschaft*. Two representatives are named by the Prussian Minister of Commerce and Industry. The representatives of the coal trade are named by the German Congress of Commerce and Industry. The representatives of the employers and employés of the industries using coal, and the representatives of the employés of gasworks are elected by their *Arbeitsgemeinschaften*. The representatives of the small industries using coal are elected by the German Chambers of Commerce and Industry. The other representatives are appointed, on the advice of those they represent, by the Minister of Public Economy of the Reich.

REGULATION OF THE COAL INDUSTRY

months. It must in addition be convened if at least ten of its members or the Minister of Public Economy of the Reich demand it. It decides by majority vote. It creates three technical committees, The Economic Committee on Mining Construction, The Economic Committee for the Utilization of Combustibles and The Social Committee of the Mines. Each member of the National Coal Council must belong to a committee. The cost of the administration of the National Coal Council and of its committees is borne by the National Colliers Associations.

Each of these organs has its own special powers.

The National Coal Council directs the economy of combustibles, in which is included importation and exportation, according to the principles of collective economy under the supervision of the Reich. It must approve the charters according to which the Colliers Associations and the National Coal Association are organized. The National Coal Council may decree general policies for the administration of combustibles, in particular for the abolition of unproductive enterprises and for the protection of consumers. It sees to it that the National Coal Association and the technical committees of the Coal Council work according to the same principles and in a coherent system. It may demand information from any of the organs that participate in the fuel industry; and the authorities and committees are obliged to give it any assistance it demands. The technical committee collect all important data based on practice and experience, study all matters that enter within their domain and prepare decisions for the National Coal Council.

The National Coal Association controls the application of the general policies and decisions decreed by the National Coal Council and regulates the details of the execution of these decrees. It must approve the general conditions of the coal deliveries of the Colliers Association. *It establishes and pub-*

lishes the selling prices of fuel, taking into account proposals made by unions and the interests of the consumers. On this point it must insure the same treatment for the consumers' societies as for the wholesalers, and see to it that each consumer, who takes at least a full carload of coal at the mine or at the point of delivery, shall obtain fuel under predetermined conditions for cash payment. Finally, the National Coal Association has authority in questions of import and export.

The Colliers Associations supervise the application of the decrees issued by the National Coal Council and by the National Coal Association, and, within the framework of these decrees, regulate the production, utilization and consumption on the part of their members. They, themselves, sell the fuel which should be put at their disposal by their members, on the account of the latter. The powers of the Association of Coal-gas Manufacturers are similar.

The mining companies may raise claims and protests against the regulations of the Associations of which they are members, appealing to the National Coal Association and beyond that to the National Coal Council.

If any measure on the part of the National Coal Council, the National Coal Association, or of the Colliers Associations violates any vested right, the individual or the association injured is entitled to suitable indemnity. This indemnity may be sued for before ordinary tribunals.

The powers of the Reich, the States, and the municipalities are fixed by the decree of August, 1919, as follows:

The Reich, through the intermediacy of the Minister of Public Economy, exercises general control over the fuel economy. The Minister may in particular lower the price of coal fixed by the National Coal Association. He may also organize a representation of fuel consumers, a representation with authority to fix the retail price of coal. The cost incurred by the Reich in the execution of the law on the regulation of coal, up to a minimum of 200,000 marks per year, must be borne by the National Coal Association.

The States represented by the Committee on Commerce and Industry in the Reichsrat are authorized to participate in the deliberations of the National Coal Council and its committees, but only with consultative powers. Fiscal authorities are authorized to demand information of the National Coal Council of the Reich and of its committees as well as of the National Coal Associations and of the Colliers Associations.

Municipalities of at least 10,000 inhabitants and groups and Unions of Municipalities, after having heard the claims of dealers and consumers, and guided by the wholesale price of coal fixed by the National Coal Association, are themselves empowered to fix the retail price within their territories.

II.—The regulation above described was far from giving complete satisfaction. It has been attacked both by the consumers and the socialists. The latter criticize it as not having gone far enough along the road of nationalization. The former, on the other hand, complain that prices are fixed by an Assembly in which coal owners form a very great majority (The National Coal Association), and that the other interests are not able to make themselves sufficiently heard. The result of this system is that the coal producers always come to agreement to the detriment of the consumers and constantly increase the price of coal.

It must be conceded to the socialists that in the system established by the law of March 23, 1919, the principles of collective economy are applied in the most parsimonious manner possible. The only Council in which there is parity between employers and workers is the National Coal Council, but the rôle of this Council is reduced to a minimum. The real directors and administrators of the coal industry are the Colliers Associations and the National Coal Association. The National Coal Council has hardly any effective power.

As for the Cabinet, the right of the Minister of Public Economy to oppose his veto to measures taken by the National Coal Association and in particular to lower by law the prices fixed by the latter, is considered by the Socialists entirely insufficient in view of the close co-operation of the coal mine owners and the dealers in league against him.

In May, 1920, a bill was elaborated by the Cabinet. It provided for the abolition of the National Coal Association and for the transfer of its powers to the National Coal Councils; in addition the influence of the consumers was to be considerably increased within the National Coal Council. But the Constituent Assembly adjourned before this project could be examined by them.

Meanwhile a change was effected. It was agreed at the end of May, 1920, that decisions of the National Coal Association would thereafter not be operative unless they were made in agreement with a "Great Commission" of the National Coal Council. If agreement is not arrived at the matter must be brought before the National Coal Council itself which thereupon decides, its decision becoming binding upon the Association.

III.—But this reform did not suffice, and the question of a complete transformation of the regulation of the coal industry was submitted to a searching examination by the Committee on Socialization. One thing was unanimously agreed upon— the existing régime could not continue. The Provisional Economic Council, in its meeting on July 24, the Cabinet of the Reich in the meeting of the Reichstag on August 5, and the Committee on Socialization declared that the coal industry must thereafter be completely subjected to the principles of collective economy; that the wage-earners and salaried employés in this industry must be included in the number of responsible directors of the industry; and that the profits obtained from the exploitation of the mines by private capital must be considerably decreased.

As for the practical means of realizing these recommendations the Committee on Socialization was not able to come to an agreement and submitted two different proposals.

The first, that of Lederer, signed by ten out of twenty-one members, demanded *immediate expropriation and nationalization of all the mines*. The owners of the mines would receive an indemnity in the form of bonds bearing a fixed interest, and the ownership of these mines would be transferred to an autonomous body, called "The German Coal Corporation." This corporation is to be governed by the National Coal Council, which appoints a "directorate" to administer affairs. The right to appoint industrial heads, as well as the responsibility for the technical exploitation, passes to the National Coal Council and to the Directorate. Bonuses for production are to be given to directors, salaried employés and workers.

The authors of this proposition insist on the fact that they are not instituting state socialism for mines with all its attendant fiscal and bureaucratic dangers; and to emphasize what it is they are aiming at, they propose that the mines now owned by the Reich and by the States be taken away from them and transferred to the German Commonwealth of Coal.

Prices will be fixed by the Reich, to whose budgets will be accounted the profits of the exploitation—and undoubtedly the losses.

The second proposition, that of Rathenau and signed by eleven members out of twenty-one, does not go as far along the road of nationalization. The present owners of mines, according to this plan, provisionally retain their property, but their rights therein are strikingly reduced. The distribution and the sale of products cease to be guaranteed by the National Coal Association—which is, in fact, done away with—and are given over to the National Coal Council and to a Directorate, four out of five of whose members are elected by the Council; the fifth, the President, is appointed by the Minister of Public Economy.

The principal innovation consists in this. Whereas formerly the sale of coal was made on the basis of the individual exploitations, according to this project every mine transfers to the National Coal Council its whole output, and the net price is averaged according to the books. The National Council, therefore, has a monopoly on the wholesale trade and it fixes the selling prices. In addition to the net cost the Council credits to the mine (1) the cost of delivery and the interest and amortization of bonds of the enterprises; (2) the interest and amortization of new investments; (3) the normal fixed interest on the operating capital employed in the exploitations; (4) bonuses, fixed according to a schedule, for the increase of output of each exploitation; or deductions in case of decrease of output.

The National Council may demand the inauguration of new projects, or exploitations may propose improvements with the approval of the Council, provided that either the Council or the entrepreneur furnishes the necessary funds. Finally, in order to retain the free play of private initiative, an entrepreneur may, even in spite of the National Council, make investment but at his own risk and peril.

By these provisions the entrepreneur loses all interest in the increase of the price of coal, for commerce in it and commercial profits are denied to him. Also the fixing of high net prices does not serve him in any way, since his books are supervised by the properly empowered auditors of the National Council. The only way left him to make big profits is to improve his exploitation in its economic and social aspects. The interest or the profit which has hitherto ruled economy is retained in form, but it can no longer work except in the common interest. The situation of the manager will depend as to-day on an objective economic success.

The Cabinet of the Reich announced its intention of soon submitting a project of law which will adopt in outline the Rathenau proposition. Already the mine owners are discussing in the press the question of the "maturity" of the mines and the mode of calculating the cost of production. But above private interest there is a collective interest and the question will come up whether the system proposed by the Committee on Socialization and the Cabinet does not incur the risk of becoming more troublesome than profitable to the community itself.

CONCLUSION

We have analyzed in the preceding pages the principal provisions of the German Constitution. There are in it a great number of other provisions, which had to be omitted from this analysis deliberately, either because they also occur in all the other Constitutions of the world, such as the principle stated by Article 102, that judges are independent—provisions which do not at all serve in characterizing the work of Weimar; or, on the other hand, because they were dictated exclusively by the necessity of solving problems created by the particular circumstances in the midst of which the Reich found itself; such as the provisions of Article 88 and those following, dealing with the post, railroads, and navigable waterways. These provisions present only a slight interest from the general constitutional point of view.

In its final draft the Constitution of 1919 bears throughout the stamp of *compromises,* which had to be effected between the parties represented in the Assembly, on practically every problem attacked. On nearly every question which the Constituent Assembly had to solve, bargains were negotiated between the conflicting interests and theories of the parties opposed. If one takes these articles of the Constitution one after another, one can draw up the balance sheet of every party, and note the points on which it has won its cause and those on which it had to compromise. The Social Democrats wanted to substitute for the federal Empire a unitary State; whereas the Centre, whose co-operation was needed for the Social Democrats to remain in power, defended the federalist idea. The final result constitutes a marked victory for the Social Democrats. But on the question of the relation of Church and State, the Centre obtained a solution that is much nearer their desires than those of the Social Democrats. Sometimes problems of a non-constitutional nature were mixed into negotiations on the Constitution. It is known, for example, that the Social Democrats secured the signature of the Centre to the Treaty of Versailles only in exchange for Social Democratic consent to the compromise clauses on education.

Nevertheless the product of these negotiations and these transactions constitutes a work whose essential characteristics are clearly enough indicated, and whose bold outline seems to respond to the demands which all constitutions of this kind make.

From the point of view of legal technique the Constitution of Weimar is, on the whole, well made. Conscientiously, scientifically, the men who drew it up studied foreign Constitutions, subjected them to the most stringent criticism, tested them by the particular exigencies of the Reich and by the special character of its people. Here they imitated, there they initiated. Naturally, they were not wholly able to detach themselves from the judgments, preferences and prejudices that prevail in their country. Perhaps from the strictly German point of view it is better that it should be so. The work is strongly marked with their traits. It is logical and fine-spun, audacious, complicated and sometimes obscure, painstakingly conceived and solidly constructed.

But whatever technical merit a legal document may present, it is worth little unless it accommodates itself to the realities for which it is created, unless, too, it is strong enough to resist the thrusts directed against it and to master them.

CONCLUSION

Has the Constitution of Weimar resistance enough to withstand all the inevitable assaults which will be aimed at it, and can it guarantee to the German people a well-ordered public life and a stable government?

We know the bases on which it is constructed; politically—unitarism, parliamentary democracy, the republic; economically—the participation of the working class in the management of industry, evolution toward the nationalization of the industries most important in the national life. The political institutions, under more or less different forms, have been tested by other peoples, who have not complained of them. Will these institutions, adapted as they have been, succeed equally for the German people? The economic institutions are new. What will be their worth?

The question is serious; for in this edifice so logically constructed all parts are mutually interdependent, and the whole will not endure unless the parts are solid. The downfall of any of them will drag down the others. Political institutions will not function unless economic provisions assure industry and commerce sufficient prosperity. But economic institutions will be swept away if the government is overwhelmed and ceases to fulfil its mission.

The Constitution begins with making the Reich a state as unitary as possible without completely suppressing every trace of the federal régime. But there are strong centrifugal tendencies. In Prussia there are several provinces that demand to be formed into distinct states. Throughout the Reich there are several states that demand the return to a purely federal régime, if not actually the complete separation from the German Reich. Will these tendencies be strong enough to bring about a relaxation of the unitary bond, if not actually the disintegration of the Reich? We have already pointed out the difference, for example, separating Catholic, peasant and conservative Bavaria from Protestant, industrial and socialist

Prussia. The States were able to endure without much difficulty the hegemony of a victorious, powerful, prosperous Prussia, a hegemony by which they profited. But the same States resent the thought that a Prussia, which they hold responsible for the defeat and which they now see much weakened, should want to keep them still under its yoke and to attempt, under the pretext of unity, to absorb the Reich. They feel this all the more strongly since the future is dark. Prussia has been dangerously stricken and it may appear more advantageous not to tie up too intimately their own interests with those of such a state.

Once more Prussia holds the fate of Germany in its hands. If, renouncing the attitude which it has maintained since the Revolution, Prussia permits a transformation of some of its provinces into states, or if it accords them an autonomy so great that they will be in effect assimilated into states, then the federalist or separatist tendencies will probably lose much of their strength, and the unitarism desired by the Constitution will be able to maintain itself and even to develop. But if Prussia, relying on its strength and prestige, diminished though they be, insists on keeping the other German states, willing or not, in a Reich dominated by it, then it may be that the federalist or separatist tendencies will prevail.

The political institutions of Germany are as strongly impregnated with the *democratic idea* as possible. The majority is sovereign. But there are minorities, to the right and to the left, that aspire to dictatorship. It seems little likely that another attempt like that of Kapp and Lüttwitz will succeed any better than the last attempt—at least unless a sudden and complete change in the political orientation of the people takes place. On the other side, the Independents, for whom even in Berlin a *coup d'état* may be perhaps easy enough, know that they would have against them the great majority of the German people, and their leaders openly declare that their hour has not yet come. If in the domain of democratic doctrine a change seems likely to come, it is probable that it will appear in the form of a right expressly accorded to economic associations or, in a still more general manner, to producers, to exercise a special and direct influence on the government. If the Provisional Economic Council succeeds, it is possible that Germany will broaden the experiment and attempt a true Economic Parliament.

Parliamentary government has been accepted but it is mistrusted. There have also been introduced a whole series of measures such as the referendum, initiative, the nomination and the impeachment of the President by the people, which are not only logical applications of the democratic principle, but which are also assurances against any possible misdeeds of parliamentarism. This is a splendid proof of trust in democracy. It is for the future to say whether it is justified.

As a matter of fact the referendum and initiative await the law which is to organize them. What will these institutions produce in a country as vast as Germany? It is easy to see that they will strikingly increase the burden of governmental machinery, and one asks oneself whether they will not incur the risk of completely impeding its functioning. For the success of these institutions, we must suppose a sufficiently firm political education and intelligence, a public that knows its wishes and how to make them prevail, a Parliament and a Cabinet skilled in recognizing the wishes of the nation and ready to submit to them. Because of the mistrust of parliamentarism, it has been decided that the President shall be elected directly by the people. He is endowed with power by the nation and placed near to the Reichstag in order to control it. But may he not become too strong, and is there not a danger that he will abuse his powers to the great injury of liberty and democracy itself? The present President has been elected by the National Assembly. Considerable as are the powers which the Constitution gives him, he is actually one of the least powerful chiefs of state in the world. Will matters be different when he is elected by the whole people? Will he be strong enough, or too strong?

This democracy which does not fear the plebiscite, has expressly excluded the *monarchical form* for the Reich and for the States. There are, nevertheless, here and there, particularly in Bavaria, monarchical plots. Will the Constitution have here, too, enough force to command obedience? It does not seem for the moment that a monarchical restoration, no matter of what dynasty its pretender, would have any serious chance of succeeding. For, until some new state of affairs, the working class, which would permit a dictatorship exercised by itself, will probably oppose every attempt at a return to the abolished personal régime.

The Economic Constitution departs much more from old customs than the political Constitution.

The idea of the Councils is probably the only really new idea that has appeared in the public law of modern states since the war. German law has given this idea solemn consecration and has embodied it in the Constitution. But up to now it has given it only the most restricted application. The Factory Workers Councils have hardly begun to function, and the working class has not yet any clear notion of the manner in which it will use the power given by the law to these new organisms.

The doctrine of the Councils leads naturally to *nationalization*. For to confide the administration of the whole of an industry to Economic Councils, in which the workers are represented by the side of the employers and consumers, is to make a direct application of the *Mitbestimmungsrecht*. But other considerations are also tending to give this system a place of increasing importance. "The free play of economic forces" is no longer being upheld. It is affirmed everywhere that classic liberalism has had its day, and that in order to improve the economic situation so extremely unfavourable in all the modern states, it is not enough that things be allowed freely to take their course. It is now thought that "let alone" leads to bankruptcy. One no longer believes in the former principles that held as absolute the right to private property, the right of work, liberty of commerce, and freedom of contract. To-day these rights are held to be limited by the general good and must be exercised by the individual in the interest of all.

As the question of principle seems to be settled the problem becomes almost exclusively a practical one. A certain number of industries have become more or less nationalized or even socialized and will become still more so, their number also probably growing. The discussion now seems to be only on the modes of application, on the degree of "maturity" necessary; on whether this or that industry is or is not ripe; on the mode of calculating the cost of exploitation; on bonuses for output, etc., etc.

Like the idea of the Councils, this doctrine of nationalization seems to gain more and more. What will come of it for Germany and for the States that will follow this road? Are not these new formulas the ephemeral result of the upheaval due to the war? Or will they, improved and tested by practice, be definitely installed in the economic organization of all modern peoples? To the countries that adopt them, will they bring ruin or economic prosperity and social peace? On these matters, one can only write interrogation marks. In any event, however, it is important to follow the German experiment with the greatest possible interest.

GLOSSARY

German	Translation
REICH	Commonwealth
REICHS-	of the Commonwealth, national
REICHSARBEITERRAT	National Workers' Council
REICHSGERICHT	National Judicial Court
REICHSKANZLER	National Chancellor
REICHSMINISTER	National Minister
REICHSMINISTERIUM, pl., -IEN	National Department
REICHSPRÄSIDENT	President of the Commonwealth, National President
REICHSRAT	National Council
REICHSREGIERUNG	National Cabinet
REICHSTAG	National Assembly
REICHSVERWALTUNGSGERICHT	National Administrative Court
REICHSWIRTSCHAFTSRAT	National Economic Council
LAND	State (an integral part of the Commonwealth)
LANDES-	of the State, State
LANDESREGIERUNG	State Cabinet
LANDTAG	State Assembly
WAHLPRÜFUNGSGERICHT	Electoral Commission
STAAT	country, state (one of the family of nations); referring to Germany, it designates the Commonwealth and separate States as a single political entity.
STAATSGERICHTSHOF	Supreme Judicial Court
STAATLICH	political
FREISTAATLICH	republican

APPENDIX

THE CONSTITUTION
OF THE
GERMAN COMMONWEALTH

PREAMBLE

The German People, united in all their branches, and inspired by the determination to renew and strengthen their Commonwealth in liberty and justice, to preserve peace both at home and abroad, and to foster social progress, have adopted the following Constitution.

PART ONE

Structure and Functions of the Commonwealth

SECTION I

COMMONWEALTH AND STATES

ARTICLE 1

The German Commonwealth is a republic.
Political authority is derived from the People.

ARTICLE 2

The territory of the Commonwealth consists of the territories of the German States. Other territories may be incorporated into the Commonwealth by national law, if their inhabitants, exercising the right of self-determination, so desire.

ARTICLE 3

The national colours are black, red and gold. The merchant flag is black, white and red, with the national colours in the upper inside corner.

ARTICLE 4

The generally recognized principles of the law of nations are accepted as an integral part of the law of the German Commonwealth.

ARTICLE 5

Political authority is exercised in national affairs by the National Government in accordance with the Constitution of the Commonwealth, and in State affairs by the State Governments in accordance with the State constitutions.

ARTICLE 6

The Commonwealth has exclusive jurisdiction over:
1. Foreign relations;
2. Colonial affairs;
3. Citizenship, freedom of travel and residence, immigration and emigration, and extradition;
4. Organization for national defence;
5. Coinage;
6. Customs, including the consolidation of customs and trade districts and the free interchange of goods;
7. Posts and telegraphs, including telephones.

ARTICLE 7

The Commonwealth has jurisdiction over:
1. Civil law;
2. Criminal law;
3. Judicial procedure, including penal administration, and official co-operation between the administrative authorities;
4. Passports and the supervision of aliens;
5. Poor relief and vagrancy;
6. The press, associations and public meetings;
7. Problems of population; protection of maternity, infancy, childhood and adolescence;
8. Public health, veterinary practice, protection of plants from disease and pests;
9. The rights of labour, social insurance, the protection of wage-earners and other employés, and employment bureaus;
10. The establishment of national organizations for vocational representation;
11. Provision for war-veterans and their surviving dependents;

12. The law of expropriation;
13. The socialization of natural resources and business enterprises, as well as the production, fabrication, distribution, and price-fixing of economic goods for the use of the community;
14. Trade, weights and measures, the issue of paper money, banking, and stock and produce exchanges;
15. Commerce in foodstuffs and in other necessaries of daily life, and in luxuries;
16. Industry and mining;
17. Insurance;
18. Ocean navigation, and deep-sea and coast fisheries;
19. Railroads, internal navigation, communication by power-driven vehicles on land, on sea, and in the air; the construction of highways, in so far as pertains to general intercommunication and the national defence;
20. Theatres and cinematographs.

ARTICLE 8

The Commonwealth also has jurisdiction over taxation and other sources of income, in so far as they may be claimed in whole or in part for its purposes. If the Commonwealth claims any source of revenue which formerly belonged to the States, it must have consideration for the financial requirements of the States.

ARTICLE 9

Whenever it is necessary to establish uniform rules, the Commonwealth has jurisdiction over:
1. The promotion of social welfare;
2. The protection of public order and safety.

ARTICLE 10

The Commonwealth may prescribe by law fundamental principles concerning:
1. The rights and duties of religious associations;
2. Education, including higher education and libraries for scientific use;
3. The law of officers of all public bodies;
4. The land law, the distribution of land, settlements and homesteads, restrictions on landed property, housing, and the distribution of population;
5. Disposal of the dead.

ARTICLE 11

The Commonwealth may prescribe by law fundamental principles concerning the validity and mode of collection of State taxes, in order to prevent:
1. Injury to the revenues or to the trade relations of the Commonwealth;
2. Double taxation;
3. The imposition of excessive burdens, or burdens in restraint of trade on the use of the means and agencies of public communication;
4. Tax discriminations against the products of other States in favour of domestic products in interstate and local commerce; or
5. Export bounties;

or in order to protect important social interests.

ARTICLE 12

So long and in so far as the Commonwealth does not exercise its jurisdiction, such jurisdiction remains with the States. This does not apply in cases where the Commonwealth possesses exclusive jurisdiction.

The National Cabinet may object to State laws relating to the subjects of Article 7, Number 13, whenever the general welfare of the Commonwealth is affected thereby.

ARTICLE 13

The laws of the Commonwealth are supreme over the laws of the States which conflict with them.

If doubt arises, or difference of opinion, whether State legislation is in harmony with the law of the Commonwealth, the proper authorities of the Commonwealth or the central authorities of the States, in accordance with more specific provisions of a national law, may have recourse to the decision of a supreme judicial court of the Commonwealth.

ARTICLE 14

The laws of the Commonwealth will be executed by the State authorities, unless otherwise provided by national law.

ARTICLE 15

The National Cabinet supervises the conduct of affairs over which the Commonwealth has jurisdiction.

In so far as the laws of the Commonwealth are to be carried into effect by the State authorities, the National Cabinet may issue general instructions. It has the power to send commissioners to the central authorities of the States, and, with their consent, to the subordinate State authorities, in order to supervise the execution of national laws.

It is the duty of the State Cabinets, at the request of the National Cabinet, to correct any defects in the execution of the national laws. In case of dispute, either the National Cabinet or that of the State may have recourse to the decision of the Supreme Judicial Court, unless another court is prescribed by national law.

ARTICLE 16

The officers directly charged with the administration of national affairs in any State shall, as a rule, be citizens of that State. The officers, employés and workmen of the national administration shall, if they so desire, be employed in the districts where they reside as far as is possible and not inconsistent with their training and with the requirements of the service.

ARTICLE 17

Every State must have a republican constitution. The representatives of the People must be elected by the universal, equal, direct and secret suffrage of all German citizens, both men and women, according to the principles of proportional representation. The State Cabinet shall require the confidence of the representatives of the People.

The principles in accordance with which the representatives of the People are chosen apply also to municipal elections; but by State law a residence qualification not exceeding one year of residence in the municipality may be imposed in such elections.

ARTICLE 18

The division of the Commonwealth into States shall serve the highest economic and cultural interests of the People after most thorough consideration of the wishes of the population affected. State boundaries may be altered and new States may be created within the Commonwealth by the process of constitutional amendment.

With the consent of the States directly affected, it requires only an ordinary law of the Commonwealth.

An ordinary law of the Commonwealth will also suffice, if one of the States affected does not consent, provided that the change of boundaries or the creation of a new State is desired by the population concerned and is also required by a preponderant national interest.

The wishes of the population shall be ascertained by a referendum. The National Cabinet orders a referendum on demand of one-third of the inhabitants qualified to vote for the National Assembly in the territory to be cut off.

Three-fifths of the votes cast, but at least a majority of the qualified voters, are required for the alteration of a boundary or the creation of a new State. Even if a separation of only a part of a Prussian administrative district, a Bavarian circle, or, in other States, a corresponding administrative district, is involved, the wishes of the population of the whole district must be ascertained. If there is no physical contact between the territory to be cut off and the rest of the district, the wishes of the population of the district to be cut off may be pronounced conclusive by a special law of the Commonwealth.

After the consent of the population has been ascertained the National Cabinet shall introduce into the National Assembly a bill suitable for enactment.

If any controversy arises over the division of property in connection with such a union or separation, it will be determined upon complaint of either party by the Supreme Judicial Court of the German Commonwealth.

ARTICLE 19

If controversies concerning the Constitution arise within a State in which there is no court competent to dispose of them, or if controversies of a public nature arise between different States or between a State and the Commonwealth, they will be determined upon complaint of one of the parties by the Supreme Judicial Court of the German Commonwealth, unless another judicial court of the Commonwealth is competent.

The President of the Commonwealth executes judgments of the Supreme Judicial Court.

SECTION II

THE NATIONAL ASSEMBLY

ARTICLE 20

The National Assembly is composed of the delegates of the German People.

ARTICLE 21

The delegates are representatives of the whole People. They are subject only to their own consciences and are not bound by any instructions.

ARTICLE 22

The delegates are elected by universal, equal, direct and secret suffrage by all men and women over twenty years of age, in accordance with the principles of proportional representation. The day for elections must be a Sunday or a public holiday.

The details will be regulated by the national election law.

ARTICLE 23

The National Assembly is elected for four years. New elections must take place at the latest on the sixtieth day after its term comes to an end.

The National Assembly convenes at the latest on the thirtieth day after the election.

ARTICLE 24

The National Assembly meets each year on the first Wednesday in November at the seat of the National Government. The President of the National Assembly must call it earlier if the President of the Commonwealth, or at least one-third of the members of the National Assembly, demand it.

The National Assembly determines the close of its session and the day of re-assembling.

ARTICLE 25

The President of the Commonwealth may dissolve the National Assembly, but only once for the same cause.

The new election occurs at the latest on the sixtieth day after such dissolution.

ARTICLE 26

The National Assembly chooses its President, Vice-President and its Secretaries. It regulates its own procedure.

ARTICLE 27

During the interval between sessions, or while elections are taking place, the President and Vice-President of the preceding session conduct its affairs.

ARTICLE 28

The President administers the regulations and policing of the National Assembly building. The management of the building is subject to his direction; he controls its receipts and expenses in accordance with the provisions of the budget, and represents the Commonwealth in all legal affairs and in litigation arising during his administration.

ARTICLE 29

The proceedings of the National Assembly are public. At the request of fifty members the public may be excluded by a two-thirds vote.

ARTICLE 30

True and accurate reports of the proceedings in public sittings of the National Assembly, of a State Assembly, or of their committees, are absolutely privileged.

ARTICLE 31

An Electoral Commission to decide disputed elections will be organized in connection with the National Assembly. It will also decide whether a delegate has forfeited his seat.

The Electoral Commission consists of members of the National Assembly, chosen by the latter for the life of the Assembly, and of members of the National Administrative Court, to be appointed by the President of the Commonwealth on the nomination of the presidency of this court.

This Electoral Commission pronounces judgment after public hearings through a quorum of three members of the National Assembly and two judicial members.

Proceedings apart from the hearings before the Electoral Commission will be conducted by a National Commissioner appointed by the President of the Commonwealth. In other respects the procedure will be regulated by the Electoral Commission.

ARTICLE 32

The National Assembly acts by majority vote unless otherwise provided in the Constitution. For the conduct of elections by the National Assembly it may, in its rules of procedure, make exceptions.

The quorum to do business will be regulated by the rules of procedure.

ARTICLE 33

The National Assembly and its committees may require the presence of the National Chancellor and of any National Minister.

The National Chancellor, the National Ministers, and Commissioners designated by them, have the right to be present at the sittings of the National Assembly and of its committees. The States are entitled to send their plenipotentiaries to these sittings to submit the views of their Cabinets on matters under consideration.

At their request the representatives of the Cabinets shall be heard during the deliberations, and the representatives of the National Cabinet shall be heard even outside the regular order of business.

They are subject to the authority of the presiding officer in matters of order.

ARTICLE 34

The National Assembly has the right, and, on proposal of one-fifth of its members, the duty to appoint committees of investigation. These committees, in public sittings, inquire into the evidence which they, or the proponents, consider necessary. The public may be excluded by a two-thirds vote of the committee of investigation. The rules of procedure regulate the proceedings of the committee and determine the number of its members.

The judicial and administrative authorities are required to comply with requests by these committees for information, and the record of the authorities shall on request be submitted to them.

The provisions of the code of criminal procedure apply as far as is suitable to the inquiries of these committees and of the authorities assisting them, but the secrecy of letter and other post, telegraph, and telephone services will remain inviolate.

ARTICLE 35

The National Assembly appoints a Standing Committee on foreign affairs which may also act outside of the sittings of the National Assembly and after its expiration or dissolution until a new National Assembly convenes. Its sittings are not public, unless the committee by a two-thirds vote otherwise provides.

The National Assembly also appoints a Standing Committee for the protection of the rights of the representatives of the People against the National Cabinet during a recess and after the expiration of the term for which it was elected.

These committees have the rights of committees of investigation.

ARTICLE 36

No member of the National Assembly or of a State Assembly shall at any time whatsoever be subject to any judicial or disciplinary prosecution or be held responsible outside of the House to which he belongs on account of his vote or his opinions uttered in the performance of his duty.

ARTICLE 37

No member of the National Assembly or of a State Assembly shall during the session, without the consent of the House to which he belongs, be subject to investigation or arrest on account of any punishable offence, unless he is caught in the act, or apprehended not later than the following day.

Similar consent is required in the case of any other restraint of personal liberty which interferes with the performance by a delegate of his duties.

Any criminal proceeding against a member of the National Assembly or of a State Assembly, and any arrest or other restraint of his personal liberty shall, at the demand of the House to which he belongs, be suspended for the duration of the session.

ARTICLE 38

The members of the National Assembly and the State Assemblies are entitled to refuse to give evidence concerning persons who have given them information in their official capacity, or to whom they have given information in the performance of their official duties, or concerning the information itself. In regard also to the seizure of papers their position is the same as that of persons who have by law the right to refuse to give evidence.

A search or seizure may be proceeded with in the precincts of the National Assembly or of a State Assembly only with the consent of its President.

ARTICLE 39

Civil officers and members of the armed forces need no leave to perform their duties as members of the National Assembly or of a State Assembly.

If they become candidates for election to these bodies, the necessary leave shall be granted them to prepare for their election.

ARTICLE 40

The members of the National Assembly shall have the right of free transportation over all German railroads, and also compensation as fixed by national law.

APPENDIX

SECTION III

THE NATIONAL PRESIDENT AND THE NATIONAL CABINET

ARTICLE 41

The National President is chosen by the whole German People.

Every German who has completed his thirty-fifth year is eligible for election.

The details will be regulated by a national law.

ARTICLE 42

The National President, on assuming his office, takes before the National Assembly the following oath:

I swear to devote all my energy to the welfare of the German People, to increase their prosperity, to protect them from injury, to preserve the Constitution and the laws of the Commonwealth, to perform my duties conscientiously, and to deal justly with all.

The addition of a religious affirmation is permitted.

ARTICLE 43

The term of the National President is seven years. He is eligible for re-election.

The President may be removed before the end of his term by vote of the People on proposal of the National Assembly. The act of the National Assembly in such case requires a two-thirds majority vote. Upon such action the President is suspended from further exercise of his office. A refusal by the People to remove the President has the effect of a new election and entails the dissolution of the National Assembly.

The National President shall not be subject to criminal prosecution without the consent of the National Assembly.

ARTICLE 44

The National President may not at the same time be a member of the National Assembly.

ARTICLE 45

The National President represents the Commonwealth in matters of international law. He concludes in the name of the Commonwealth, alliances and other treaties with foreign powers. He accredits and receives ambassadors.

War is declared and peace concluded by national law.

Alliances and treaties with foreign States, relating to subjects within the jurisdiction of the Commonwealth, require the consent of the National Assembly.

ARTICLE 46

The President appoints and dismisses the civil and military officers of the Commonwealth if not otherwise provided by law. He may delegate this right of appointment or dismissal to other authorities.

ARTICLE 47

The National President has supreme command over all the armed forces of the Commonwealth.

ARTICLE 48

If any State does not perform the duties imposed upon it by the Constitution or by national laws, the National President may hold it to the performance thereof by force of arms.

If public safety and order in the German Commonwealth is materially disturbed or endangered, the National President may take the necessary measures to restore public safety and order, and, if necessary, to intervene by force of arms. To this end he may temporarily suspend, in whole or in part, the fundamental rights established in Articles 114, 115, 117, 118, 123, 124 and 153.

The National President must immediately inform the National Assembly of all measures adopted by authority of Paragraphs 1 or 2 of this Article. These measures shall be revoked at the demand of the National Assembly.

If there is danger from delay, the State Cabinet may for its own territory take provisional measures as specified in Paragraph 2. These measures shall be revoked at the demand of the National President or of the National Assembly.

The details will be regulated by a national law.

ARTICLE 49

The National President exercises the right of pardon for the Commonwealth.

National amnesties require a national law.

ARTICLE 50

All orders and directions of the National President, including those concerning the armed forces, require for their validity the countersignature of the National Chancellor or of the appropriate National Minister. By the countersignature responsibility is assumed.

ARTICLE 51

The National President is represented temporarily in case of disability by the National Chancellor. If such disability seems likely to continue for any considerable period, he shall be represented as may be determined by a national law.

The same procedure shall be followed in case of a premature vacancy of the Presidency until the completion of the new election.

ARTICLE 52

The National Cabinet consists of the National Chancellor and the National Ministers.

ARTICLE 53

The National Chancellor and, on his proposal, the National Ministers are appointed and dismissed by the National President.

ARTICLE 54

The National Chancellor and the National Ministers require for the administration of their offices the confidence of the National Assembly. Each of them must resign if the National Assembly by formal resolution withdraws its confidence.

ARTICLE 55

The National Chancellor presides over the National Cabinet and conducts its affairs in accordance with rules of procedure, which will be framed by the National Cabinet and approved by the National President.

ARTICLE 56

The National Chancellor determines the general course of policy and assumes responsibility therefor to the National Assembly. In accordance with this general policy each National Minister conducts independently the particular affairs intrusted to him and is held individually responsible to the National Assembly.

ARTICLE 57

The National Ministers shall submit to the National Cabinet for consideration and decision all drafts of bills and other matters for which this procedure is prescribed by the Constitution or by law, as well as differences of opinion over questions which concern the departments of several National Ministers.

ARTICLE 58

The National Cabinet will make its decisions by majority vote. In case of a tie the vote of the presiding officer will be decisive.

ARTICLE 59

The National Assembly is empowered to impeach the National President, the National Chancellor, and the National Ministers before the Supreme Judicial Court of the German Commonwealth for any wrongful violation of the Constitution or laws of the Commonwealth. The proposal to bring an impeachment must be signed by at least one hundred members of the National Assembly and requires the approval of the majority prescribed for amendments to the Constitution. The details will be regulated by the national law relating to the Supreme Judicial Court.

SECTION IV

THE NATIONAL COUNCIL

ARTICLE 60

A National Council will be organized to represent the German States in national legislation and administration.

ARTICLE 61

In the National Council each State has at least one vote. In the case of the larger States one vote is accorded for every million inhabitants. Any excess equal at least to the population of the smallest State is reckoned as equivalent to a full million. No State shall be accredited with more than two-fifths of all votes.

[German-Austria after its union with the German Commonwealth will receive the right of participation in the National Council with the number of votes corresponding to its population. Until that time the representatives of German-Austria have a deliberate voice.][1]

---

[1] Stricken out at the demand of the Supreme Council of the Allied and Associated Powers. The Supreme Council addressed the following demand to Germany on September 2, 1919:

"The Allied and Associated Powers have examined the German Constitution of August 11, 1919. They observe that the provisions of the second paragraph of Article 61 constitute a formal violation of Article 80 of the Treaty of Peace signed at Versailles on June 28, 1919. This violation is twofold:

"1. Article 61 by stipulating for the admission of Austria to the Reichsrat assimilates that Republic to the German States composing the German Em-

The number of votes is determined anew by the National Council after every general census.

ARTICLE 62

In committees formed by the National Council from its own members no State will have more than one vote.

ARTICLE 63

The States will be represented in the National Council by members of their Cabinets. Half of the Prussian votes, however, will be at the disposal of the Prussian provincial administrations in accordance with a State law.

The States have the right to send as many representatives to the National Council as they have votes.

pire—an assimilation which is incompatible with respect to the independence of Austria.

"2. By admitting and providing for the participation of Austria in the Council of the Empire Article 61 creates a political tie and a common political action between Germany and Austria in absolute opposition to the independence of the latter.

"In consequence the Allied and Associated Powers, after reminding the German Government that Article 178 of the German Constitution declares that 'the provisions of the Treaty of Versailles can not be affected by the Constitution,' invite the German Government to take the necessary measures to efface without delay this violation by declaring Article 61, Paragraph 2, to be null and void.

"Without prejudice to subsequent measures in case of refusal, and in virtue of the Treaty of Peace (and in particular Article 29), the Allied and Associated Powers inform the German Government that this violation of its engagements on an essential point will compel them, if satisfaction is not given to their just demand within 15 days from the date of the present note, immediately to order the extension of their occupation on the right bank of the Rhine."

Article 29 of the Treaty of Peace refers to Map No. 1 which shows the boundaries of Germany and provides that the text of Articles 27 and 28 will be final as to those boundaries. Article 80 reads as follows:

"Germany acknowledges and will respect strictly the independence of Austria, within the frontiers which may be fixed in a Treaty between that State and the Principal Allied and Associated Powers; she agrees that this independence shall be inalienable, except with the consent of the Council of the League of Nations."

A diplomatic act was signed at Paris on September 22, 1919, by the representatives of the Principal Allied and Associated Powers and Germany in the following terms:

"The undersigned, duly authorized and acting in the name of the German Government, recognizes and declares that all the provisions of the German Constitution of August 11, 1919, which are in contradiction of the terms of the Treaty of Peace signed at Versailles on June 28, 1919, are null.

"The German Government declares and recognizes that in consequence Paragraph 2 of Article 61 of the said Constitution is null, and that in particular the admission of Austrian representatives to the Reichstag could only take place in the event of the consent of the Council of the League of Nations to a corresponding modification of Austria's international situation.

"The present declaration shall be approved by the competent German legislative authority, within the fortnight following the entry into force of the Peace Treaty.

"Given at Versailles, September 22, 1919, in the presence of the undersigned representatives of the Principal Allied and Associated Powers."

ARTICLE 64

The National Cabinet must summon the National Council on demand by one-third of its members.

ARTICLE 65

The chairmanship of the National Council and of its committees is filled by a member of the National Cabinet. The members of the National Cabinet have the right and on request [of the National Council] the duty to take part in the proceedings of the National Council and its committees. They must at their request be heard at any time during its deliberations.

ARTICLE 66

The National Cabinet, as well as every member of the National Council, is entitled to make proposals in the National Council.

The National Council regulates its order of business through rules of procedure.

The plenary sittings of the National Council are public. In accordance with the rules of procedure the public may be excluded during the discussion of particular subjects.

Decisions are taken by a majority of those present.

ARTICLE 67

The National Council shall be kept informed by the National Departments of the conduct of national business. At deliberations on important subjects the appropriate committees of the National Council shall be summoned by the National Departments.

SECTION V

NATIONAL LEGISLATION

ARTICLE 68

Bills are introduced by the National Cabinet or by members of the National Assembly.

National laws are enacted by the National Assembly.

ARTICLE 69

The introduction of bills by the National Cabinet requires the concurrence of the National Council. If an agreement between the National Cabinet and the National Council is not reached, the National

Cabinet may nevertheless introduce the bill, but must state the dissent of the National Council.

If the National Council resolves upon a bill to which the National Cabinet does not assent, the latter must introduce the bill in the National Assembly together with a statement of its attitude.

ARTICLE 70

The National President shall compile the laws which have been constitutionally enacted and within one month publish them in the National Bulletin of Laws.

ARTICLE 71

National laws go into effect, unless otherwise specified, on the fourteenth day following the date of their publication in the National Bulletin of Laws at the national capital.

ARTICLE 72

The promulgation of a national law may be deferred for two months, if one-third of the National Assembly so demands. Laws which the National Assembly and the National Council declare to be urgent may be promulgated by the National President regardless of this demand.

ARTICLE 73

A law enacted by the National Assembly shall be referred to the People before its promulgation, if the National President so orders within a month.

A law whose promulgation is deferred at the demand of at least one-third of the National Assembly shall be submitted to the People, if one-twentieth of the qualified voters so petition.

A popular vote shall further be resorted to on a measure initiated by the People if one-tenth of the qualified voters so petition. A fully elaborated bill must accompany such petition. The National Cabinet shall lay the bill together with a statement of its attitude before the National Assembly. The popular vote does not take place if the desired bill is enacted without amendment by the National Assembly.

A popular vote may be taken on the budget, tax laws, and laws relating to the classification and payment of public officers only by authority of the National President.

The procedure in connection with the popular referendum and initiative will be regulated by national law.

ARTICLE 74

The National Council has the right to object to laws passed by the National Assembly.

The objection must be filed with the National Cabinet within two weeks after the final vote in the National Assembly and must be supported by reasons within two more weeks at the latest.

In case of objection, the law is returned to the National Assembly for reconsideration. If an agreement between the National Assembly and the National Council is not reached, the National President may within three months refer the subject of the dispute to the People. If the President makes no use of this right, the law does not go into effect. If the National Assembly disapproves by a two-thirds majority the objection of the National Council, the President shall promulgate the law in the form enacted by the National Assembly within three months or refer it to the People.

ARTICLE 75

An act of the National Assembly may be annulled by a popular vote, only if a majority of those qualified take part in the vote.

ARTICLE 76

The Constitution may be amended by process of legislation. But acts of the National Assembly relating to the amendment of the Constitution are effective only if two-thirds of the legal membership are present, and at least two-thirds of those present give their assent. Acts of the National Council relating to the amendment of the Constitution also require a two-thirds majority of all the votes cast. If an amendment to the Constitution is to be adopted by the People by popular initiative, the assent of a majority of the qualified voters is required.

If the National Assembly adopts an amendment to the Constitution against the objection of the National Council, the President may not promulgate this law, if the National Council within two weeks demands a popular vote.

ARTICLE 77

The National Cabinet issues the general administrative regulations necessary for the execution of the national laws so far as the laws do not otherwise provide. It must secure the assent of the National Council if the execution of the national laws is assigned to the State authorities.

SECTION VI

THE NATIONAL ADMINISTRATION

ARTICLE 78

The conduct of relations with foreign countries is exclusively a function of the Commonwealth.

The States, in matters subject to their jurisdiction, may conclude treaties with foreign countries; such treaties require the assent of the Commonwealth.

Agreements with foreign countries regarding changes of national boundaries will be concluded by the Commonwealth with the consent of the State concerned. Changes of boundaries may be made only by authority of a national law, except in cases where a mere adjustment of the boundaries of uninhabited districts is in question.

To assure the representation of interests arising from the special economic relations of individual States to foreign countries or from their proximity to foreign countries, the Commonwealth determines the requisite arrangements and measures in agreement with the States concerned.

ARTICLE 79

The national defence is a function of the Commonwealth. The organization of the German People for defence will be uniformly regulated by a national law with due consideration for the peculiarities of the people of the separate States.

ARTICLE 80

Colonial policy is exclusively a function of the Commonwealth.

ARTICLE 81

All German merchant ships constitute a unified merchant marine.

ARTICLE 82

Germany forms a customs and trade area surrounded by a common customs boundary.

The customs boundary is identical with the international boundary. At the seacoast the shore of the mainland and of the islands belonging to the national territory constitutes the customs boundary. Deviations may be made for the course of the customs boundary at the ocean and at other bodies of water.

Foreign territories or parts of territories may be incorporated in the customs area by international treaties or agreements.

Portions of territory may be excluded from the customs area in accordance with special requirements. In the case of free ports this exclusion may be discontinued only by an amendment to the Constitution.

Districts excluded from the customs area may be included within a foreign customs area by international treaties or agreements.

All products of nature or industry, as well as works of art, which are subjects of free commerce within the Commonwealth, may be transported in any direction across State and municipal boundaries. Exceptions are permissible by authority of national law.

ARTICLE 83

Customs duties and taxes on articles of consumption are administered by the national authorities.

In connection with national tax administration by the national authorities, arrangements shall be provided which will enable the States to protect their special agricultural, commercial, trade and industrial interests.

ARTICLE 84

The Commonwealth has authority to regulate by law:

1. The organization of the State tax administrations so far as is required for the uniform and impartial execution of the national tax laws;

2. The organization and functions of the authorities charged with the supervision of the execution of the national tax laws;

3. The accounting with the States;

4. The reimbursement of the costs of administration in connection with the execution of the national tax laws.

ARTICLE 85

All revenues and expenditures of the Commonwealth must be estimated for each fiscal year and entered in the budget.

The budget is adopted by law before the beginning of the fiscal year.

Appropriations are ordinarily granted for one year; in special cases they may be granted for a longer period. Otherwise, provisions extending beyond the fiscal year or not relating to the national revenues and expenditures or their administration, are inadmissible in the national budget law.

The National Assembly may not increase appropriations in the budget bill or insert new items without the consent of the National Council.

The consent of the National Council may be dispensed with in accordance with the provisions of Article 74.

ARTICLE 86

In the following fiscal year the National Minister of Finance will submit to the National Council and to the National Assembly an account concerning the disposition of all national revenue so as to discharge the responsibility of the National Cabinet. The auditing of this account will be regulated by national law.

ARTICLE 87

Funds may be procured by borrowing only in case of extraordinary need and in general for expenditures for productive purposes only. Such procurement of funds as well as the assumption by the Commonwealth of any financial obligation is permissible only by authority of a national law.

ARTICLE 88

The postal and telegraph services, together with the telephone service, are exclusively functions of the Commonwealth.

The postage stamps are uniform for the whole Commonwealth.

The National Cabinet, with the consent of the National Council, issues the regulations prescribing the conditions and charges for the use of the means of communication. With the consent of the National Council it may delegate this authority to the Postmaster General.

The National Cabinet, with the consent of the National Council, establishes an advisory council to co-operate in deliberations concerning the postal, telegraph and telephone services and rates.

The Commonwealth alone concludes treaties relating to communication with foreign countries.

ARTICLE 89

It is the duty of the Commonwealth to acquire ownership of the railroads which serve as means of general public communication, and to operate them as a single system of transportation.

The rights of the States to acquire private railroads shall be transferred to the Commonwealth on its demand.

ARTICLE 90

With the taking over of the railroads the Commonwealth also acquires the right of expropriation and the sovereign powers of the States pertaining to railroad affairs. The Supreme Judicial Court decides controversies relating to the extent of these rights.

ARTICLE 91

The National Cabinet, with the consent of the National Council, issues the regulations governing the construction, operation and traffic of railroads. With the consent of the National Council it may delegate this authority to the appropriate national minister.

ARTICLE 92

The national railroads, irrespective of the incorporation of their budget and accounts in the general budget and accounts of the Commonwealth, shall be administered as an independent economic enterprise which shall defray its own expenses, including interest and the amortization of the railroad debt, and accumulate a railroad reserve fund. The amount of the amortization and of the reserve fund, as well as the purpose to which the reserve fund may be applied, shall be regulated by special law.

ARTICLE 93

The National Cabinet with the consent of the National Council establishes advisory councils for the national railroads to co-operate in deliberations concerning railroad service and rates.

ARTICLE 94

If the Commonwealth takes over the operation of railroads which serve as means of general public communication in any district, additional railroads to serve as means of general public communication within this district may only be built by the Commonwealth or with its consent. If new construction or the alteration of existing national railroad systems encroaches upon the sphere of authority of the State police, the national railroad administration, before its decision, shall grant a hearing to the State authorities.

Where the Commonwealth has not yet taken over the operation of the railroads, it may lay out on its own account by virtue of national law railroads deemed necessary to serve as means of general public communication or for the national defence, even against the opposition of the States, whose territory they will traverse, without, however, impairing the sovereign powers of the States, or it may turn over the construction to another to execute, together with a grant of the right of expropriation if necessary.

Each railroad administration must consent to connection with other roads at the expense of the latter.

ARTICLE 95

Railroads serving as means of general public communication which are not operated by the Commonwealth are subject to supervision by the Commonwealth.

The railroads subject to national supervision shall be laid out and equipped in accordance with uniform standards established by the Commonwealth. They shall be maintained in safe operating condition and developed according to the requirements of traffic. Facilities and equipment for passenger and freight traffic shall be maintained and developed in keeping with the demand.

The supervision of rates is designed to secure non-discriminatory and moderate railroad charges.

ARTICLE 96

All railroads, including those not serving as means of general public communication, must comply with the requirements of the Commonwealth so far as concerns the use of the roads for purposes of national defence.

ARTICLE 97

It is the duty of the Commonwealth to acquire ownership of and to operate all waterways serving as means of general public communication.

After they have been taken over, waterways serving as means of general public communication may be constructed or extended only by the Commonwealth or with its consent.

In the administration, development, or construction of such waterways the requirements of agriculture and water-supply shall be protected in agreement with the States. Their improvement shall also be considered.

Each waterways administration shall consent to connection with other inland waterways at the expense of the latter. The same obligation exists for the construction of a connection between inland waterways and railroads.

In taking over the waterways the Commonwealth acquires the right of expropriation, control of rates, and the police power over waterways and navigation.

The duties of the river improvement associations in relation to the development of natural waterways in the Rhine, Weser, and Elbe basins shall be assumed by the Commonwealth.

ARTICLE 98

Advisory national waterways councils will be formed in accordance with detailed regulations issued by the National Cabinet with the consent of the National Council to co-operate in the management of the waterways.

ARTICLE 99

Charges may be imposed on natural waterways only for such works, facilities, and other accommodations as are designed for the relief of traffic. In the case of state and municipal public works they may not exceed the necessary costs of construction and maintenance. The construction and maintenance costs of works designed not exclusively for the relief of traffic, but also for serving other purposes, may be defrayed only to a proportionate extent by navigation tolls. Interest and amortization charges on the invested capital are included in the costs of construction.

The provisions of the preceding paragraph apply to the charges imposed for artificial waterways and for accommodations in connection therewith and in harbours.

The total costs of a waterway, a river basin, or a system of waterways may be taken into consideration in determining navigation tolls in the field of inland water transportation.

These provisions apply also to the floating of timber on navigable waterways.

Only the Commonwealth imposes on foreign ships and their cargoes other or higher charges than on German ships and their cargoes.

For the procurement of means for the maintenance and development of the German system of waterways the Commonwealth may by law call on the shipping interests for contributions also in other ways [than by tolls].

ARTICLE 100

To cover the cost of maintenance and construction of inland navigation routes any person or body of persons who in other ways than through navigation derives profit from the construction of dams may also be called upon by national law for contributions, if several

States are involved or the Commonwealth bears the costs of construction.

ARTICLE 101

It is the duty of the Commonwealth to acquire ownership of and to operate all aids to navigation, especially lighthouses, lightships, buoys, floats and beacons. After they are taken over, aids to navigation may be installed or extended only by the Commonwealth or with its consent.

SECTION VII

THE ADMINISTRATION OF JUSTICE

ARTICLE 102

Judges are independent and subject only to the law.

ARTICLE 103

Ordinary jurisdiction will be exercised by the National Judicial Court and the courts of the States.

ARTICLE 104

Judges of ordinary jurisdiction are appointed for life. They may against their wishes be permanently or temporarily removed from office, or transferred to another position, or retired, only by virtue of a judicial decision and for the reasons and in the forms provided by law. The law may fix an age limit on reaching which judges may be retired.

Temporary suspension from office in accordance with law is not affected by this Article.

If there is a re-organization of the courts or of the judicial districts, the State department of justice may order involuntary transfers to another court or removal from office, but only with allowance of full salary.

These provisions do not apply to judges of commercial tribunals, lay associates, and jurymen.

ARTICLE 105

Extraordinary courts are illegal. No one may be removed from the jurisdiction of his lawful judge. Provisions of law relating to military courts and courts-martial are not affected hereby. Military courts of honour are abolished.

ARTICLE 106

Military jurisdiction is abolished except in time of war and on board war-vessels. Details will be regulated by national law.

ARTICLE 107

There shall be administrative courts both in the Commonwealth and in the States, in accordance with the laws, to protect the individual against orders and decrees of administrative authorities.

ARTICLE 108

In accordance with a national law a Supreme Judicial Court will be established for the German Commonwealth.

PART TWO

Fundamental Rights and Duties of Germans

SECTION I

THE INDIVIDUAL

ARTICLE 109

All Germans are equal before the law.

Men and women have fundamentally the same civil rights and duties.

Privileges or discriminations due to birth or rank and recognized by law are abolished. Titles of nobility will be regarded merely as part of the name and may not be granted hereafter.

Titles may be conferred only when they designate an office or profession; academic degrees are not affected by this provision.

Orders and honorary insignia may not be conferred by the state.

No German may accept a title or order from a foreign Government.

ARTICLE 110

Citizenship in the Commonwealth and in the States will be acquired and lost in accordance with the provisions of a national law. Every citizen of a State is at the same time a citizen of the Commonwealth.

Every German has the same rights and duties in each State of the Commonwealth as the citizens of that State.

ARTICLE 111

All Germans enjoy the right to travel and reside freely throughout the whole Commonwealth. Every one has the right of sojourn and settlement in any place within the Commonwealth, the right to acquire land and to pursue any gainful occupation. No limitations may be imposed except by authority of a national law.

ARTICLE 112

Every German has the right to emigrate to foreign countries. Emigration may be limited only by national law.

All German citizens, both within and without the territory of the Commonwealth, have a right to its protection with respect to foreign countries.

No German may be surrendered to a foreign Government for prosecution or punishment.

ARTICLE 113

Those elements of the People which speak a foreign language may not be interfered with by legislative or administrative action in their free and characteristic development, especially in the use of their mother tongue in the schools or in matters of internal administration and the administration of justice.

ARTICLE 114

Personal liberty is inviolable. An interference with or abridgement of personal liberty through official action is permissible only by authority of law.

Persons, who are deprived of their liberty, shall be informed at latest on the following day by what authority and on what grounds they have been deprived of liberty, and they shall without delay receive an opportunity to present objections against such loss of liberty.

ARTICLE 115

The house of every German is his sanctuary and is inviolable. Exceptions are permissible only by authority of law.

ARTICLE 116

An act can be punishable only if the penalty was fixed by law before the act was committed.

ARTICLE 117

The secrecy of postal, telegraphic, and telephonic communications is inviolable. Exceptions may be permitted only by national law.

ARTICLE 118

Every German has a right within the limits of the general laws to express his opinion freely by word, in writing, in print, by picture, or in any other way. No relationship arising out of his employment may hinder him in the exercise of this right, and no one may discriminate against him if he makes use of this right.

There is no censorship, although exceptional provisions may be made by law in the case of moving pictures. Legal measures are also permissible for combating obscene and indecent literature as well as for the protection of youth at public plays and spectacles.

SECTION II

COMMUNITY LIFE

ARTICLE 119

Marriage, as the foundation of family life and of the maintenance and increase of the nation, is under the special protection of the Constitution. It is based on the equal rights of both sexes.

The maintenance of the purity, the health, and the social advancement of the family is the task of the state and of the municipalities. Families with numerous children have a claim to equalizing assistance.

Motherhood has a claim to the protection and care of the State.

ARTICLE 120

The physical, mental, and moral education of their offspring is the highest duty and the natural right of parents, whose activities are supervised by the political community.

ARTICLE 121

Illegitimate children shall be provided by law with the same opportunities for their physical, mental, and moral development as legitimate children.

ARTICLE 122

Youth shall be protected against exploitation as well as against neglect of their moral, mental, or physical welfare. The necessary arrangements shall be made by state and municipality.

Compulsory protective measures may be ordered only by authority of the law.

ARTICLE 123

All Germans have the right of meeting peaceably and unarmed without notice or special permission.

Previous notice may be required by national law for meetings in the open, and such meetings may be forbidden in case of immediate danger to the public safety.

ARTICLE 124

All Germans have the right to form associations or societies for purposes not contrary to the criminal law. This right can not be limited by preventive measures. The same provisions apply to religious associations and societies.

Every association has the right of incorporation in accordance with the civil law. No association may be denied this right on the ground that it pursues a political, social-political, or religious object.

ARTICLE 125

The liberty and secrecy of the suffrage are guaranteed. Details will be regulated by the election laws.

ARTICLE 126

Every German has the right to petition or to complain in writing to the appropriate authorities or to the representatives of the People. This right may be exercised by individuals as well as by several persons together.

ARTICLE 127

Municipalities and unions of municipalities have the right of self-government within the limits of the laws.

ARTICLE 128

All citizens without distinction are eligible for public office in accordance with the laws and according to their ability and services.

All discriminations against women in the civil service are abolished.

The principles of the official relation shall be regulated by national law.

ARTICLE 129

Civil officers are appointed for life, in so far as is not otherwise provided by law. Pensions and provisions for surviving dependents will be regulated by law. The duly acquired rights of the civil officers are inviolable. Claims of civil officers based upon property rights may be established by process of law.

Civil officers may be suspended, temporarily or permanently retired, or transferred to other positions at a smaller salary only under the legally prescribed conditions and forms.

A process of appeal against disciplinary sentence and opportunity for reconsideration shall be established. Reports of an unfavorable character concerning a civil officer shall not be entered in his official record, until he has had the opportunity to express himself. Civil officers shall also be permitted to inspect their official records.

The inviolability of the duly acquired rights and the benefit of legal processes for the establishment of claims based on property rights are also assured especially to regular soldiers. In other respects their position is regulated by national law.

ARTICLE 130

The civil officers are servants of the whole community, not of a part of it.

To all civil officers freedom of political opinion and of association are assured.

The civil officers receive special representation in their official capacity in accordance with more precise provisions of national law.

ARTICLE 131

If a civil officer in the exercise of the authority conferred upon him by law fails to perform his official duty toward any third person, the responsibility is assumed by the state or public corporation in whose service the officer is. The right of redress [by the state or public corporation] against the officer is reserved. The ordinary process of law may not be excluded.

Detailed regulations will be made by the appropriate law-making authority.

ARTICLE 132

Every German, in accordance with the laws, has the duty of accepting honorary offices.

ARTICLE 133

All citizens are obliged, in accordance with the laws, to render personal services to the state and the municipality.

The duty of military service will be defined in accordance with the provisions of the national defence law. This will determine also how far particular fundamental rights shall be restricted in their application to the members of the armed forces in order that the latter may fulfil their duties and discipline may be maintained.

ARTICLE 134

All citizens, without distinction, contribute according to their means to the support of all public burdens, as may be provided by law.

SECTION III

RELIGION AND RELIGIOUS SOCIETIES

ARTICLE 135

All inhabitants of the Commonwealth enjoy complete liberty of belief and conscience. The free exercise of religion is assured by the Constitution and is under public protection. This Article leaves the general laws undisturbed.

ARTICLE 136

Civil and political rights and duties are neither conditioned upon nor limited by the exercise of religious liberty.

The enjoyment of civil and political rights as well as eligibility to public office is independent of religious belief.

No one is under any obligation to reveal his religious convictions.

The authorities have a right to inquire about religious affiliation only so far as rights and duties are dependent thereon or in pursuance of a statistical enumeration prescribed by law.

No one may be forced to attend any church ceremony or festivity, to take part in any religious exercise, or to make use of any religious oath.

ARTICLE 137

There is no state church.

Freedom of association in religious societies is guaranteed. The combination of religious societies within the Commonwealth is not subject to any limitations.

Every religious society regulates and administers its affairs independently within the limits of the general law. It appoints its officers without interference by the state or the civil municipality.

Religious societies may be incorporated in accordance with the general provisions of the civil law.

Existing religious societies remain, to the same extent as heretofore, public bodies corporate. The same rights shall be accorded to other religious societies if by their constitution and the number of their members they offer a guaranty of permanence. If a number of such public religious societies unite, this union is also a public body corporate.

The religious societies, which are recognized by law as bodies corporate, are entitled on the basis of the civil tax rolls to raise taxes according to the provisions of the laws of the respective States.

The associations, which have as their aim the cultivation of a system of ethics, have the same privileges as the religious societies.

The issuance of further regulations necessary for carrying out these provisions comes under the jurisdiction of the States.

ARTICLE 138

State contributions to religious societies authorized by law, contract, or any special grant, will be commuted by State legislation. The general principles of such legislation will be defined by the Commonwealth.

The property of religious societies and unions and other rights to their cultural, educational, and charitable institutions, foundations, and other possessions are guaranteed.

ARTICLE 139

Sundays and legal holidays remain under the protection of law as days of rest and spiritual edification.

ARTICLE 140

The members of the armed forces shall be granted the necessary leave for the performance of their religious duties.

ARTICLE 141

In so far as there is need for religious services and spiritual care in hospitals, prisons or other public institutions, the religious societies shall be permitted to perform the religious offices, but all compulsion shall be avoided.

SECTION IV

EDUCATION AND SCHOOLS

ARTICLE 142

Art, science and the teaching thereof are free. The state guarantees their protection and takes part in fostering them.

ARTICLE 143

The education of the young shall be provided for through public institutions. In their establishment the Commonwealth, States and municipalities co-operate.

The training of teachers shall be regulated in a uniform manner for the Commonwealth according to the generally recognized principles of higher education.

The teachers in the public schools have the rights and duties of state officers.

ARTICLE 144

The entire school system is under the supervision of the state; it may grant a share therein to the municipalities. The supervision of schools will be exercised by technically trained officers who must devote their time principally to this duty.

ARTICLE 145

Attendance at school is obligatory. This obligation is discharged by attendance at the elementary schools for at least eight school years and at the continuation schools until the completion of the eighteenth year. Instruction and school supplies in the elementary and continuation schools are free.

ARTICLE 146

The public school system shall be systematically organized. Upon a foundation of common elementary schools the system of secondary and higher education is erected. The development of secondary and higher education shall be determined in accordance with the needs of all kinds of occupations, and the acceptance of a child in a particular school shall depend upon his qualifications and inclinations, not upon the economic and social position or the religion of his parents.

Nevertheless, within the municipalities, upon the petition of those entitled to instruction common schools shall be established of their faith or ethical system, in so far as this does not interfere with a system of school administration within the meaning of Paragraph 1. The wishes of those entitled to instruction shall be considered as much as possible. Details will be regulated by State laws in accordance with principles to be prescribed by a national law.

To facilitate the attendance of those in poor circumstances at the secondary and higher schools, public assistance shall be provided by the Commonwealth, States, and municipalities, particularly, assistance to the parents of children regarded as qualified for training in the secondary and higher schools, until the completion of the training.

ARTICLE 147

Private schools, as a substitute for the public schools, require the approval of the state and are subject to the laws of the States. Approval shall be granted if the private schools do not fall below the public schools in their educational aims and equipment as well as in the scientific training of their teachers, and if no separation of the pupils according to the wealth of their parents is fostered. Approval shall be withheld if the economic and legal status of the teachers is not sufficiently assured.

Private elementary schools shall be only permissible, if for a minority of those entitled to instruction whose wishes are to be considered according to Article 146, Paragraph 2, there is no public elementary school of their faith or ethical system in the municipality, or if the educational administration recognizes a special pedagogical interest.

Private preparatory schools shall be abolished.

The existing law remains in effect with respect to private schools which do not serve as substitutes for public schools.

ARTICLE 148

All schools shall inculcate moral education, civic sentiment, and personal and vocational efficiency in the spirit of German national culture and of international conciliation.

In the instruction in public schools care shall be taken not to hurt the feelings of those of differing opinion.

Civics and manual training are included in the school curriculum. Every pupil receives a copy of the Constitution on completing the obligatory course of study.

The common school system, including university extension work, shall be cherished by the Commonwealth, States and municipalities.

ARTICLE 149

Religious instruction is included in the regular school curriculum, except in the nonsectarian (secular) schools. The imparting of religious instruction is regulated by the school laws. Religious instruction is imparted in accordance with the principle of the religious society concerned, without prejudice to the right of supervision of the state.

The imparting of religious instruction and the use of ecclesiastical ceremonies is optional with the teachers, and the participation of the pupils in religious studies and in ecclesiastical ceremonies and festivities is left to the decision of those who have the right to control the religious education of the child.

The theological faculties in the universities will be continued.

ARTICLE 150

The artistic, historical and natural monuments and scenery enjoy the protection and care of the state.

The prevention of the removal of German art treasures from the country is a function of the Commonwealth.

SECTION V

ECONOMIC LIFE

ARTICLE 151

The regulation of economic life must conform to the principles of justice, with the object of assuring humane conditions of life for all.

Within these limits the economic liberty of the individual shall be protected.

Legal compulsion is permissible only for safeguarding threatened rights or in the service of predominant requirements of the common welfare.

The freedom of trade and industry is guaranteed in accordance with the national laws.

ARTICLE 152

Freedom of contract prevails in economic relations in accordance with the laws.

Usury is forbidden. Legal practices which conflict with good morals are void.

ARTICLE 153

The right of private property is guaranteed by the Constitution. Its nature and limits are defined by law.

Expropriation may be proceeded with only for the benefit of the community and by due process of law. There shall be just compensation in so far as is not otherwise provided by national law. If there is a dispute over the amount of the compensation, there shall be a right of appeal to the ordinary courts, in so far as not otherwise provided by national law. The property of the States, municipalities, and associations of public utility may be taken by the Commonwealth only upon payment of compensation.

Property-rights imply property-duties. Exercise thereof shall at the same time serve the general welfare.

ARTICLE 154

The right of inheritance is guaranteed in accordance with the civil law.

The share of the state in inheritances is determined in accordance with the laws.

ARTICLE 155

The distribution and use of the land is supervised by the state in such a way as to prevent its misuse and to promote the object of insuring to every German a healthful dwelling and to all German families, especially those with numerous children, homesteads corresponding to their needs. War-veterans shall receive special consideration in the enactment of a homestead law.

Landed property, the acquisition of which is necessary to satisfy the demand for housing, to promote settlement and reclamation, or to improve agriculture, may be expropriated. Entailments shall be dissolved.

The cultivation and utilization of the soil is a duty of the landowner toward the community. An increase of the value of land arising without the application of labour or capital to the property shall inure to the benefit of the community as a whole.

All mineral resources and all economically useful forces of nature are subject to the control of the state. Private royalties shall be transferred to the state, as may be provided by law.

ARTICLE 156

The Commonwealth may by law, without impairment of the right to compensation, and with a proper application of the regulations relating to expropriation, transfer to public ownership private business enterprises adapted for socialization. The Commonwealth itself, the States, or the municipalities may take part in the management of business enterprises and associations, or secure a dominating influence therein in any other way.

Furthermore, in case of urgent necessity the Commonwealth, if it is in the interest of collectivism, may combine by law business enterprises and associations on the basis of administrative autonomy, in order to insure the co-operation of all producing elements of the people, to give to employers and employés a share in the management, and to regulate the production, preparation, distribution, utilization and pecuniary valuation, as well as the import and export, of economic goods upon collectivistic principles.

The co-operative societies of producers and of consumers and associations thereof shall be incorporated, at their request and after consideration of their form of organization and peculiarities, into the system of collectivism.

ARTICLE 157

Labour is under the special protection of the Commonwealth.
The Commonwealth will adopt a uniform labour law.

ARTICLE 158

Intellectual labour, the rights of the author, the inventor and the artist enjoy the protection and care of the Commonwealth.

The products of German scholarship, art, and technical science shall also be recognized and protected abroad through international agreement.

Article 159

The right of combination for the protection and promotion of labour and economic conditions is guaranteed to everybody and to all professions. All agreements and measures which attempt to limit or restrain this liberty are unlawful.

Article 160

Any one employed on a salary or as a wage-earner has the right to the leave necessary for the exercise of his civil rights and, so far as the business is not substantially injured thereby, for performing the duties of public honorary offices conferred upon him. To what extent his right to compensation shall continue will be determined by law.

Article 161

For the purpose of conserving health and the ability to work, of protecting motherhood, and of guarding against the economic effects of age, invalidity and the vicissitudes of life, the Commonwealth will adopt a comprehensive system of insurance, in the management of which the insured shall predominate.

Article 162

The Commonwealth commits itself to an international regulation of the legal status of the workers, which shall strive for a standard minimum of social rights for the whole working class of the world.

Article 163

Every German has, without prejudice to his personal liberty, the moral duty so to use his intellectual and physical powers as is demanded by the welfare of the community.

Every German shall have the opportunity to earn his living by economic labour. So long as suitable employment can not be procured for him, his maintenance will be provided for. Details will be regulated by special national laws.

ARTICLE 164

The independent agricultural, industrial, and commercial middle class shall be fostered by legislation and administration, and shall be protected against oppression and exploitation.

ARTICLE 165

Wage-earners and salaried employés are qualified to co-operate on equal terms with the employers in the regulation of wages and working conditions, as well as in the entire economic development of the productive forces. The organizations on both sides and the agreements between them will be recognized.

The wage-earners and salaried employés are entitled to be represented in local workers' councils, organized for each establishment in the locality, as well as in district workers' councils, organized for each economic area, and in a National Workers' Council, for the purpose of looking after their social and economic interests.

The district workers' councils and the National Workers' Council meet together with the representatives of the employers and with other interested classes of people in district economic councils and in a National Economic Council for the purpose of performing joint economic tasks and co-operating in the execution of the laws of socialization. The district economic councils and the National Economic Council shall be so constituted that all substantial vocational groups are represented therein according to their economic and social importance.

Drafts of laws of fundamental importance relating to social and economic policy before introduction [into the National Assembly] shall be submitted by the National Cabinet to the National Economic Council for consideration. The National Economic Council has the right itself to propose such measures for enactment into law. If the National Cabinet does not approve them, it shall, nevertheless, introduce them into the National Assembly together with a statement of its own position. The National Economic Council may have its bill presented by one of its own members before the National Assembly.

Supervisory and administrative functions may be delegated to the workers' councils and to the economic councils within their respective areas.

The regulation of the organization and duties of the workers' councils and of the economic councils, as well as their relation to other social bodies endowed with administrative autonomy, is exclusively a function of the Commonwealth.

SECTION VI

TRANSITIONAL AND FINAL PROVISIONS

ARTICLE 166

Until the establishment of the National Administrative Court, the National Judicial Court takes its place in the organization of the Electoral Commission.

ARTICLE 167

The provisions of Article 18, Paragraphs 3 to 6, become effective two years after the promulgation of the national Constitution.

ARTICLE 168

Until the adoption of the State law as provided in Article 63, but at the most for only one year, all the Prussian votes in the National Council may be cast by members of the State Cabinet.

ARTICLE 169

The National Cabinet will determine when the provisions of Article 83, Paragraph 1, shall become effective.

Temporarily, for a reasonable period, the collection and administration of customs-duties and taxes on articles of consumption may be left to the States at their discretion.

ARTICLE 170

The Postal and Telegraphic Administrations of Bavaria and Wurtemberg will be taken over by the Commonwealth not later than April 1, 1921.

If no understanding has been reached over the terms thereof by October 1, 1920, the matter will be decided by the Supreme Judicial Court.

The rights and duties of Bavaria and Wurtemberg remain in force as heretofore until possession is transferred to the Commonwealth. Nevertheless, the postal and telegraphic relations with neighbouring foreign countries will be regulated exclusively by the Commonwealth.

Article 171

The state railroads, canals and aids to navigation will be taken over by the Commonwealth not later than April 1, 1921.

If no understanding has been reached over the terms thereof by October 1, 1920, the matter will be decided by the Supreme Judicial Court.

Article 172

Until the national law regarding the Supreme Judicial Court becomes effective its powers will be exercised by a Senate of seven members, four of whom are to be elected by the National Assembly and three by the National Judicial Court, each choosing among its own members. The Senate will regulate its own procedure.

Article 173

Until the adoption of a national law according to Article 138, the existing state contributions to the religious societies, whether authorized by law, contract or special grant, will be continued.

Article 174

Until the adoption of the national law provided for in Article 146, Paragraph 2, the existing legal situation will continue. The law shall give special consideration to parts of the Commonwealth where provision for separate schools of different religious faiths is not now made by law.

Article 175

The provisions of Article 109 do not apply to orders and decorations conferred for services in the war-years 1914-1919.

Article 176

All public officers and members of the armed forces shall be sworn upon this Constitution. Details will be regulated by order of the National President.

ARTICLE 177

Wherever by existing laws it is provided that the oath be taken in the form of a religious ceremony, the oath may be lawfully taken in the form of a simple affirmation by the person to be sworn: "I swear." Otherwise the content of the oath provided for in the laws remains unaltered.

ARTICLE 178

The Constitution of the German Empire of April 16, 1871, and the law of February 10, 1919, relating to the provisional government of the Commonwealth, are repealed.

The other laws and regulations of the Empire remain in force, in so far as they do not conflict with this Constitution. The provisions of the Treaty of Peace signed on June 28, 1919, at Versailles, are not affected by the Constitution.

Official regulations, legally issued on the authority of laws heretofore in effect, retain their validity until superseded by other regulations or legislation.

ARTICLE 179

In so far as reference is made in laws or executive orders to provisions and institutions which are abolished by this Constitution, their places are taken by the corresponding provisions and institutions of this Constitution. In particular, the National Assembly takes the place of the National Convention, the National Council that of the Committee of the States, and the National President elected by authority of this Constitution that of the National President elected by authority of the law relating to the provisional government.

The power to issue executive orders, conferring upon the Committee of the States in accordance with the provisions heretofore in effect, is transferred to the National Cabinet; in order to issue executive orders it requires the consent of the National Council in accordance with the provisions of this Constitution.

ARTICLE 180

Until the convening of the first National Assembly, the National Convention will function as the National Assembly. Until the inauguration of the first National President the office will be filled by the National President elected by authority of the law relating to the provisional government.

ARTICLE 181

The German People have ordained and established this Constitution by their National Convention. It goes into effect upon the day of its promulgation.

SCHWARZBURG, August 11, 1919

(Signed)

The National President
EBERT

The National Cabinet
BAUER

ERZBERGER	HERMANN MÜLLER	DR. DAVID
NOSKE	SCHMIDT SCHLICKE	GIESBERTS
	DR. MAYER	DR. BELL